Make Your Own Dress Patterns

A Primer in Patternmaking for Those Who Like to Sew

ADELE P. MARGOLIS

Illustrated by
Judy Skoogfors

Dover Publications, Inc. Mineola, New York

To my editor and very good friend
HAROLD KUEBLER
who has borne up nobly through decades of darts

Bibliographical Note

This Dover edition, first published in 2006, is an unabridged republication of
*Make Your Own Patterns: A Primer in Patternmaking for Those Who Like to
Sew*, originally published by Doubleday & Company, Inc., Garden City, New
York, in 1985.

International Standard Book Number: 0-486-45254-9

Manufactured in the United States of America
Dover Publications, Inc., 31 East 2nd Street, Mineola, N.Y. 11501

CONTENTS

Introduction

For many sewers, creativity is often blocked by dependence on ready-made patterns. One has visualized something that cannot be found for all the looking in pattern books. There's such a time lag between the moment an exciting style triggers the imagination and that faraway day when a pattern for it is commercially available—if it ever is. Some sewers give up and settle for what they can get. Many begin apprehensively to take liberties with existing patterns. Timidly, they attempt to combine one pattern with another but are too fearful to make much progress. How they wish they knew more about patterns!

If you are one who has been scared to death to move a dart (you think it is put there by an act of Congress) or one who is awed by the seeming complexity of a pattern (the professionals in the field like to keep you that way) or one who doubts his or her ability to create ("I'm really not an artist")—relax! The basic principles of patternmaking are neither too mysterious, too numerous, nor too difficult for the home sewer. Anyone who can work through the labyrinthian directions for sewing that accompany the commercial pattern can surely learn the comparatively simple and clear rules for patternmaking. What's more, the rules work alike for skirts, pants, jackets, and coats and for men's, women's, and children's clothing. For the I-can't-draw-a-straight-line-myself crowd, there are plenty of helpful drafting tools.

Even for the sewer who prefers the timesaving use of commercial patterns to developing one's own, a knowledge of patternmaking is essential. Without it, one is slave to the bought pattern; with it, free to make such changes as one desires. Most important of all, understanding what you are working with will give an independence in design, construction, and, yes, even in fitting.

It is my hope that the simple nontechnical instructions for patternmaking contained in this book will open the door to a new world in which sewers may find creative excitement in executing their own designs.

Adele Pollock Margolis

Philadelphia, Pennsylvania

PART I

PATTERN WHYS

Fig. 1

Chapter 1

Geometric Gems

COVER OR CONFORM

The simplest patterns to make are for clothes designed merely to cover, not to conform to the wearer's contours. Such designs were in times past and are still a favored way of dressing. Patterns for them are derived from geometric shapes.

For a nonconforming body covering, ease of construction and ease of fit are more important considerations than individualized shaping. While the wearer lends a degree of dash and animation to the garment, its handsomeness depends largely on the beauty and character of the fabric of which it is made. Individualization of such a one-size-fits-all garment is more a matter of style than of the relationship of its lines to the lines of the figure—how one drapes it, wraps it, winds it, belts it, trims it, accessorizes it.

All one really needs to know to make the pattern for such clothes is the length and width and which geometric shape to use.

CONSIDER THE POSSIBILITIES

There are rectangles, squares, circles, semicircles, and triangles with which to work.

Cut as long and as wide as you wish, a *rectangle* becomes a fashionable stole (Fig. 1a). Cut wide enough and long enough for controlled fullness (gathers, pleats, smocking, shirring, and the like), the rectangle can serve as a skirt (Fig. 1b), a collar and cuffs (Fig. 1c and 1d), a trimming (Fig. 1e), and so on.

Fold a rectangle in half, slash an opening in front, and fling one end over your shoulder (Fig. 2a). Carve out sleeves and behold! a caftan (Fig.

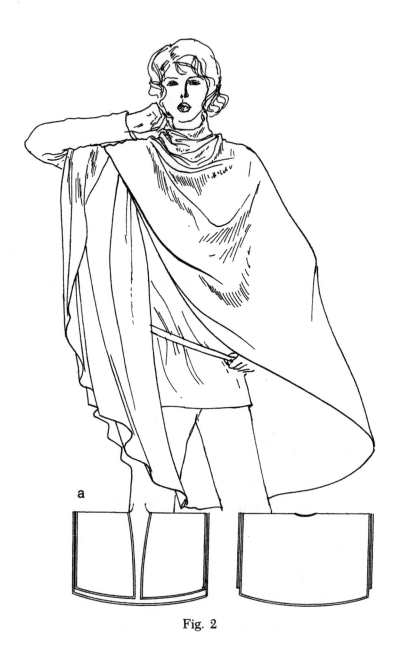

a

Fig. 2

2b). For a slip-on shape, simply cut out a neckline (Fig. 2c). (Make a neckline large enough to slip over the head but not so large as to slip off the shoulders. If necessary to piece the fabric, plan a center seam.)

b

c

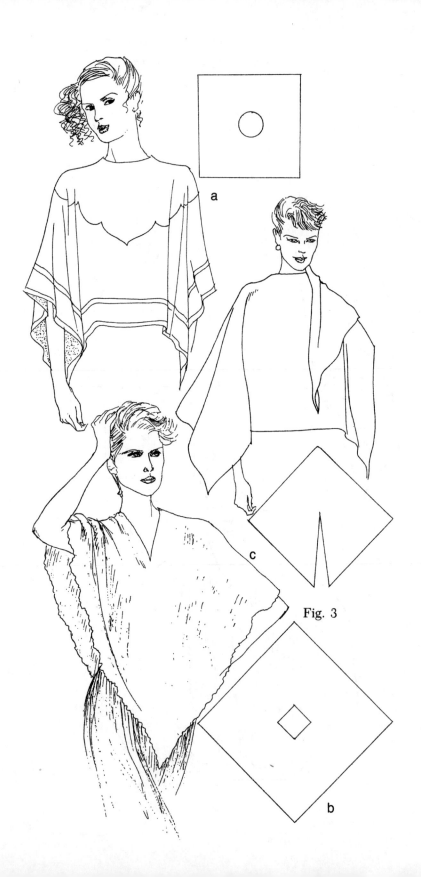

a

c

Fig. 3

b

With a hole to slip over your head, a *square* becomes a capelet (Figs. 3a and 3b). Or slash an opening from one corner of the square for an unusual shoulder drape to a cape (Fig. 3c).

A *circle* with (Fig. 4a) or without (Fig. 4b) a front opening can also become a cape. Or a collar (Fig. 4c) or cuffs (Fig. 4d). With a placket and a waistband, it could be a skirt (Fig. 4e).

Fig. 4

A *semicircle* (Fig. 5a) or triangle (Fig. 5b) of either single or double thickness, trimmed or untrimmed, makes an elegant shawl.

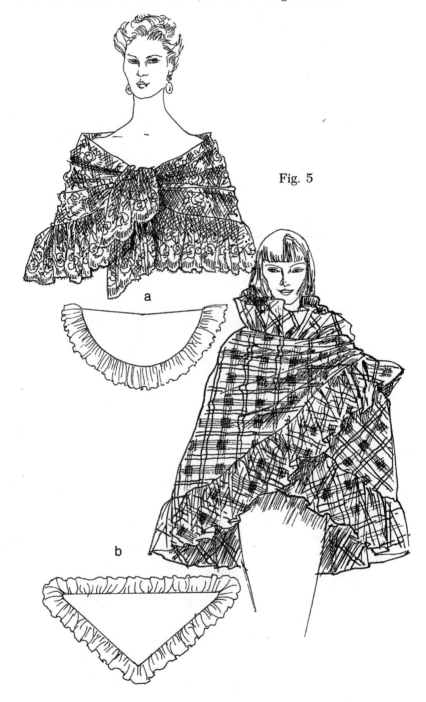

Fig. 5

GENERAL DIRECTIONS FOR MAKING A PATTERN FROM A GEOMETRIC SHAPE

Before making the pattern, see Chapter 3, "It's a Pattern!"

1. Determine the size and shape of the garment (or part of it).

2. Use a length of pattern paper of sufficient length and width. (Tissue, shelf, or wrapping paper will do.) Piece the paper where necessary.

3. Sketch in the desired shape of the pattern.

4. True the lines with an appropriate drafting tool: ruler, yardstick, triangle, French curve, compass, or any circular shape of appropriate size (in a pinch, a bowl or plate works well).

5. Fold the pattern in half lengthwise and/or crosswise to even out both sides of a balanced design.

6. Add seam allowances where necessary. Indicate the grain of the fabric with a double-headed arrow.

7. Test the pattern in some trial material to perfect it for size, shape, fullness.

GEOMETRIC FORMS AND BLOCK PATTERNS

To make patterns for clothes designed to conform to the figure, one must know length, width, and figure (rather than geometric) shape. Such garments and those with more intricate styling than that offered by a simple geometric shape are developed by *drafting* or *draping*. Draping is a highly personal, slow, often costly method of producing patterns. Flat-pattern drafting is a simple, standard, fast, comparatively inexpensive method. Therefore, the latter is (understandably) more widely used today than draping. (Directions for draping will be found in Chapter 15.)

Flat patterns start with and are variations of a "block" pattern—a geometric shape again. (The block pattern is also called a *sloper* or *basic pattern.*)

Accustomed as they were to dealing with rectangular lengths of cloth, those inventive souls who devised the flat-pattern system saw the rectangle as a logical starting point. By measuring a certain amount down, up, or over, within the rectangle, they found it possible to construct a "block" pattern for a bodice, a skirt, sleeves, slacks, and the like. This was, in fact, the method used (still used by many) for producing style patterns as well as slopers.

Great as it is, a pattern is flat while you are not and thereby hangs a tale.

Chapter 2

An Art to a Dart

The body has height, width, and depth. Within this roughly cylindrical framework there are a series of secondary curves and bulges, each with its high point, or apex—more in a woman, less in a man, and differently placed in a child. These concern the patternmaker for the pattern must provide enough length and width of fabric to cover the high points (where the body is fullest, the measurements largest, and the fabric requirements greatest) while at the same time providing some means of controlling the excess material in a smaller adjoining area. *Dart control* is the means by which this is accomplished.

Wherever on the body there is a difference between two adjoining measurements (bust or chest and waist, hips and waist, lower shoulder blades and waist, upper shoulder blades and shoulders) or wherever movement creates a bulge (as at the elbow), you will find that some form of shaping by dart control is necessary.

Dart control is the basic structure of all fitted and semifitted clothing whatever the design. *The rules for dart control apply equally to children's, boys', and men's clothing as well as to girls' and women's. The needs of a woman's figure are most marked, so the principles of dart control can be more clearly demonstrated by it. There is this too: there are more variations in design in women's clothing than in men's. Therefore, the illustrations in this book are largely limited to women's clothing.*

DART CONTROL, A SYSTEM FOR SHAPING FABRIC TO FIT THE FIGURE

This is how dart control works. Say your hips measure 37 inches and your waist measures 27 inches. The garment must fit at both waist and hips despite their difference in measurement. That 10-inch differential comes out in dart control.

The greater the difference, the larger the amount of control. The smaller the difference, the smaller the amount of control. It is not

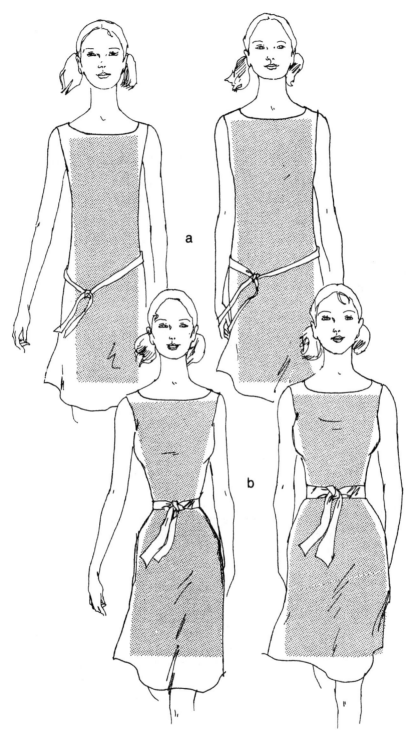

a

b

Fig. 6

whether a figure is short or tall, heavy or slim, which determines that amount. It is always the *relationship between the two adjoining measurements*.

DART CONTROL FOR COLUMNAR FIGURES

However heavy, slim, short, or tall, columnar figures *need less shaping* because there is less difference between adjoining measurements (Fig. 6a).

DART CONTROL FOR HOURGLASS FIGURES

However heavy, slim, short, or tall, hourglass figures *need more shaping* because there is more difference between adjoining measurements (Fig. 6b).

DART CONTROL FOR ALL FIGURE TYPES

There is this, too: the larger the amount of stitched dart control, the larger the resulting bulge. The smaller the amount of stitched dart control, the smaller the resulting bulge. This means that the shaping will be greater in those areas of the body that have the greatest need. Gentler shaping is reserved for those areas where the needs are less.

All of this vital information—the amount and the placement of the dart control—is contained in the basic pieces of a sloper (Fig. 7). (See page 204 for children's sloper. For boys' and men's slopers, use simple basic patterns.)

Note that the total amount of dart control is divided three ways—front, back, and side. In the bodice, since the bust needs the most shaping, the largest amount of control is placed in front. In the skirt (or pants), since the buttocks require the most shaping, the largest amount of control is placed in back. If you place the front and back bodices and skirts side by side so that the center fronts and center backs are parallel to each other, you can readily see the dart control on the side seams (Fig. 8).

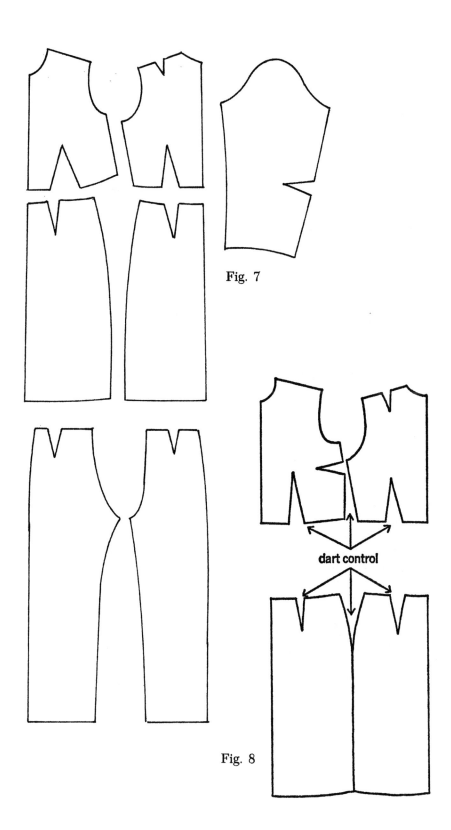

Fig. 7

dart control

Fig. 8

PINWHEEL PATTERNS

The fascinating thing about dart control is that while the amount of control remains constant (established by standard or personal measurements), it may be shifted or divided so that it appears anywhere on bodice, skirt, or sleeve. There is only one rule: the dart control must originate at an outside seam and end up at or pass over the crest (apex) of a figure curve. It's as if the high point of the curve were the pivot of a pinwheel from which the control can be swung in any direction (Fig. 9).

Fig. 9

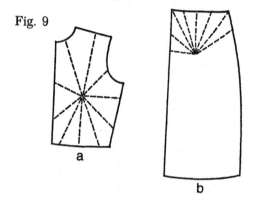

a

b

DESIGN BY DARTS

The simplest and most usual form in which dart control appears is in darts. Material is stitched to take in an amount needed to fit the smaller dimension. As it tapers off the high point (the dart point), it releases enough material to fit the larger dimension.

A different position for a dart means a new design for a garment. The shaping is in no way altered by the position of the control. It doesn't make any difference whether the darts come from the center, sides, top, or bottom. Exactly the same shaping results though it does alter the shape of the pattern piece.

In many designs, the simple waistline dart is used in the same position and in the same amount as in the sloper. It is elementary but effective shaping (Fig. 10).

You may not get any superior shaping by shifting the dart to another position but you will get some welcome variety. Wouldn't it be dreary to have the same old waistline dart in all one's clothes?

Shifting the dart control to a new position is the first and easiest way to design by darts.

Fig. 10

HERE'S WHAT YOU'LL NEED TO GET STARTED

Some of these tools are already in your sewing equipment. A few special ones can be purchased at an art store, a dressmaker's or tailor's supply
store, or a well-equipped notions counter of a general store or from a
mail-order house. The latter often advertise in the pattern books. These
are by no means all the tools which a pattern drafter uses but will be quite
sufficient for those who don't make their living at it.

*For doing the exercises in this book
with quarter-scale models*

For developing full-scale patterns

Colored construction paper for the
patterns and a notebook of white, un-
lined paper for the record.

Blank paper tough enough for the construction and final patterns; shelf
paper (join pieces for width) or wrap-

ping paper, both good and easily obtainable; tissue paper, less bulky for a final pattern but more of a problem in pattern construction; pattern paper.

Soft paper napkins for testing fullness or drapery.

Unbleached muslin or cotton for testing the pattern; use the same degree of firmness as intended for the design; test fullness and drapery in voile or other soft fabric. Use tricot or other inexpensive knit fabric to test designs for knit styles.

Scissors—sharp and reserved exclusively for cutting paper.

Scotch tape

Several pencils of medium-soft lead sharpened to fine points; a colored pencil.

An eraser (it is possible to make mistakes).

A gauge for determining seam allowances, facings, and other small measurements.

A small ruler.

A 12-inch ruler; a yardstick; an L-square or a T-square.

Curved ruler.

French curves #16, #17, and any other suitable for your design.

A 45-degree triangle for determining the grain of the fabric.

A tracing wheel with sharp prongs for use on paper (as opposed to the blunt-pronged tracing wheel used for marking fabric with dressmaker's tracing paper).

Scale models.

A full-scale sloper (basic pattern).

For your convenience in working with the quarter-scale patterns in this book, trace the 45-degree triangle and the French curve shown in Fig. 11. Cut them out of stiff paper or cardboard.

Should you be unable to secure the French curves #16 and #17, use the neck-and-armhole guide provided in Fig. 12.

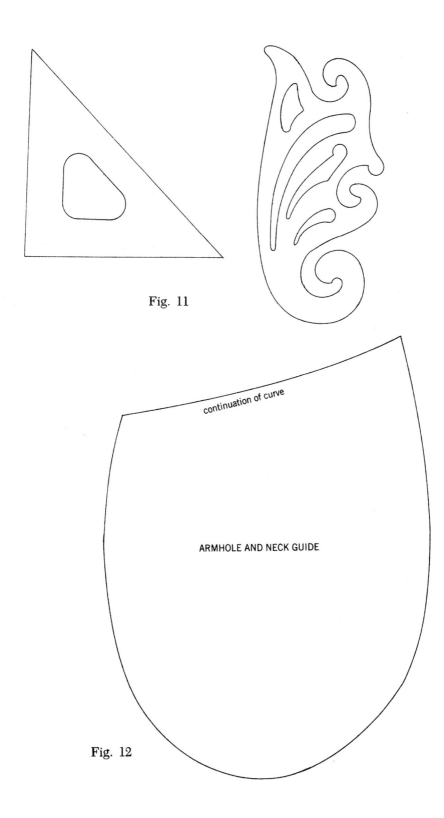

Fig. 11

continuation of curve

ARMHOLE AND NECK GUIDE

Fig. 12

SLOPERS FOR STARTING

The sloper is a basic pattern cut to standard size from a table of standard body measurements. It contains all the necessary information about the shaping, contour seams, and ease that will make the sloper fit a particular size. It has no fullness, design details, or seam allowances. It is used as the basis for creating new designs.

In the clothing industry, the sloper is drafted in accord with a set of body measurements developed by manufacturers, distributors, and users in cooperation with the National Bureau of Standards and issued by the Department of Commerce. While this does establish a uniform criteria, the use of the standard is voluntary.

Many manufacturers gain their reputations on particular cut and fit for what they consider a "standard" size. They may arrive at this judgment via personnel, experience, or sales. Americans are great name-brand buyers. If the cut and fit of So-and-So's size 10 are great for you, that's the brand you'll buy whether the sizing conforms to the standard or not.

BASIC PATTERNS AVAILABLE
FOR HOME SEWERS

Each of the major pattern companies makes a basic pattern. You may find them listed in the pattern catalogues by various names—foundation pattern, master pattern, try-on pattern, shell pattern, basic-fitting pattern, etc. Each pattern was drafted to a set of body measurements approved by the Measurement Standard Committee of the Pattern Industry.

While all pattern companies have accepted these body measurements as a base, they vary in the amounts of ease added. This makes for slight differences in basic patterns of the same size.

If a basic pattern is not available, buy from your favorite pattern company a simple fitted dress pattern with plain round neck, straight skirt, and long, straight, set-in sleeves. For slacks, buy a simple, straight-legged, fitted slacks pattern. These will serve the same purpose. See also Chapter 7, "A Set of Slopers."

STANDARD SLOPER FOR
STANDARD-SIZE PATTERN

Use the commercial basic pattern for the creation of new designs in standard sizes. Any alterations to make the pattern fit an individual figure can be made after the new design has been developed. (This is the same procedure as if you had bought the pattern instead of creating it.)

PERSONALIZED SLOPER FOR
INDIVIDUAL PATTERN

Many home sewers prefer to create their designs from an individual basic pattern made to their measurements and fitted to their figures. This type of basic pattern has built into it all the many little departures from the standard that say "You." Designs developed from a personalized basic pattern need no further alterations.

SCALE MODELS FOR THE EXERCISES
IN THIS BOOK

Simply because it is a more practical way to do the exercises in this book we will use the quarter-scale models in Fig. 13. Trace and cut out the necessary five pieces: bodice front, bodice back, skirt front, skirt back, and sleeve. Use heavy paper, oaktag, or lightweight cardboard. These slopers are going to get a lot of use; they are the basis of all new designs.

Even when you feel confident enough to produce full-scale patterns, you will find it convenient to develop the new patterns to scale. After all the problems have been solved in miniature, it is easy enough to transfer the information to life size.

All dimensions given throughout this book are for full-scale patterns. You will have to quarter them for your quarter-scale patterns.

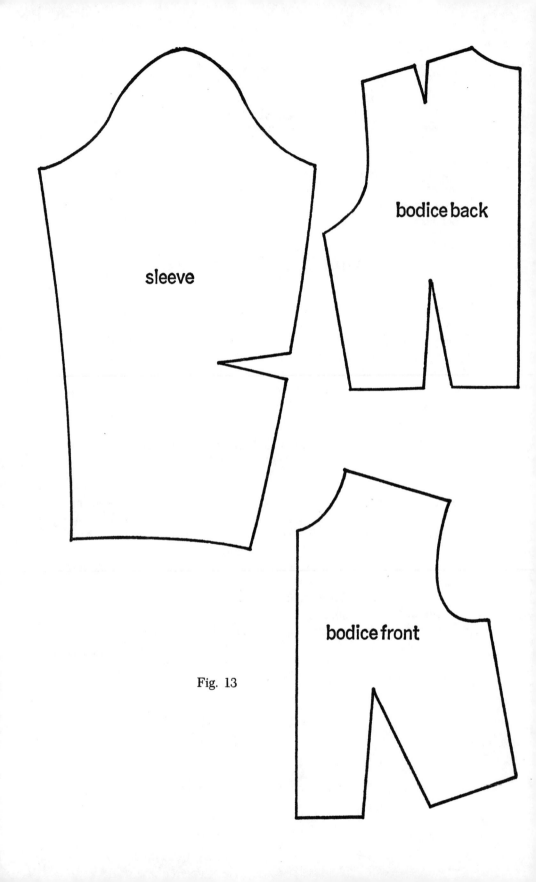

sleeve

bodice back

bodice front

Fig. 13

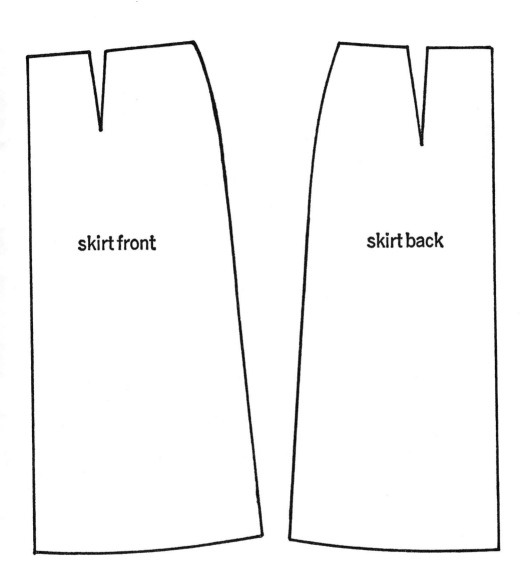

skirt front

skirt back

Quarter-scale slopers for your convenience

HOW TO SHIFT THE SLOPER DART CONTROL TO NEW POSITIONS

The *French underarm dart* is a favorite for understandable reasons. The direction of the dart line suggests the lift one associates with a high youthful figure (Fig. 14).

1. Trace the bodice-front sloper.

2. Cut out the tracing and the dart. (You may want to make a batch of these cut-out bodices to keep handy for the following exercises.)

3. Locate the position of the new dart on the side seam. This may be a point anywhere up from the waistline 2 inches to 2½ inches. Any dart above this becomes an underarm dart. Mark the point A.

4. Using a ruler, draw a line from point A to the dart point (Fig. 14a). This is the new dart line.

5. Slash the dart line to the dart point. Start the slashing at the side seam.

6. Close the original dart and fasten it with Scotch tape. Notice that the waistline dart control is shifted to the new position (Fig. 14b). It automatically contains the right amount of dart control.

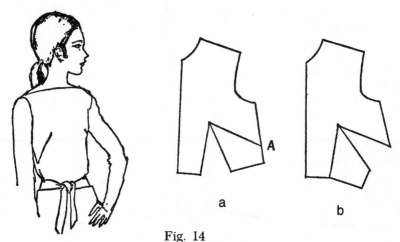

Fig. 14

Are you surprised at the magic? Does this new dart that looks so different actually create the same shaping? For an answer try this little experiment with a *bulging block*.

1. Using one of your bodice-front slopers, close the waistline dart and fasten it with Scotch tape. This produces half a bodice front shaped to fit a quarter-scale figure. Instead of a flat block pattern, it is now a bulging block.

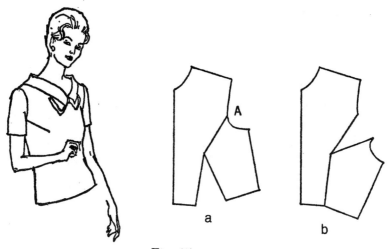

Fig. 15

2. Take your newly created French underarm dart pattern. Close the dart and fasten it with Scotch tape. Now you have another bulging block.

3. Superimpose one block over the other. Though the position of the darts is different, the shaping (bulge) has changed not at all. *Shifting the dart control in no way changes the size, fit, or bulge of the pattern.*

The *dart that emerges from the armhole* is an interesting one (Fig. 15).

1. Trace the bodice-front sloper.

2. Cut out the tracing and the dart.

3. Locate the position of the new dart on the armhole anywhere that appeals to your eye. Just remember that a longer line at an angle is more graceful than a squat, horizontal line. Mark the new point A.

4. From A draw a line to the dart point (Fig. 15a).

5. Slash the dart line to the dart point. Start the slashing at the armhole.

6. Close the original dart. Fasten it with Scotch tape. The correct dart control is automatically shifted to the new position (Fig. 15b).

If you need further convincing, convert this flat pattern to a bulging block and test it over your previous blocks. Once again, nothing has changed except the position of the dart.

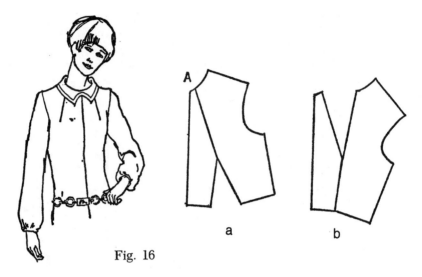

Fig. 16

A *neckline dart* is produced by the same procedure (Fig. 16).

1. Trace the bodice-front sloper.
2. Cut out the tracing and the dart.
3. Locate position of the new dart at the neckline. Mark the point A.
4. Draw a line from A to the dart point (Fig. 16a).
5. Slash the dart line to the dart point. Start slashing at neckline.
6. Close the original dart, shifting the control to the new position (Fig. 16b). Fasten with Scotch tape.

A *dart* may originate *at center front* (Fig. 17).

1. Trace the bodice-front sloper. Cut out the tracing and the dart.
2. Position the new dart at center front. Mark the point A.
3. Draw a slash line from A to the dart point (Fig. 17a).
4. Slash the dart line to the dart point. Start slashing at center front.
5. Close the original dart, shifting the control to the new position (Fig. 17b). Fasten with Scotch tape.

SWING-AROUND-THE-SLOPER

Using this technique, you can make patterns with darts emerging from any point on the circumference of the sloper. There are only two rules which must be followed:

1. You must use the dart point as a pivot for swinging the control into its new position.
2. The new dart must start at some seam line and extend to the dart point.

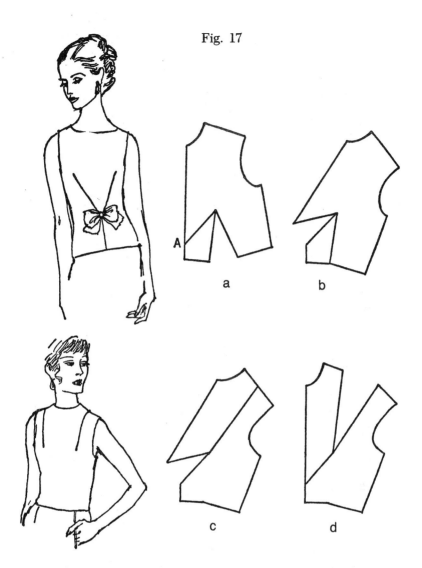

Fig. 17

A

a   b

c   d

One does not always have to start the shifting from the sloper waistline dart. It is possible to start with the dart in any position and shift to another. This would be true if you wished to use a pattern other than your sloper as a basis for the new design or if you changed your mind about the position of the dart in a design. For instance, to shift the center-front dart of the pattern in Fig. 17 to a shoulder dart:

1. Draw the new dart line from the shoulder to the dart point (Fig. 17c).

2. Slash the dart line to the point. Start the slashing at the shoulder.

3. Close the center-front dart, thereby shifting the control to the shoulder (Fig. 17d). The amount of dart control is in no way affected by this type of change.

As in any art, when you have mastered all the rules you may take some liberties with them. In real patterns, it is not likely that you would shift *all* of the dart control to a new position particularly in a fashion period when clothes are easy and relaxed in fit. This will be discussed in later chapters.

The shifting of dart control works the same way on all the basic pattern pieces—bodice front and back, skirt or pants front and back, and the sleeve.

HOW TO SHIFT THE SKIRT DART

1. Trace the skirt-front sloper.

2. Cut out the tracing and the dart. (Cut a batch of these slopers for future exercises so you won't have to stop each time.)

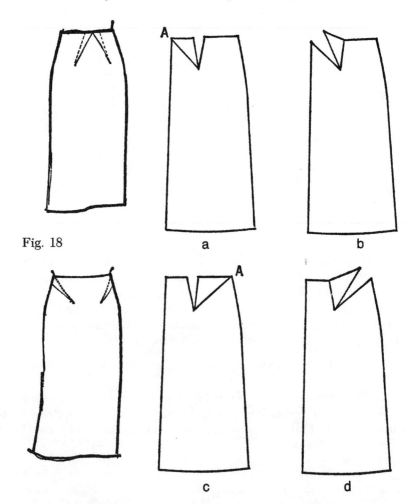

Fig. 18

a

b

c

d

3. Locate the position of the new dart at the waistline either at center front (Fig. 18a) or at the side (Fig. 18c). Mark the point A.

4. Draw a slash line from A to the dart point.

5. Slash the dart line to the dart point. Start the slashing at the waistline.

6. Close the original waistline dart, shifting the control to the new position (Figs. 18b and 18d). Fasten with Scotch tape.

HOW TO SHIFT THE SLEEVE DART

1. Trace the sleeve sloper.

2. Cut out the tracing and the dart. (Cut a batch of these slopers for future exercises.)

3. Locate the position of the new dart at the wrist (either one third or one fourth of the way up from the back underarm seam). Mark the point A.

4. Draw a slash line from A to the dart point (Fig. 19a).

5. Slash the dart line to the dart point. Start the slashing from the wrist.

6. Close the elbow dart, shifting the control to the new position (Fig. 19b). Fasten with Scotch tape.

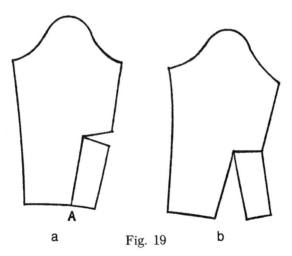

a   Fig. 19   b

CURVED DARTS

Darts need not always be straight lines. They may be curved for interest. For instance, a French underarm dart looks quite pretty when it is a curved rather than a straight line (Fig. 20).

1. On the cut-out sloper with the cut-out dart, locate the position of the new dart. Mark the point A.

2. Draw a curved line from A to the dart point. You may draw the line freehand for eye appeal, then true the line with an appropriate curved instrument or you may draw directly with any of the instruments that may have a curve that appeals to you (Fig. 20a).

3. Slash the curved dart line.

4. Close the original dart, shifting the control to the new curved dart (Fig. 20b). Fasten with Scotch tape.

Convert this pattern into a bulging block. Compare it with your original waistline-dart block. Does the curve make any difference in the amount of control? None whatever. You merely have a new design that utilizes the original control.

Just for fun, go back and try all the darts you've done with curved instead of straight lines.

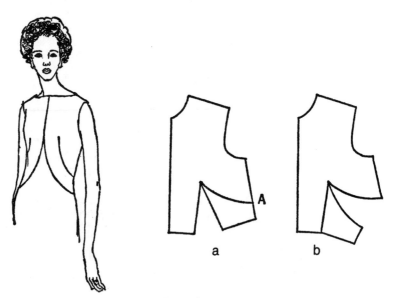

Fig. 20

ASYMMETRIC DESIGNS

All of the foregoing patterns were designed for a balanced effect, that is, half a pattern to be cut on a fold of fabric. When opened out, the darts will be exactly the same on either side of the center front or back. This is a formal or symmetrical balance (Fig. 21a). It is the one most generally used in clothing design.

Balance can be achieved in another way. The right and left sides may be different though equal. This is a balance of uneven parts, a "felt" balance, the type most seen in nature. It is called an informal or asymmetrical balance (Fig. 21b). In clothing design, this is a more sophisticated type of balance and requires great skill in handling. It is so easy to push it to a point of imbalance.

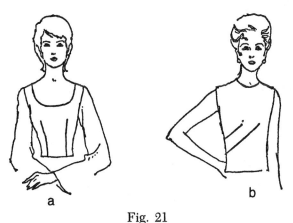

Fig. 21

TO MAKE THE PATTERN FOR FIGURE 21b

1. Use two bodice-front slopers fastened at center front with Scotch tape (Fig. 21c). Asymmetric patterns must be developed from a complete sloper.

2. Close both waistline darts and fasten them with Scotch tape creating a complete bulging block.

3. Rest the bulging block on the table and draw the position of the darts on the inside of the pattern. It is easier to work on the inside of the bulge. The right dart starts at the right side seam and goes to the right dart point. The left dart starts at the right side seam and goes to the left

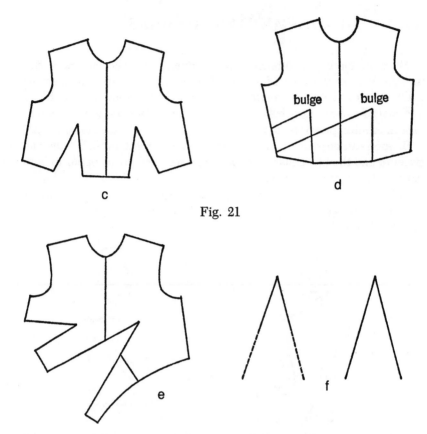

c

d

Fig. 21

e

f

dart point. Make the two dart lines parallel to each other; they'll look prettier that way (Fig. 21d).

4. Slash the new dart lines so the pattern opens out flat (Fig. 21e). Note that the left dart appears larger. This is only because it is longer. In reality, *the amount of dart control is equal in both darts.* Were the right dart extended to the same length as the left dart it would appear the same size (Fig. 21f).

BULGING BLOCK TO THE RESCUE

If ever you are puzzled about what to do with a dart while you are developing a new design, use the bulging-block method. It is an easy way to eliminate any darts that get in the way of the new style lines. There is another method for freeing the area of darts in a flat pattern while designing: shift them temporarily to an out-of-the-way position (see page 81).

STRUCTURAL DESIGN VS. ADDED DECORATION

When it comes to designing (any form of designing), there are two current schools of thought. One believes in the beauty of undisguised structure, purity of line, handsome materials. The other doesn't go along with this austerity. It prefers the enrichment of additional ornamentation.

Both are acceptable in clothing design. There are outstanding designers in each category. If you are a purist, then continue to be. Should you prefer to gild the lily, go right ahead. You have plenty of company in both camps.

Often some discreet detail consistent with the structural line can provide added interest (Fig. 22).

In Fig. 22a the neck dart is emphasized with topstitching.

In Fig. 22b ribbon ending in a tiny, flat bow has been superimposed on the dart concealing the structure.

In Fig. 22c a curved welt has been inserted into the curved dart.

In Fig. 22d both bodice and skirt close on the darts.

SHAPING SHOULD SUIT THE FABRIC, TOO

When you are using a solid-color fabric, the position of the dart control is no problem. Your chief concern in deciding dart placement is which best carries out your design idea. When you are using a figured material (a spaced print of either large or small units); a stripe; a check; a plaid; a visible vertical or horizontal weave; a diagonal weave or print, then the choice of dart position becomes more complex.

Any dart when stitched into the garment will interrupt the continuity of the fabric design. Therefore, you must choose darts which will do so with the least disturbing effect.

Consider *the simple vertical waistline dart.*

In a solid-color fabric, the dart shows clearly and effectively and can even be a part of the design (Fig. 23a).

The waistline dart in Fig. 23b cuts right into the floral motif of the fabric. How silly when this is the chief beauty of the dress. A better solution would be to shift the darts to an area that contains no design unit.

Fig. 22

Fig. 23

In a horizontally striped fabric, the horizontal stripes, easily matched, are little affected by the vertical waistline dart (Fig. 23c).

A chevron design results when vertically striped material is stitched in a vertical dart (Fig. 23d). Whether this is objectionable or not depends on the nature of the stripes.

Fabrics with diagonal stripes are just plain difficult. When a vertical dart is stitched into the diagonal print or weave, the resulting distortion is vivid (Fig. 23e). No darts or darts that follow the diagonal line of the fabric are possible solutions.

The French underarm dart with its long diagonal line is a problem in some fabrics.

In a solid color, the line is striking (Fig. 24a).

The diagonal stripe of the bias bodice of Fig. 24b can be worked into a pleasing little design.

Fig. 24

The diagonal line of the French underarm dart in a horizontal or vertical stripe, a check or plaid, results in a complete mismatching of the fabric design (Fig. 24c).

If you are planning to use a diagonal fabric, make the stripes an integral part of the design (Fig. 25).

When a commercial pattern says "Striped, plaid, or obvious diagonal fabrics are not suitable," better heed the admonition. The professional patternmakers know whereof they speak. The pattern has been carefully tested for the effect of the darts on the fabric.

Fig. 25

THE MORAL IS CLEAR

If fabric is the inspiration for your design, use darts that will be consistent with the surface design of the material. If you start with your pattern design, choose fabric that will best conform to the position of the darts.

LOOK, MA, NO DARTS

Dart control need not be a dart! Any device will do as long as it "takes in" the amount needed to make the garment fit the smaller measurement and "lets it out" at the right place to fit the larger measurement. A pleat (Fig. 26a), gathering (Fig. 26b), or smocking (Fig. 26c) will work just as well as a dart and often with more interest.

Fig. 26

When you plan to use the dart control for gathers (or shirring or smocking), the amount of the control must be spread over a wider area. Were you to limit your gathering to the space allotted to the dart, you would have to draw up the entire amount so as not to alter the length of the original seam line. Can you imagine the impossible bunching that would result? Here is how to remedy the situation.

HOW TO SHIFT THE DART CONTROL FOR GATHERS, SHIRRING, OR SMOCKING

Neckline Fullness

1. On the cut-out bodice-front sloper with the cut-out dart, locate the outside limits of the neckline fullness. Mark points A and B on the neckline. For continuous fullness across the neck (as illustrated), place A at the center front (Fig. 27a).

2. Draw slash lines from A and B to the dart point. Draw several additional slash lines between A and B (Fig. 27a).

3. Slash all slash lines.

4. Shift all or part of the waistline control to the neckline. Spread the sections so the spaces between are equal and half the amount is added at the center front (Fig. 27b). (The full amount will result when the completed pattern is opened out.)

5. Trace the new pattern. Draw the new neckline with a smooth,

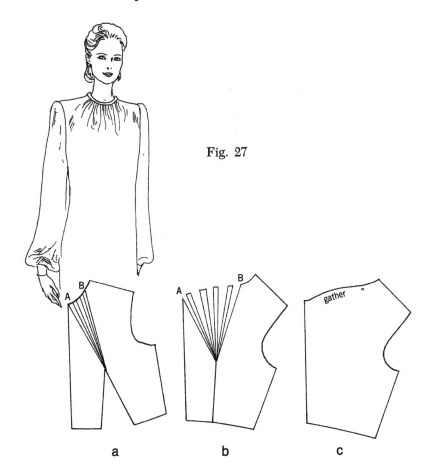

Fig. 27

a   b   c

curved freehand line, correcting any irregularities. Indicate the area to be gathered (Fig. 27c).

This multiple-slash method not only produces the spread necessary for the gathers, it also *provides a guide for the new seam line.* Were you simply to shift the dart control to the new position by a single slash line as in the first of our exercises, you would have an opening for the fullness but no way of knowing where the new seam line should be. A straight line across the opening would not allow sufficient material to be included in the seam. A freehand curved line would only be guessing. A pattern must be precise.

Actually, the more lines slashed and the more sections spread, the more accurate the seam line. Since we are working with such a small sloper, the few slash lines we have used will do. However, on a full-scale sloper, one would have to use many more.

Skirt Hemline Fullness

1. On the cut-out skirt-front sloper with the cut-out dart, draw a slash line from the dart point to the hemline parallel to the center front.

2. Draw several additional lines on either side of the first slash line (Fig. 28a). (There will be room for more of them toward the side seam.)

3. Slash all slash lines.

4. Close the waistline dart, shifting the control to the hemline.

5. Spread all sections so the spaces between are equal (Fig. 28b).

6. Trace the new pattern, correcting the hemline with a smooth curve (Fig. 28c).

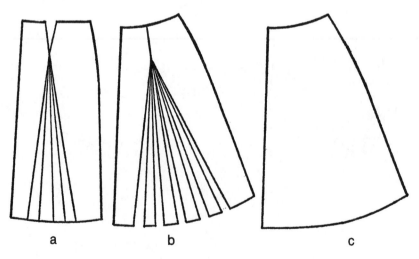

a   b   c

Fig. 28

Elbow Dart Converted to Gathers

1. On the cut-out sleeve sloper with the cut-out dart, locate the outside limits of the fullness (a total area of 2½ to 3 inches should suffice). Mark points A and B (Fig. 29a). Draw slash lines from A and B to the dart point.

2. Draw several slash lines on either side of the dart (Fig. 29a).

3. Slash and spread so spaces between sections are equal (Fig. 29b).

4. Trace the new pattern correcting any irregularities on the seam line. Note area to be gathered (Fig. 29c).

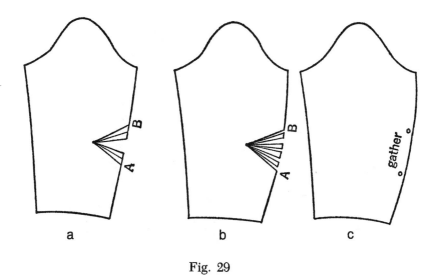

a   b   c

Fig. 29

Such fullness can be created in similar ways on any seam line of any pattern section.

NOTE: The only fullness in these designs is that of the dart control. There is no additional fullness. Directions for adding fullness are given in Chapter 6.

DART-FREE PATTERNS

A dart-free pattern is a wonderful way to keep an elaborate or fascinating fabric design intact (Fig. 30a). It is a good basis for décolleté and form-fitting evening or sun dresses for slight figures (Fig. 30b). Often additional fullness can be worked more easily on a dartless sloper than one complicated by the original dart control (Fig. 30c).

Dart-free patterns can be handled in one of several ways. The dart control can simply be left unstitched. (See "Unstitched Dart Control," below.) The dart can be eliminated entirely or shifted to some seam. (See "Dart-free Bodice Sloper," page 42, and "Dart-free Skirt Sloper," page 44).

Fig. 30

Unstitched Dart Control

Use the bodice or hip-length sloper (see page 191).

Bodice with Unstitched Dart Control

Treat the waistline dart control as for gathers (Figs. 31a and 31b).

Hip-length Sloper with Unstitched Dart Control

1. Extend the underarm dart to the center front (Fig. 31c). Either cut it out and close the dart completely, or fold out the dart.
2. Ignore the double-pointed waistline dart in the finished pattern. Correct the center front with a straight line that starts at the neckline and ends at the waist, cutting off the jog that forms because of the closed underarm dart (Fig. 31d).

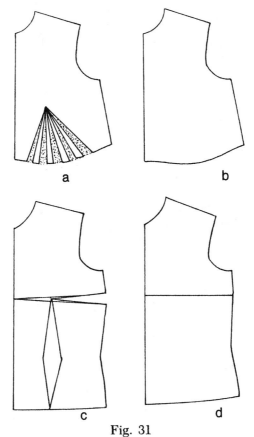

Fig. 31

Dart-free Bodice Sloper *(for figures that require very little shaping)*

1. Trace the bodice-front and bodice-back slopers. Cut out the tracings *but do not cut out the darts.*

2. Starting at the ends of the dart legs, draw new darts (front and back) whose points are on the underarm curve of the armhole about 1 inch to 2 inches in from the side seams (Fig. 32a).

3. Fold in all but ¼ inch of the new dart and fasten with Scotch tape (Fig. 32b). The ¼ inch remains as a little ease.

4. Take off just enough length at center front and center back to give a

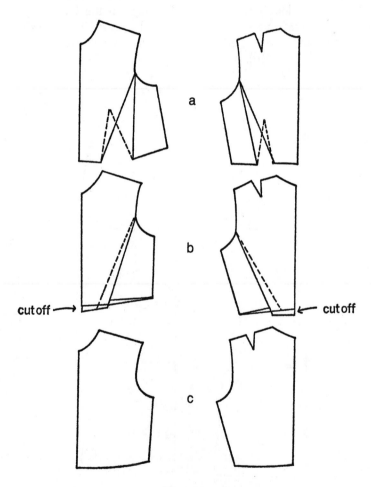

Fig. 32

pleasing slightly curved waistline.* In doing so, you will be correcting the jog that results from the folding of the dart (Fig. 32b).

5. Trace the new dartless sloper (Fig. 32c).

Bias-cut woven material or knit fabric cut from this pattern can be blocked over a tailor's ham to provide just enough swell for a slightly shaped figure.

AN "EASY" WAY TO ELIMINATE A DART

Too many dart lines in any one area can be confusing and aesthetically jarring. Or perhaps a "no-dart" look is desired even though some shaping is required. If the amount of dart control is relatively small and the fabric cooperative (that is, it "eases" readily), the control may be eased into a joining seam rather than stitched as a dart. There are a number of places in a garment where this is frequently done.

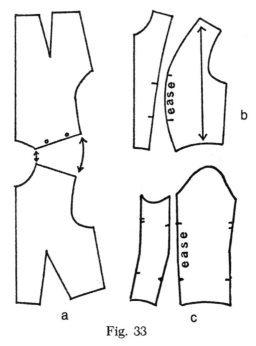

Fig. 33

* A bulge requires length to go over it as well as width to go around it. In removing the dart in this pattern, we have eliminated the bulge and reduced the width. It follows that we do not need all the length, either.

The back shoulder dart can be eased into the front shoulder seam by gathering, ease stitching, or steam pressing (Fig. 33a).

The side-front bodice dart can be eased into a shaping seam at the bust by the same methods (Fig. 33b).

As can what's left of the elbow dart in a two-piece sleeve (Fig. 33c).

DART-FREE SKIRT SLOPER

Trace the skirt-front sloper. Cut out the tracing but do not cut out the dart. How you proceed from this point depends on the purpose for which you will use the sloper.

If the sloper is to be used for fitting a flat abdomen or for preserving the flow of the fabric design, use Method 1. If the sloper is to be used for adding fullness, use Method 2.

Method 1

1. Starting at the ends of the dart legs, draw new legs ending at the side seam (Fig. 34a). Note that the dart leg closest to the side seam is slightly shorter.

2. Fold out or cut out and close the new dart (Fig. 34b).

3. Trace the new pattern, correcting the waistline (Fig. 34c).

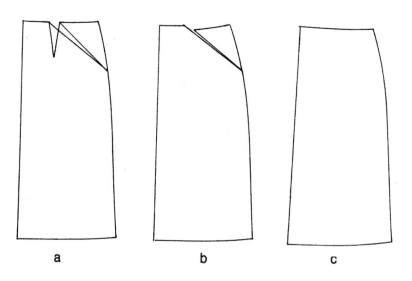

a   b   c

Fig. 34

Method 2

1. Starting at the ends of the dart legs, draw new dart legs ending at the hem (Fig. 35a). The dart legs should be equal in length.

2. Fold out or cut out and close the new dart. Correct the waistline (Fig. 35b).

3. Trace the new pattern (Fig. 35c).

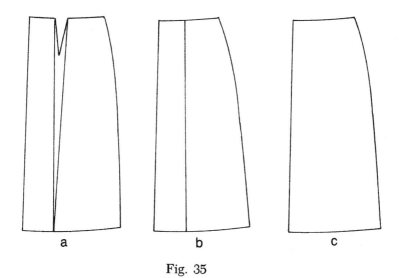

a   b   c

Fig. 35

By this method, the hip measurement is somewhat diminished by the closing of the dart but the fullness yet to be added will provide plenty of hip room.

Back-skirt slopers can be handled in the same way, by either Method 1 or Method 2.

THERE'S AN ART TO A DART

Even in these first elementary exercises you can begin to see the design possibilities of dart control. You must admit there's an art to that dart you've been taking for granted.

Chapter 3

It's a Pattern!

If you run true to form, you are (after just one chapter in pattern design) overwhelmed with your prowess as a patternmaker. You can hardly restrain yourself from fishing out those patterns you've been stashing away for years and shifting all their darts. What's more, you feel certain you know how to get the dart you observed on that dress you saw in the window, or in a fashion magazine, or on that attractively dressed woman who sat beside you on the bus.

This is all very fine—but hold on! We haven't made a *real* pattern yet. What we have done needs a little work on it before it can earn that name.

FROM PATTERN EXERCISE
TO FINISHED PATTERN

Patterns go through a step-by-step progression. All patterns start with a *sloper*. The *construction pattern* (the working pattern) may go through many changes before it becomes the desired design. The *final pattern* (the one we really mean when we say "pattern") must include all the information needed for cutting and assembling the garment.

Thus far, we have worked with the first two types of patterns. We can take all of the exercises in Chapter 2 and convert them into finished patterns by giving them the treatment described in this chapter.

REFINING THE PATTERN

How to Correct a Line Distorted by Pattern Changes

As you have discovered by now, there are many times in patternmaking when the process of shifting or dividing the dart control will produce angularity (Fig. 36a), distortion (Fig. 36b), no line at all (Fig. 36c), or a jog

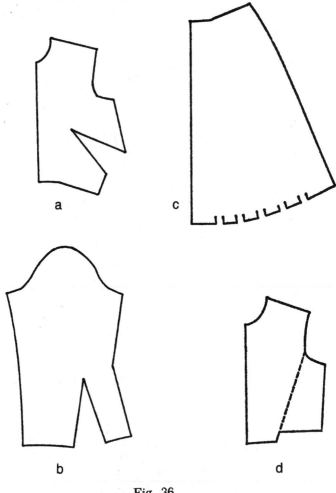

Fig. 36

(Fig. 36d). There will be others that you will come across as your patternmaking becomes more complex.

Patterns are never allowed to remain this way. The angularity of the
waistline seam in Fig. 36a would not fit the curve of the body. The distortion of the sleeve seam of Fig. 36b could not accurately be matched and
stitched to the other sleeve seam. There is no hemline in Fig. 36c—only
vague open spaces and intermittent lines of skirt. How would you know
where to cut the pattern? If you left the jog in Fig. 36d, a section of your
side bodice would be missing. All of these need correction.

To correct Fig. 36a (angularity), draw a curved line either freehand or
with any of the curved instruments. You need not use the entire curve of

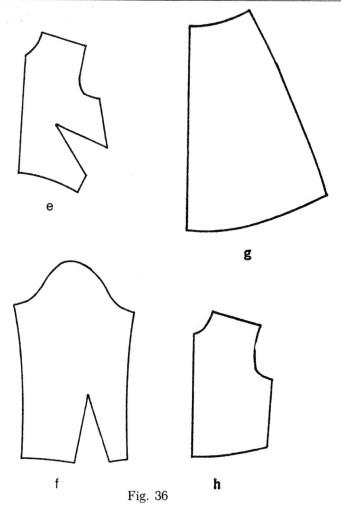

Fig. 36

the instrument. Slide it along until you find that part of it that comes closest to the construction pattern. Use as much of the curve as you need to complete or correct a line (Fig. 36e).

To correct Fig. 36b (distortion), fold the sleeve pattern in half, matching the underarm seam at the armhole and the wrist. Correct the distorted seam by making it match the other. Either trace or cut to shape (Fig. 36f).

To correct Fig. 36c (no line), draw a curved line starting at the beginning of the original line and ending at the end of the original line. Use what lines you do have as a guide and keep the new line close to them (Fig. 36g).

To correct Fig. 36d (jog), draw a new line which fills in the missing section. Start at the beginning of the original line and stop at the end of it (Fig. 36h).

USE YOUR JUDGMENT IN CORRECTING A PATTERN

Remember that while a pattern may be designed to bypass the body for style, it must at the same time conform to body contours in some places in order for it to fit. Style lines may be angular but circumference lines (those that go around the body) are curved, however slightly.

Make certain that joining seams match so they really can be joined.

DESIGNER'S DARTS VS. DRESSMAKER'S DARTS

The darts in your basic pattern (sloper) which extend to the high points of the curve being considered are called *designer's darts*. As you have learned, all changes in dart control are made from these darts.

Only in very small or youthful figures and only in very form-revealing garments are darts stitched to the dart point. That would be asking too much of most figures.

Generally, in dressmaking and tailoring, the darts are shortened somewhat to give a sculptured, soft effect and a little more ease. These shortened darts are called *dressmaker's darts*.

Designer's darts are used in *making a pattern*. *Dressmaker's darts* are used in *making a garment*.

All darts in commercial patterns are shortened darts. Should you wish to relocate such a dart you would first have to extend it to the designer's dart point.

All darts in the patterns you are creating are unshortened darts. For your final pattern, these will have to be shortened to dressmaker's darts.

HOW TO SHORTEN A DART

1. Measure down from the dart point (Fig. 37a) the amount you wish to shorten the dart. Mark the new dart point in the center of the space.

2. Draw new dart legs starting at the ends of the original darts and ending at the lowered dart point (Fig. 37b). It is not the amount of control you wish to change, merely the length of the dart.

HOW TO LENGTHEN (EXTEND) A DART

1. Measure directly up from the dart point (Fig. 37c) the amount you wish to lengthen the dart. Mark the new dart point.

2. Draw new dart legs starting at the ends of the original darts and ending at the raised dart point (Fig. 37d).

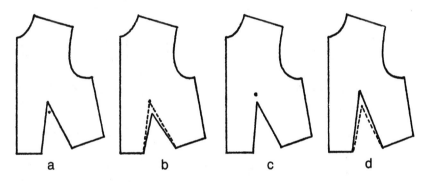

Fig. 37

The broken lines in Fig. 37 represent the original darts; the solid lines, the new darts.

HOW MUCH?

Here is a guide for shortening designer's darts to convert them into dressmaker's darts. Keep in mind that "standards" may be meaningless when applied to individual requirements. Shorten the darts the amount that looks best and feels most comfortable.

Bodice: The front-waistline dart is shortened ½ inch from bust-point height,* the back-waistline dart is shortened 1 inch from the shoulder-blade height.

The underarm dart is shortened 2 inches or more from the bust point. (This dart is *at* bust-point height. Should it be on a slight angle, it must end at bust-point height no matter where it originates on the side seam.) Heavy-bosomed figures may bring the underarm dart closer to the bust point for additional shaping.

A front-shoulder dart is shortened 2 inches or more from the bust point. It, too, may be brought closer to the bust point in heavy-bosomed figures. The back-shoulder dart is usually stitched to a finished length of 3 inches.

The French underarm dart is an exception. It may be stitched to the bust point except in larger figures when it is shortened ½ inch or more.

Sleeve: The elbow dart is usually stitched to a finished length of 2½ inches.

Skirt and Pants: The front dart is shortened 2 inches from the high point of the front hipbone.

The back dart is shortened 1 inch from the high point of the buttocks.

Frequently skirt and pants darts fit better when unshortened (or shortened very little) so that the dart releases the greatest amount of material where the figure is fullest.

* The terms "height" and "point" refer to the highest point of the curve.

A PAIR OF SHAPELY DART LEGS

Straight dart legs must always be equal in length, AB equals BC (Fig. 38a). If they are not, make them so. Wherever possible, balance the dart on the grain to avoid puckering the material when stitched.

When the dart legs are curved, one (AB) may be a little longer than the other (BC) (Fig. 38b). Ease AB into BC. Because of the angle, it is comparatively easy to "ease" a curve.

Straight dart legs ending just short of the high point (ADC dressmaker's dart) provide ease in the bulge area (Fig. 38c). Dart legs stitched to the dart point remove the ease (ABC) (Fig. 38c).

When the dart legs are "bowed" for closer fit (as in an evening or cocktail dress), the ease is removed (Fig. 38d).

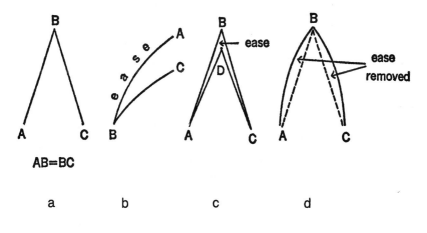

Fig. 38

SIGNS AND SYMBOLS

A finished pattern contains certain signs and symbols which make cutting accurate and assembling the garment easier.

Commercial patterns leave very little to chance or misinterpretation. They use not only signs and symbols but printed directions as well: PLACE ON FOLD, CUT TWO. For your patterns you may use as many or as few markings as will be useful and understandable. Be sure to include enough information but don't overload the pattern with signs, symbols, and notations. This would only make for confusion.

Fig. 39 illustrates the markings that generally appear on a pattern. Not every pattern will need all of them. Some will need more.

There is an established system of marking. If you choose to use your own secret code, make certain that you have the legend noted somewhere. The whole idea of markings is to simplify your work, not to complicate it with deciphering woes.

THE NAME OF THE PATTERN PIECE

When the pattern piece has a simple and characteristic shape, there is no problem in identifying it. For instance, you would have no trouble recognizing a bodice front if it looked like the sloper or any of the fairly simple variations of it in Chapter 2. Intricate patterns with more unusual shapes may not be so easy to identify. There is no need for guessing if the pattern is labeled.

Write the name of the pattern clearly on it. Commercial patterns have the name printed on the pattern. Often they identify the piece by number—1, 2, 3, 4, 5, etc.—or by letter—A, B, C, D, E, etc. This indicates the order in which the pattern piece is used.

TO FOLD OR NOT TO FOLD

Patterns generally come in halves, that is, half a front, half a back, etc. This makes cutting easier, faster, and more accurate (right and left sides are cut alike). It also saves space and tissue both for storing and for cutting on a normal table. It precludes tangling with yards of pattern and fabric in the layout stage.

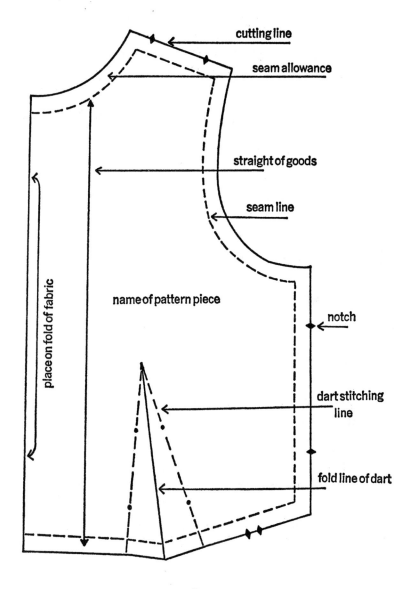

cutting line

seam allowance

straight of goods

seam line

name of pattern piece

place on fold of fabric

notch

dart stitching line

fold line of dart

a

Fig. 39

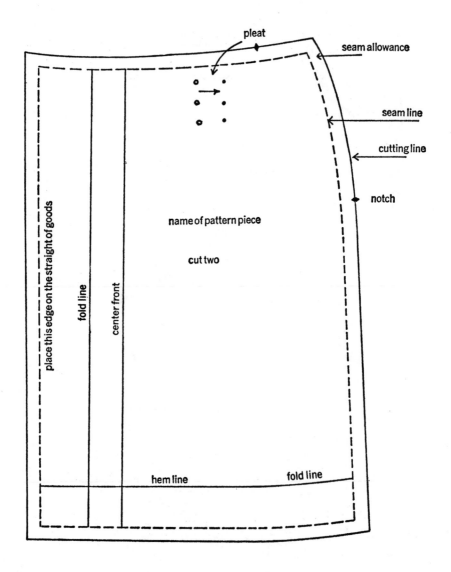

b

Fig. 39

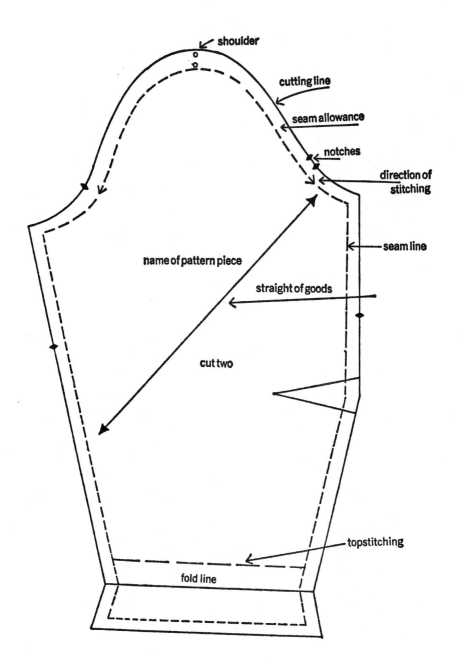

shoulder

cutting line

seam allowance

notches

direction of stitching

name of pattern piece

seam line

straight of goods

cut two

topstitching

fold line

c

Fig. 39

Half a pattern may be laid on a fold to produce a complete unit when the fabric is unfolded (Fig. 39a). Two or more separate but identical pieces may be cut at the same time. For example, two skirt fronts (Fig. 39b), two sleeves (Fig. 39c).

The symbol for a fold of fabric is two medium-sized perforations or two medium-sized circles ($\substack{\circ\\\circ}$) placed at the center of the fold line. You may instead write along the fold line the following: PLACE ON FOLD OF FABRIC or simply FOLD OF FABRIC.

For separate but identical pieces, write CUT TWO or CUT FOUR or whatever the required number.

GRAIN LINE (Straight of Goods)

Whatever the fiber, whatever the texture, whatever the weave or knit, cloth has grain. Grain is a lengthwise or crosswise yarn or thread of woven fabric, the lengthwise rib or horizontal course of knitted fabric. All woven or knit fabrics and therefore all garments hang with the grain.

The designer uses the "hang" of the fabric as part of the design. Because the fabric is woven or knit as it is, it hangs best with the lengthwise grain and most fabrics are used in this way (Fig. 40a).

Sometimes for a special decorative effect a garment is cut in whole or in part on the horizontal grain (Fig. 40b).

The line that cuts diagonally across the lengthwise and crosswise grain is the *bias*. Bias-cut fabric has considerable flexibility. It is used when body-conforming fit, roundness or curviness, or easy movement or flare is wanted. It is essential for drapery. Bias can also be used for decorative effect in striped, blocked, or plaid fabric (Fig. 40c).

In most patterns, the grain is indicated by a long line with an arrowhead at each end (Figs. 39a and 39c).

Sometimes the grain is indicated along one edge of the pattern with the printed or lettered direction, PLACE THIS EDGE ON THE STRAIGHT OF GOODS. A decorative selvage is often utilized in this way (Fig. 39b).

Unless otherwise noted, a center fold of fabric is placed on the lengthwise grain.

Whatever the grain, *the grain line should extend throughout the entire length of the pattern to ensure accurate placement of pattern on fabric.*

Theoretically, placing the pattern on the fabric so that the grain line is an equal distance from the selvage at both ends should guarantee that

Fig. 40

fabric will be cut on the straight of goods. It is on this principle that most commercial patterns provide a short grain line. Unfortunately, this cannot be true unless the material is anchored so firmly in correct position that it cannot slide off grain. Otherwise what may be accurate at the two points measured may be completely wrong in other places. Don't take chances. It is easy enough to draw a long grain line.

HOW TO ESTABLISH THE LENGTHWISE GRAIN
(Fig. 41a)

From the center front or center back of the pattern, measure over equal distances in two or more places. Draw a line connecting these points and extending the entire length of the pattern. This places the grain parallel to the center line.

HOW TO ESTABLISH THE CROSSWISE GRAIN
(Fig. 41b)

At the widest part of the pattern, place the right angle (90 degrees) of your triangle against the center-front or center-back line with one leg of the triangle directly over it. "Square" a line across the entire width of the pattern (Fig. 41d). This is the crosswise grain.

A right angle, or "square," may also be established by using the tailor's square (Fig. 41e) or a T-square (Fig. 41f) in the same way as the triangle.

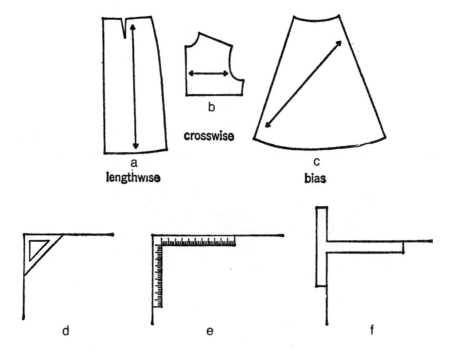

a
lengthwise

b
crosswise

c
bias

d   e   f

Fig. 41

HOW TO ESTABLISH THE BIAS GRAIN (Fig. 41c)

With the triangle in the same position as for the horizontal grain (Fig. 41d) draw the diagonal line opposite the 90-degree angle.

STITCHING LINES—SEAMS

When you have developed the construction pattern so it is just the way you want it to be for your finished pattern, trace all the outside edges, correcting them as necessary. This is the stitching (seam) line (Figs. 39a, b, and c).

To preserve the designated shape of the cut fabric it is stitched with the grain. Often a pattern will indicate the direction of the stitching with an arrow (Fig. 39c) or a simplified drawing of a presser foot.

STITCHING LINES—DARTS

Trace the stitching lines of all darts. Missing thus far is the stitching line at dart's end. It is drafted in the following way:

1. Fold the darts on the underside of the pattern in the position in which they will be pressed in the garment (wearing position). All vertical darts are pressed toward the center; all horizontal darts are pressed down.

Here is an easy way to do it. For a vertical dart: crease the dart leg nearest the center; bring it over to meet the other dart leg (Fig. 42a). This

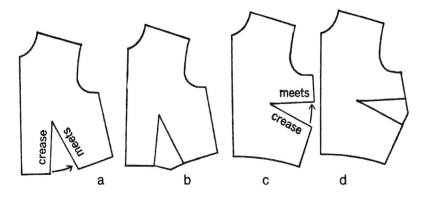

Fig. 42

closes the dart as if it were stitched. For a horizontal dart: crease the lower dart leg; bring it up to meet the upper dart leg (Fig. 42c).

2. Using the tracing wheel, trace the seam line. When the pattern is opened out, you will see a more or less pointed shape (depending on the size and position of the dart). This represents the amount of material necessary to catch the dart in the seam (Figs. 42b and 42d).

When the design calls for *pleats* or *folds,* the seam line of the pattern is arrived at by the same method.

Darts may be indicated by lines, perforations, or by perforations on lines (Fig. 39a). Perforations are useful when the marking must be tailor's tacks.

Narrow darts are generally indicated by a straight line bearing the instruction ¼-INCH DART or ⅛-INCH DART.

DECORATIVE TOPSTITCHING

Decorative topstitching must be indicated with a line of its own. Decide how far in from the edge you want the topstitching to be. Usually this is anywhere from ⅜ inch to 1 inch, but it could be any measurement you determine best for your design. Set the gauge for the amount you have decided on. Slide the gauge along the pattern following the outline of the stitching line. Make a broken line in from the stitching line or a fold to indicate the topstitching (Fig. 39c). You may label it TOPSTITCHING for clarity.

SEAM ALLOWANCE

Between the stitching line and the cutting line is the seam allowance. In most commercial patterns and in most places on the pattern the seam allowance is ⅝ inch. When you are making your own pattern you may make the seam allowance any amount you wish. One-half inch would do quite well for most patterns. If the pattern is designed for a sheer fabric, and/or if you plan to trim away the seam allowance after stitching, then you may use less. A heavy fabric will require more seam allowance. If you are uncertain about the fit, you will surely want more seam allowance.

In industry every fraction of an inch counts. Wide seam allowances can add up to greater cost or less profit.

THE CUTTING LINE

The cutting line (like the topstitching) is an even distance from the stitching line and follows its outline (Fig. 39a, b, and c). Where the *topstitching* was marked *in* from a stitching line or a fold, the *cutting line* is marked *out* from the stitching line to the amount of the seam allowance. Use your gauge.

In many commercial patterns, the direction of cutting (to preserve the grain) is indicated by a scissors symbol with blades pointed in the direction of cutting.

NOTCHES

Notches make the assembling of a garment quicker, easier, and more accurate. Were they not there, you would have to make constant decisions about which sections are intended to be joined.

Since two edges are involved, notches come in pairs (Fig. 43). In the construction pattern, notches are indicated by cross lines (Fig. 43a). In the final pattern, they may be little triangular cutouts in the seam allowance (Fig. 43b) or diamond-shaped symbols on the cutting line (Fig. 43c). You may use either. If you are not certain of the fit or the fabric (a cut in some fabrics may cause them to ravel dangerously close to the stitching line), use the latter method. It's safer. Where there is no problem, use the former.

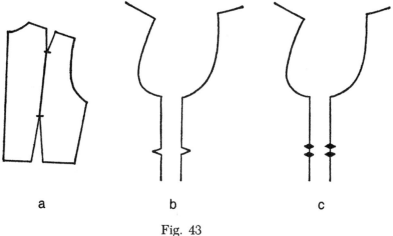

a   b   c

Fig. 43

Place the notches where you think they will facilitate the matching of seams. Notches may be used singly or in groups of two or three. Varying the number and placement of pairs of notches makes them easier to spot. Were you to use all single notches (or double or triple) and were you to place them all the same distance up or down from an edge, you'd have an awful time figuring out which seams go together.

In commercial patterns notches are numbered in the sequence of matching.

GUIDELINES

There is always a long guideline to show where the garment closes. The center front and center back are marked with long guidelines to aid in fitting (Fig. 39b).

A short horizontal guideline close to center front or center back marks the position of the natural waistline in any garment that extends below it.

SHOULDER AND UNDERARM MARKINGS

The shoulder marking is usually one of these—a notch (Fig. 44a) or a perforation or circle (Fig. 44b). On the underarm section of a two-piece sleeve, a notch or three small circles may be used to mark the underarm (Fig. 44c).

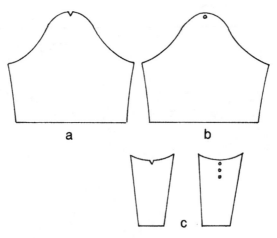

a   b

c

Fig. 44

PLACEMENT MARKS

The manner of closing a garment must always be indicated.

For a zippered closing, a notation plus notch or spot marking is used. The pattern may read LEAVE OPEN ABOVE NOTCH (Fig. 45a) or STITCH TO O (Fig. 45b).

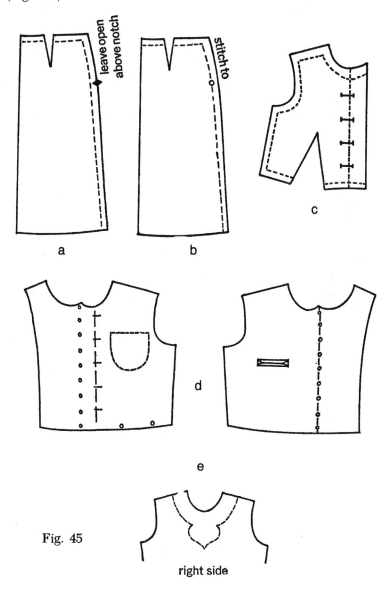

Fig. 45

For a buttoned closing, the length, size, and placement of buttonholes and buttons are drawn on the garment (Fig. 45c).

Pocket and welt placement lines, stitching lines, slash marks, and clipping lines are always shown (Fig. 45d).

Any *decorative detail* (band, trimming, appliqué, etc.) applied to the outside of the garment must be outlined (Fig. 45e).

SPOT MARKINGS

The pattern symbols in Fig. 46 are special markings that indicate matching points in a garment. For example, the spot at which a collar joins the garment, the point where the gusset joins the underarm slash, the place on which a welt is set, etc.

$$\bigcirc \circ \triangle \square$$

Fig. 46

FOLD LINES

Fold lines are placed wherever the material is to be folded back against itself as in a facing (Fig. 39b) or a hem (Figs. 39b and 39c).

Often the fold line of a dart is indicated (Fig. 39a).

Pleats are designated by a fold line and the line to which the fold is brought. The line may be a solid one or a series of medium and small circles (Fig. 39b). In addition, the direction of the fold may be shown by an arrow or a notation PLEAT MEETS (Fig. 39b).

HEMS

In the finished pattern the width of the hem is always included. The amount of the hem allowance depends on the fabric, the style of the garment, and whether the hem is straight or curved.

The depth of a turned-up hem should be no more than can be made to lie flat against the inside of the garment. If it does not, the fullness must be removed or the width of the hem reduced.

Lightweight or gauzy fabrics generally need wider hems than heavy fabrics. Stretchy fabrics require narrow hems. Opaque fabrics can have narrower hems than sheer fabrics. Sheer fabrics can have it both ways—either very narrow or very deep hems. In recent years some designers have dispensed with hems altogether.

Straight Hems

Skirts, whether of dresses or separates, have hems that range from 2 inches in opaque fabric to 12 inches in transparent fabric.

Pants or *trousers* have hems that are 2 inches.

Tuck-in shirts or *blouses* have hems that are narrow.

Overblouses have hems that range from ½ inch to 2 inches.

Jackets have hems that range from 1½ to 2 inches.

Coats have hems that are generally 2½ to 3 inches.

Straight Sleeve Hems

Dresses or *blouses,* whether short- or long-sleeved, have hems that are generally 1 inch.

Jacket sleeves have 1½-inch hems; *coat* sleeves have 2-inch hems.

NOTE: Even when a garment hem is classified as "straight," its true hemline is a slight curve. That is because all circumference lines curve to follow the natural contour of the body.

However, there are exceptions. For appearance's sake, it is often advisable to follow the straight line of a stripe, plaid or large check rather than the curved line of an accurate hemline setting. In small, tubular constructions like a sleeve or pant leg, the hem is generally turned back in a straight line.

Flared hems on any of the above are narrower in width. The more flare, the narrower.

Circular hems have little (1 inch at most) or no turnback. Some decorative edge finish is required. When the curve of the hem is too circular to fit without bumps, pleats, or darts, the hem is rolled or faced.

ANYTHING THAT WILL HELP

In addition to all of the usual signs and symbols, you are free to make any notations or write any little messages to yourself that will make the pattern easier to identify and understand, that will facilitate the layout of the pattern on the fabric, and that will make the cutting and assembling of the garment accurate.

The pattern should be so clearly marked that were you to set it aside now and pick it up again next year, you would still know how to get exactly the effect you had in mind when you designed it.

Now it might be fun to go back over some of your construction patterns and convert them into finished patterns.

Chapter 4

Divided Darts, Added Interest

One dart can be good. Two darts can be better. More darts may be better yet. Only the normal restrictions of good design set the limit to the number of divisions of the dart control.

Sometimes the amount of dart control needed is just too much burden for a single dart. It produces too great a bulge. It greatly interferes with the continuity of the fabric design. It throws a seam line very much off grain, with straining and puckering of the material as the result.

From the standpoint of fit, almost any combination of darts is better than a single dart. The more darts, the more opportunity for gradual fitting.

From the standpoint of fabric design, a division of dart control reduces the unpleasant breaking of design units.

From the standpoint of grain, a division of dart control can make the seam lines of two adjoining sections more compatible.

There are several ways in which dart control can be divided.

METHOD 1—DIVIDED DARTS

Any amount of the original dart control can be thrown into another position in the pattern as long as it starts on a seam line and extends to the dart point.

Waistline-Underarm Combination

One of the most frequent divisions of the dart control is a waistline-underarm combination (Fig. 47). In this design, the underarm dart is hidden by the position of the arm and the waistline dart is so reduced in size that the break in the fabric design is minimized.

1. On the cut-out bodice-front sloper with the cut-out dart, locate the position of the new underarm dart—anywhere from 1½ inches below the armhole to 2½ inches above the waistline. Mark the point A (Fig. 47a). (Too close to the armhole will interfere with the setting and fitting of the sleeve. Too close to the waistline makes the dart a French underarm dart, which generally does not share honors with any other dart.)

2. Draw a line from A to the dart point (Fig. 47a).

3. Slash the new dart line.

4. Close *part* of the original dart. The remaining control is automatically shifted to the new dart (Fig. 47b). Generally, most of the control remains in the waistline dart; a lesser amount is shifted to the underarm dart. Shorten both darts.

5. Complete the pattern by adding all the necessary signs, symbols, and notations.

Fig. 47

Waistline-Shoulder Dart Combination

Another common division of dart control is between waistline and shoulder darts.

1. On the cut-out bodice-front sloper with the cut-out dart, locate the position of the new shoulder dart. When there is a dart on the back shoulder, it is a fine point in design to match the location of the two. Place the front sloper against the back shoulder. Mark the position of the front shoulder dart. Label the point A (Fig. 48a).

2. Draw the new dart line from shoulder to dart point (Fig. 48a).

3. Slash the dart line.

4. Close *part* of the original dart; the remaining control is automatically shifted to the new dart (Fig. 48b). Shorten both darts.

5. Complete the pattern by adding all the necessary signs, symbols, and notations.

Fig. 48

How much dart control is shifted to a new position depends on what is appropriate for the material, what is kind to the grain, and what provides a subtle fit.

You can see how divided dart control would be a good way to handle a check or a plaid (Fig. 49).

Fig. 49

Stitched Dart-Unstitched Dart Combination

Stitching the full amount of dart control into any garment results in a fitted garment with a standard amount of ease.

In periods when a more relaxed look is fashionable, some of the divided dart control may appear as unstitched fullness.

For instance, in a bodice with dart control divided between waistline and underarm, the underarm dart is stitched for fit while the waistline dart is left unstitched for fullness (Fig. 50a).

In Fig. 50b, the dart control is divided between a stitched dart originating at the armhole and unstitched dart control at the waistline giving it some fullness.

The utilization of divided dart control—some stitched and some unstitched—is the basis of semifitted styles such as the shift or skimmer dress.

Fig. 50

HOW TO MAKE THE PATTERNS FOR
FIGS. 50a AND 50b

For Fig. 50a:

1. Divide the dart control between waistline and underarm (Fig. 51a). (The waistline dart control is handled as for gathers.)

2. Trace the pattern allowing the underarm dart to remain as a dart. Draw a line across the waistline as for a seam (Fig. 51b).

3. Complete the pattern.

For Fig. 50b:

1. Divide the dart control between waistline and armhole (Fig. 51c). (The waistline dart control is handled as in Fig. 51a).

2. Trace the pattern allowing the armhole dart to remain as a dart. Draw a line across the waistline as for a seam (Fig. 51d).

3. Complete the pattern.

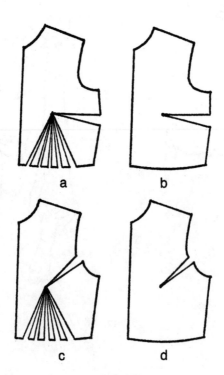

Fig. 51

Sleeve Dart Control

Sleeve dart control can be treated in the same manner.

1. On the cut-out sleeve sloper with the cut-out elbow dart, locate the position of the new control at the wrist. Mark point A one third or one fourth of the way up from the back underarm seam.

2. Draw a line from A to the elbow dart point. Draw several slash lines and slash them starting at the wrist on either side of this (Fig. 52a).

3. Close *part* of the elbow dart control. The remaining control is shifted to the wrist as for gathers (Fig. 52b).

4. Trace the new pattern leaving the diminished elbow dart as a dart. The wrist control appears as unstitched fullness (Fig. 52c).

5. Complete the pattern.

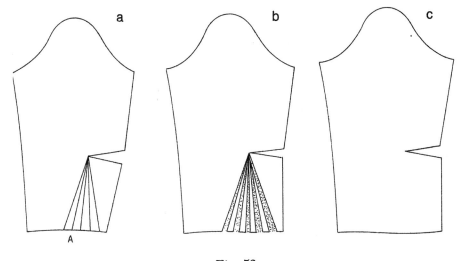

Fig. 52

The above one-piece dress sleeve becomes the basis of the one-piece suit sleeve and the one-piece coat sleeve, both of which also require the ease provided by the unstitched fullness. See page 197.

METHOD 2—MULTIPLE DARTS OR DART TUCKS

The division of dart control need not be limited to a two-way split. Dart control can be divided three ways, or four ways, or more. Theoretically, you could divide the control in many places around the perimeter of a sloper (Fig. 53). The question is, "Who would want to?" The resulting design would be pretty cluttered.

Fig. 53

Fig. 54

a

b

You will have to admit that dividing the dart control so it comes from many different directions, each vying for attention, can be very distracting (Fig. 54a). However, an equal number of darts on the *same seam line* are another matter. Repetition in a row is a time-honored method of achieving harmony and interest in design (Fig. 54b).

Dart control may be divided into multiple darts or dart tucks.

Like a single dart or divided dart control, *multiple darts* (Fig. 55a) can also produce a fitted garment but one more subtle in shaping than the former and more interesting in design than the latter.

Fig. 55

Dart tucks are parts of darts. They begin as darts but are stitched only part way. The fullness released by this construction produces a soft, full effect (Fig. 55b) or a draped effect (Fig. 55c). Dart tucks require careful and subtle designing. There's a very fine line between a chic look and a matronly one.

In doing the following exercises in this chapter, trace the construction pattern on either tissue paper or a paper napkin. You'll find them much easier to manipulate than stiff paper when folding the tiny multiple darts and dart tucks to position.

There are several ways of developing a pattern for multiple darts or dart tucks. Which you choose depends on the position of the original dart control in relation to the position of the desired darts or tucks.

MULTIPLE DARTS

Across the Neckline and Shoulders

1. Trace the bodice-front sloper. Cut out the tracing and the dart.
2. Locate the number and length of the new darts. Make them ½ to 1 inch short of the dart point. Should you wish to make continuous darts across the entire neckline, use the center-front line for the center dart (Fig. 56a). Connect the ends of each dart to the dart point. No change can be made in the sloper unless this is done.
3. Slash all dart and connecting lines.
4. Close all or part of the waistline dart shifting the control to the neckline and shoulder. Divide the dart control evenly among the new darts except for the center-front dart, which gets half the amount because it will appear on a center fold of fabric (Fig. 56b).
5. Locate the new dart points in the center of each space at the designated length of the dart. Draw new dart legs. Make sure that each pair is equal in length (Fig. 56c).
6. Fold the darts into wearing position. Trace the neckline and shoulder seams (Fig. 56d).
7. Complete the pattern.

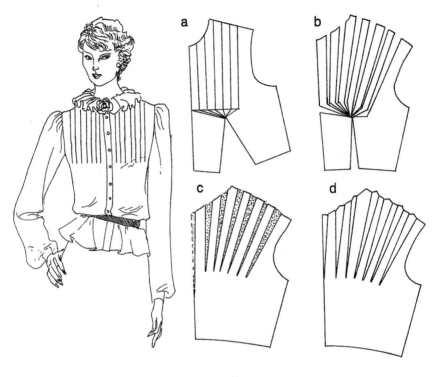

Fig. 56

At the Waistline

Do you recall the exercises that utilized the bulging block (page 23) as a method of eliminating the waistline dart so that we had an uninterrupted area in which to design? Here is another device that serves the same purpose. Using the flat pattern, shift the dart control out of the way. Do your designing. Shift it back again to the newly designed control. It's like moving furniture out of the way temporarily so you can clean under the rug.

Fig. 57

a   b   c

1. Trace the bodice-front sloper. Cut out the tracing and the dart. Shift the waistline dart control to the shoulder. Fasten with Scotch tape.

2. Locate the number and length of the new waistline darts. If you make them somewhat shorter than the sloper dart you will be shortening the darts at the same time you are dividing the control. Draw the dart lines and connect them with the dart point (Fig. 57a).

3. Slash all slash lines.

4. Close the shoulder dart, returning the control to the waistline. Fasten with Scotch tape.

5. Divide the dart control into equal darts with equal spaces between them (Fig. 57b). Trace the pattern.

6. Locate the new dart points in the center of each space at the designated height. Draw new dart legs. Make sure that each pair is equal in length.

7. Fold the darts in position. Correct the waistline and trace it (Fig. 57c).

8. Complete the pattern.

In Fig. 58, a series of *graduated darts* are distributed across the entire front bodice.

1. Shift the waistline dart control to the shoulder as in the previous exercise.

2. Draw a guide line to designate the graduated points of the darts. Use the center front as the center dart. Draw dart lines and connect the ends of each to the dart point (Fig. 58a). Numbering the darts is helpful.

3. Slash each line to the dart point. Close the shoulder dart, returning the dart control to the waistline. Divide the control into equal darts with equal spaces between them. Reserve half the amount for the center-front dart (Fig. 58b). When the pattern is placed on a fold of fabric, you will have the complete front dart.

4. Extend the center-front line of the bodice to the waistline. Locate new dart points in the center of each space at the designated height. Draw new dart legs. Make sure each pair is equal in length (Fig. 58c).

5. Fold the darts to wearing position and trace the waistline seam (Fig. 58d).

6. Complete the pattern.

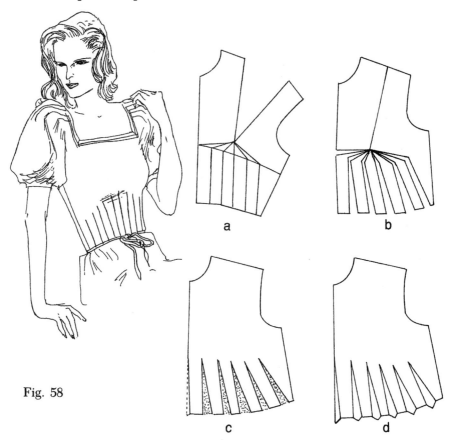

Fig. 58

At the Side Seam, Multiple French Darts

1. Trace the bodice-front sloper. Cut out the tracing and the dart.

2. Decide where and how many French darts you wish. Draw new dart lines on the sloper (Fig. 59a). Connect the end of each new dart line with the dart point (Fig. 59b).

3. Slash along each line *to the dart point*.

4. Close the waistline dart and fasten with Scotch tape. Divide the dart control evenly for the new darts (Fig. 59c). Scotch-tape to position.

5. Locate new dart points in the center of each spread area. Draw new dart legs making each pair equal in length (Fig. 59d).

6. Fold the darts into wearing position and trace the side seam (Fig. 59d). Correct the waistline with a gently curved line.

7. Complete the pattern.

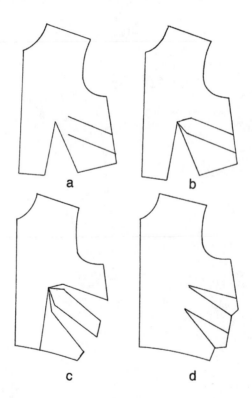

a   b

c   d

Fig. 59

An interesting design for a dress results from using related dart control in bodice and skirt (Fig. 60). The French darts of the bodice are developed as in Fig. 59. The skirt pattern is developed as directed below.

Fig. 60

Related Multiple Darts in the Skirt

1. Trace the skirt-front sloper. Cut out the tracing.

2. Draw the position of the new darts on the sloper. Make the angle of the darts comparable to those of the bodice. Extend the waistline dart to a length compatible with the new dart lines (Fig. 61a). Cut out the waistline dart.

3. Connect the end of each new dart line with the dart point (Fig. 61b).

4. Cut along each line *to the dart point*.

5. Close the original dart and fasten with Scotch tape. Divide the dart control evenly between the new darts (Fig. 61c). Scotch tape to position.

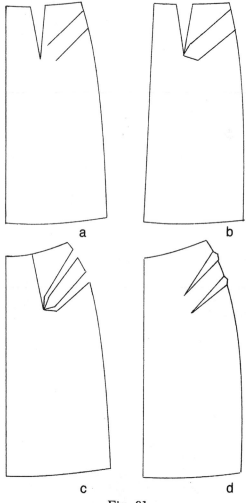

Fig. 61

6. Locate new dart points in the center of each spread area. Draw new dart legs, making certain that each pair is equal in length (Fig. 61d).

7. Fold the darts to wearing position and trace the side seam (Fig. 61d).

8. Complete the pattern.

MULTIPLE ELBOW DARTS

Here is still another method for dividing the control into multiple darts using the sloper dart control in its original position.

1. Trace the sleeve sloper. Cut out the tracing and the dart.

2. Locate the position of the new darts on each side of the elbow dart and ½ inch away from it. Make the slash lines parallel to the dart legs. Since the elbow dart is already a shortened dart, it needs no further shortening. Connect the ends of the slash lines with the point of the elbow dart (Fig. 62a).

3. Slash all slash lines.

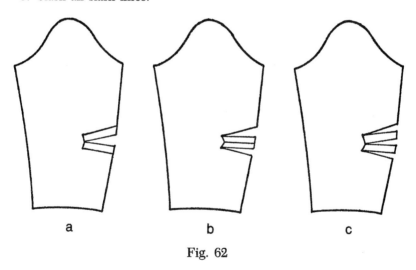

a   b   c

Fig. 62

For Two Darts (Fig. 62b)

4. Close the elbow dart completely, throwing the control to both sides of it. Make the new darts equal. Fasten with Scotch tape.

5. Trace the pattern. Locate new dart points in the center of each opening. Draw the dart legs. Make certain that each pair is equal in length.

6. Fold the darts to wearing position and trace the seam line.

7. Complete the pattern.

For Three Darts (Fig. 62c)

The method for developing three elbow darts is the same as for two with the exception of Step 4. Substitute the following:

Close *part* of the elbow dart, dividing the control equally into three darts.

SKIRT OR PANTS MULTIPLE DARTS

Use the same method as that for the sleeve.

1. Trace the skirt or pants sloper. Cut out the tracing and the dart.

2. Locate the position of the new dart lines on each side of the waistline dart and at least ½ inch away from it. Draw the dart lines parallel to the original dart legs. Connect the end of each dart line with the original dart point (Fig. 63a).

3. Slash all dart lines to the dart point. Close the original dart, throwing the control to the new darts. Distribute the waistline dart control equally. Fasten with Scotch tape (Fig. 63b).

4. Trace the pattern. Locate the new dart points in the center of each spread area. Draw the new dart legs. Make certain that each pair is the same length. Fold the darts to wearing position and trace the waistline seamline (Fig. 63c).

5. Complete the pattern.

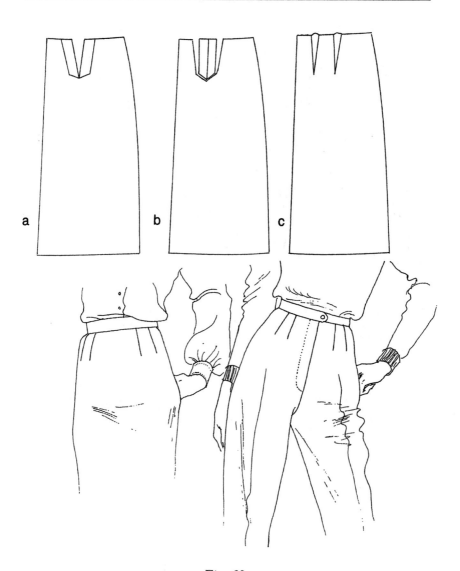

Fig. 63

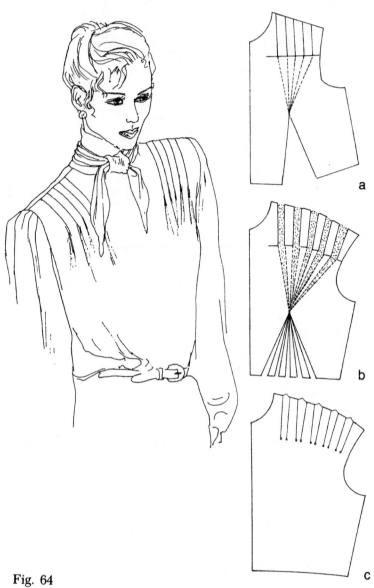

Fig. 64

MULTIPLE DART TUCKS

Multiple dart tucks are developed in much the same way as multiple darts. However, instead of stitching the darts to a point, the stitching stops part way at a designated spot. This provides both a degree of shaping and fullness at the released ends of the tucks.

At the Shoulder

1. Trace the bodice-front sloper. Cut out the tracing and the dart.

2. Locate the position of and draw the lines for the dart tucks. Designate the length of each by a cross line (Fig. 64a).

3. Connect the ends of the dart tucks to the dart point (the broken lines in Fig. 64a). Each entire line from shoulder to dart point (jog and all) becomes a slash line.

4. Slash all slash lines.

5. Close the waistline dart in whole or in part (as for gathers), throwing the dart control to the shoulder. Arrange the sections so the spaces between are equal (Fig. 64b). Fasten with Scotch tape.

6. Trace the pattern. When you come to the dart tucks, trace only to the end of each tuck as designated in Step 2. Mark end of stitching with small o's (Fig. 64c). Notice that the dart tuck legs *are not* parallel lines. Being parts of darts, they are tapered. They must be stitched so.

7. Fold the tucks into wearing position (the same rule as for darts). Trace the shoulder seam (Fig. 64c).

8. Complete the pattern.

At the Neckline

1. Trace the bodice-front sloper. Cut out the tracing and the dart.

2. Lightly draw an arc as a guideline for positioning the dart tucks. Make it a distance from the neckline equal to the length you desire for the dart tucks. They may be of equal length or graduated. Draw the lines for the dart tucks showing the number and position of each one (Fig. 65a).

3. Connect the ends of the dart tucks with the original dart point (Fig. 65a). All lines from neck to dart point (crooked though they are) become slash lines.

4. Slash all slash lines.

5. Close all or part of the original dart control. Spread the sections so the spaces between are equal (Fig. 65b). Fasten with Scotch tape.

6. Trace the pattern. When you come to the dart tucks, trace only to the end of each tuck as designated (Fig. 65b). Mark the end of the stitching with small o's.

7. Fold the dart tucks into wearing position (same rule as for darts). In folding, start matching the tucks at the neckline so the original neckline is restored. Trace the neckline (Fig. 65c).

8. Complete the pattern.

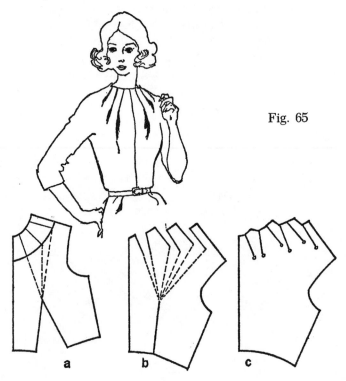

Fig. 65

a   b   c

Combination Shoulder and Neck Dart Tucks

Such a combination makes an interesting design. Can you follow the diagram in Fig. 66 for producing this pattern?

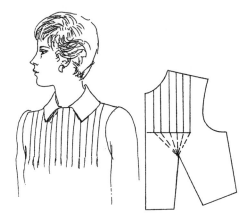

Fig. 66

At Center Front

As with darts, it doesn't matter where the dart tucks are placed as long as they begin on some seam and are connected with the dart point. However, in order to improve the design, it is possible to take some slight liberties with the position of the dart point. It may be moved in any direction up to, but no more than 1 inch. Since the released fullness of dart tucks covers a comparatively wide area, the fit of the garment is not affected. One would have to be a little more careful in moving a dart.

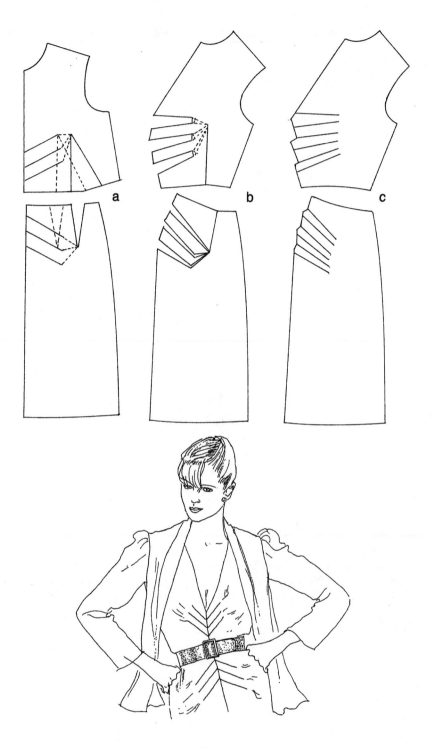

Fig. 67

1. Move the bodice and skirt darts closer to the side seams. Extend the skirt dart to a point in line with the widest measurement at the hips. The broken lines in Fig. 67a indicate the original dart. The solid lines show the darts in their new positions.

2. Locate the positions of the dart tucks above and/or below the dart point. Connect them with the new dart points (Fig. 67a).

3. Slash all slash lines.

4. Close the sloper darts. Spread the sections in the new control area (Fig. 67b).

5. Trace the pattern showing the new dart tucks and center-front seam-line (Fig. 67c).

6. Complete the pattern.

Multiple Skirt or Pants Dart Tucks

These are developed in the same way as multiple darts except that they stop part way. Follow the diagrams in Fig. 68.

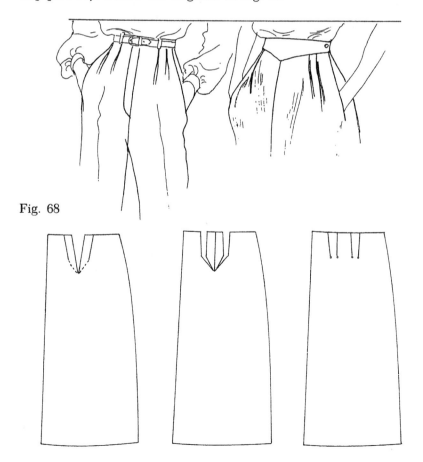

Fig. 68

SUGGESTIONS FOR NEW PATTERNMAKERS

In looking at fashions, many people lose all sense of objectivity. When a particular style doesn't fit into a personal formula for glamour, they are apt to discard it—often with unkind words.

As a pattern designer, your interest must extend to all fashions whether you would be inclined to wear them or not. Look at window fashion displays. Watch people passing. Examine the fashion magazines.

Study the darts from the standpoint of design, fit, and appropriateness to fabric.

How has the dart control been used as design?

Why has a particular control been used on a particular fabric?

Do the darts fit the people who are wearing them? Are they in the right amount—not too much or too little, considering the curves they must shape? Are they in the right place? Do they release their greatest amount of fullness where needed?

Make "shorthand" sketches of any dart treatments that interest you. The sketches don't have to be works of art. Just so you know what they mean. The rest can be done with drafting tools.

Chapter 5

Control Is What It Seams

There is no disguising a dart. From the standpoint of design it is what it is: a short jab into an otherwise unbroken area. It is obvious in function and elementary in control. Many fine patterns remain on this simple level of design by darts. And many beautiful garments are made from them, depending for their effect on handsome fabric and perfect fit.

To many a designer, however, a dart is an incomplete line. Which is very frustrating. For the designer uses *line* to express ideas as a painter uses color, a musician the notes of a scale, or a writer words. The designer of clothes approaches the space within the outline seams as a painter approaches an empty canvas. With subtle or dramatic lines, he or she seeks to divide the space into interesting areas (Fig. 69).

Fig. 69

The designer must also find a way to shape *and* style at one and the same time. How to do it? Incorporate the dart control in the design lines of the garment—a neat trick. When successfully accomplished, there is no better-fitting or more attractive garment.

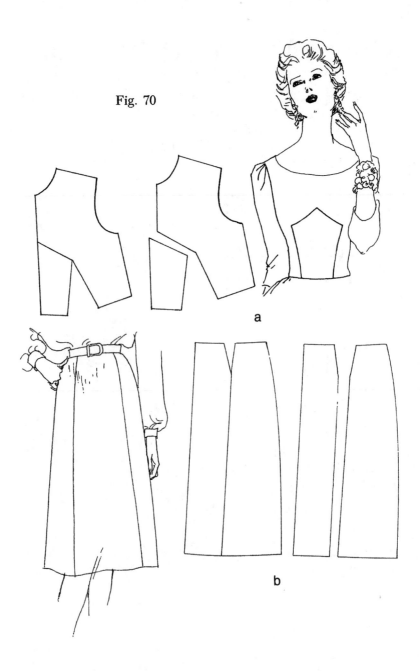

Fig. 70

a

b

CONTROL SEAMS

When a design line falls across a high point (apex) of the body, the dart control may be concealed in the seam that joins the sections. This is called a *control seam*.

The Dart Part of the Seam

The most obvious way in which seam shaping can be achieved is to use the existing dart legs as part of the style line as in Figs. 70a and 70b. When the garment is joined on this line, the control is concealed in the seam.

When there are two darts, their dart points may be connected to provide the style line as in Fig. 71. Shaping is hidden in the seam that joins the sections.

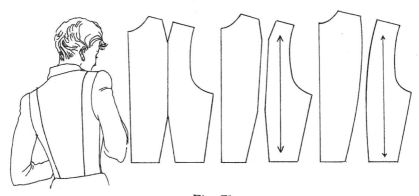

Fig. 71

Fig. 72

Divided Dart Control in the Seam

The control seam frequently works on the principle of divided dart control as in Figs. 72 and 73. For design purposes, the dart legs may be curved to conform to the style line.

Fig. 73

In Fig. 73 the remaining waistline dart control is used as unstitched fullness for a semi-fitted design. Should you wish a more fitted look, close the waistline dart so that half the amount of dart control comes off at a center-front seam, the other half at the side seam.

Fig. 74

In a *princess-style* garment, where the control is divided between shoulder and waistline, the use of the sloper dart control will result in a fitted garment (Fig. 74a). For an easier fit, use less dart control and/or shorten the shoulder and waistline darts before connecting them for a style line (Fig. 74b). Or add more seams at center front and center back using less control in each of the many seams (Fig. 74c).

To convince yourself that shaping can be done by seams instead of darts, Scotch-tape the style lines of any or all of these patterns to create bulging blocks. Test the new designs over a bulging block of closed darts. Note that the amount of dart control and the shaping have been changed in no way. Only the styling is different.

TO CONVERT THE CONTROL-SEAM
PRINCIPLE INTO A PATTERN

All of the foregoing exercises illustrate the principle of shaping by seams. To convert the exercises into patterns, follow the procedure below.

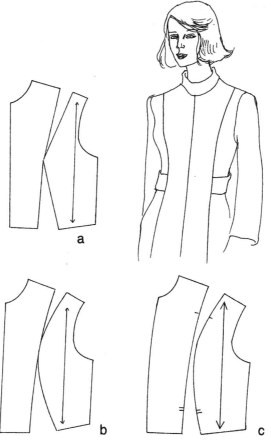

Fig. 75

1. Trace the appropriate sloper. Draw the style line incorporating the dart control. Place notches where they will facilitate assembling. (These are indicated by cross lines.)

2. Cut apart the pattern on the style line and divide the dart control in the desired amount. Fasten with Scotch tape (Fig. 75a). Establish the

grain line in each section. That of the side section is parallel to the center front.

3. Cut apart the pattern on the style line and separate the sections. Trace each on fresh paper correcting any jogs or undesired angularity (Fig. 75b). Trace the grain lines with the tracing wheel (Fig. 75c). Add seam allowances, notches, and fold of fabric.

NOTE: Since the two sections of the pattern are to be separated and cut individually in fabric, you must know how to place the side section (or any other cut-apart section) on the grain of the fabric and at what points to match the sections.

Notches are marked *before* the control is divided.

Generally, the *grain line* is marked *after* the control has been divided. It is the grain line that is the clue to how much control is in each dart. If you change the position of the grain line, you change the amount of control in the darts.

When the division of dart control does not affect the center front or center back as in the horizontal control seam of Fig. 81, the grain line may be marked *before or after* the control is divided.

When no divided dart control is involved in a control seam, the grain line is established *before* cutting apart as in Fig. 70.

THE CONTROL SEAM MOVED
OFF THE DART POINT

As with so many other rules, there are exceptions in patternmaking too. For design purposes one may take a few liberties with the position of the style line off the dart point.

For instance, *in a skirt,* the dart may be moved slightly to the center (Fig. 76a) or to the side (Fig. 76b) to create more pleasing proportions for the resulting panels.

In pants, the dart may be moved to the center front or back (Fig. 76c) to create a style line where the pants crease would ordinarily be. Such a control seam is an excellent fitting device for hard-to-fit figures.

When a control seam is moved off the dart point *in a bodice,* some auxiliary or compensatory shaping must be provided to accommodate the more pronounced body curves (Fig. 77 and Fig. 78).

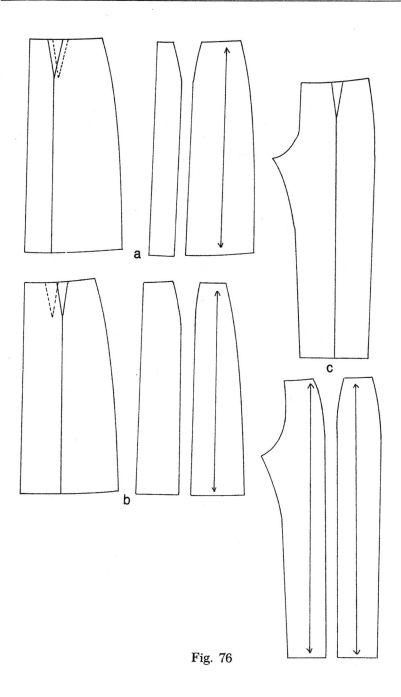

Fig. 76

THE CONTROL SEAM MOVED

Toward the Center Front

1. On the cut-out bodice-front sloper with the cut-out dart, draw the style line off the dart point toward the center front—no more than 1 inch (Fig. 77a).

2. Since no shifting of dart control is possible unless the new line is connected with the dart point, draw the connecting line at right angles to the center front. Place notch marks on the style line above and below the connecting line (Fig. 77a).

3. Slash all slash lines.

4. Close all (Fig. 77b) or part (Fig. 77c) of the waistline dart, shifting some or all of the control to the style line and the connecting line. Establish the grain in the side-front bodice parallel to the center front.

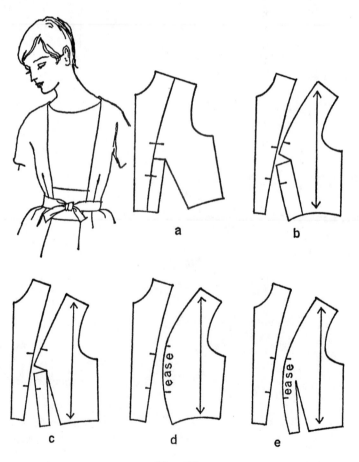

Fig. 77

5. Separate the sections. Correct any angularity.

6. Complete the pattern.

In Fig. 77b, the dart control shifted to the connecting line is eased into the center-front section between the notches (Fig. 77d).

In Fig. 77c, a small amount of dart control on the connecting-line dart is eased into the style line between the notches. The remaining waistline control is used as a dart (Fig. 77e).

As you can see, in both cases some control is retained in the side-front section to assist with the shaping that has been moved off the high point.

Toward the Side Seam

1. On the cut-out bodice-front sloper with the cut-out dart, draw the style line 2 inches or more off the dart point toward the side seam. Connect the style line with the dart point. Place notch marks on the style line as indicated (Fig. 78a).

2. Cut the sections apart. Slash the connecting line. Close the waistline dart, shifting the dart control to the style line, where it is divided between waistline and armhole, and to the connecting line, where it becomes a new dart (Fig. 78b).

3. Establish the grain in the side-front section parallel to the center front (Fig. 78b).

4. Complete the pattern.

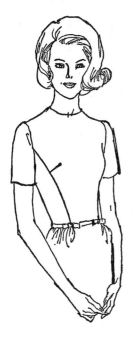

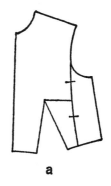

a   b

Fig. 78

NONVERTICAL CONTROL SEAMS

A control seam need not be vertical. It may be diagonal (Fig. 79a) or horizontal (Fig. 79b).

Diagonal control seams produce unusual shapes such as the diamond seaming in Fig. 79a.

A horizontal control seam creates a yoke (Fig. 79b). There are many interesting design possibilities in this kind of control. See "The Versatile Yoke," page 116.

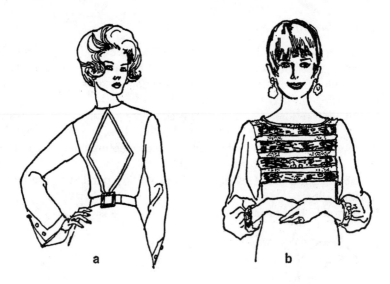

a   b

Fig. 79

A PATTERN FOR DIAGONAL CONTROL SEAMING
(as in Fig. 79a)

1. On the cut-out bodice-front sloper with the cut-out dart, draw the style line, from neck to dart point, from dart point to center-front waist-line. Place notch marks as indicated (Fig. 80a).

2. Slash the style lines.

3. Close the waistline dart, throwing the control to the style line and dividing it between neckline and waistline. Establish the grain line in both sections (Fig. 80b). If only part of the waistline dart is closed, the rest may be used as unstitched fullness as in the fashion sketch of Fig. 80.

4. Complete the pattern.

a   b

Fig. 80

A PATTERN WITH HORIZONTAL CONTROL
SEAMING (as in Fig. 79b).

1. On the cut-out bodice front with the cut-out dart, draw the horizontal style line at right angles to the center front. Make it pass across the dart point. Place notch marks on the style line as indicated (Fig. 81a).

2. Slash the style line.

3. Close all or part of the waistline dart, throwing the control to the seam line (Fig. 81b). If only part of the waistline dart is closed, the rest may be used as unstitched fullness as in the fashion sketch of Fig. 81 (Fig. 81c).

4. Complete the pattern.

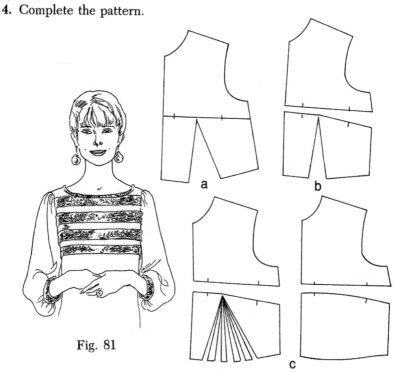

Fig. 81

A ONE-SIDED AFFAIR

Control seams may be asymmetric as they are in the clever seaming of the design in Fig. 82. Start with a complete bodice front sloper.

1. Draw the style lines, making each touch a dart. The center front of this design is on the straight grain (Fig. 82a).

Fig. 82

2. Slash the pattern on both style lines.

3. Close the waistline dart entirely for a fitted design. Divide the dart control on the style lines (Fig. 82b).

4. Close part of each dart (an equal amount) throwing some of the waistline control to each control seam. Treat the remainder as unstitched fullness (Fig. 82c).

5. Complete the pattern.

CONTROL SEAMS IN BACK, SKIRT, AND SLEEVE

The foregoing discussion of control seams has dealt with the bodice front. The principles illustrated work just as well in a bodice back, in a skirt, and in a sleeve.

THE BODICE BACK YOKE

1. On the cut-out bodice-back sloper with the cut-out darts, draw the style line for the yoke. Make it at right angles to the center back. Notch the style line (Fig. 83a).

2. Extend the shoulder dart to the style line (Fig. 83a).

3. Slash the style line.

4. Cut out the extended dart and close it. Note that the shoulder dart control is shifted to the control seam at the armhole (Fig. 83b).

5. Correct the shoulder line and the seam lines as necessary. Consider using the waistline dart control as dart tucks or gathers.

6. Complete the pattern.

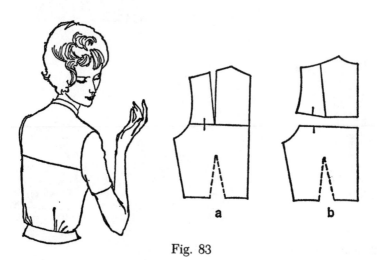

Fig. 83

FABRIC—A CONSIDERATION

The amount of dart control on the yoke seam can be placed where it will least show in the fabric.

If the yoke material is a solid color or overall design, divide the amount of the control between the yoke and the lower bodice. This will balance the grain on either side of the seam. Each seam line will then have a similar curve, making it easier to stitch (Fig. 84a).

If the fabric for the yoke is horizontally striped while the lower bodice is a solid color, overall design, or a vertical stripe, straighten the yoke seam line so it is in keeping with the straight lines of the fabric. Move all of the dart control over to the lower bodice, whose curved style line will not affect the fabric design (Fig. 84b). (This is the pattern of Fig. 81.)

If the yoke fabric is a solid color, overall design, or a vertical stripe while the lower bodice is horizontally striped, move the dart control to the yoke and straighten the seam line of the lower bodice (Fig. 84c).

The amount of the dart control remains the same whether it is placed above, placed below, or straddles the style line.

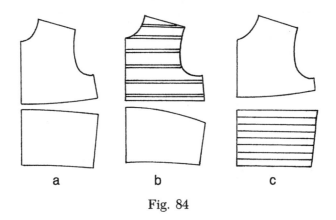

Fig. 84

. . . AND SKIRTS, TOO

The Six-Gored Skirt—three gores front, three gores back

1. Trace the skirt-front and skirt-back slopers but do not trace the darts. Eliminate the flare by straightening the side seams from the hips to hem.

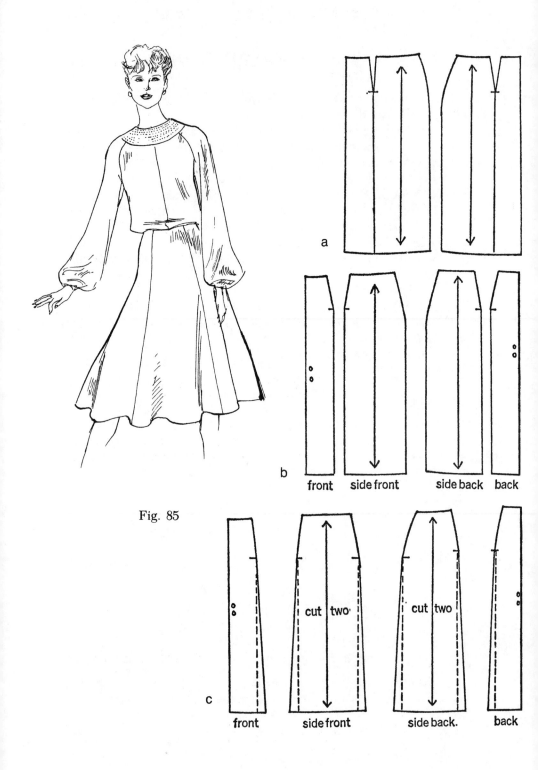

a

b

front   side front   side back   back

Fig. 85

cut two   cut two

c

front   side front   side back.   back

2. Draw gore lines one-third over from center front and center back and parallel to them (Fig. 85a).

3. Center the front and back darts on the gore lines and trace (Fig. 85a).

4. Place notch marks at the dart points. Establish the grain parallel to the center front and center back in each side-skirt section (Fig. 85a).

5. Cut out the pattern. Cut out the darts. Slash the style lines. The control now rests in the seams that join the gores—front, side front, side back, and back (Fig. 85b).

6. A more graceful skirt will result from a small amount of flare (1 to 2 inches) added at the hem of each control seam (Fig. 85c). The flare starts at the hips and extends to the hem.

7. Trace the pattern, correcting the control seam lines with slightly curved lines from the hips to waistline.

8. Label each section. The center gores are placed on a fold of fabric; cut two of each side gore (Fig. 85c).

9. Complete the pattern.

The Eight-Gored Skirt—four gores front, four gores back

Make the pattern for this skirt (Fig. 86) by the same method as the six-gored skirt with these exceptions:

1. Divide each skirt sloper in half. Divide the dart control so that two thirds of the amount is placed on the gore line and one third at the center seam. This will make for an even distribution of the control when all front and all back sections are stitched together.

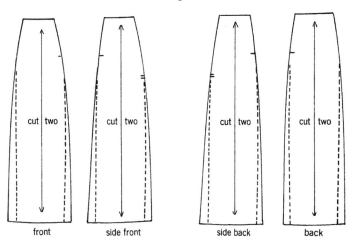

front   side front   side back   back

Fig. 86

Fig. 86

2. The center front and center back become seam lines instead of folds of fabric.

3. Add flare at center front and center back to balance the flare on the opposite control seams.

4. The grain line in each gore is parallel to the original center front and center back.

5. Cut two of each section.

6. Complete the pattern.

CONTROL SEAM IN A TWO-PIECE SLEEVE

The elbow dart control of a one-piece sleeve can be divided and shifted to the control seam of a two-piece sleeve.

1. Trace the sleeve sloper. Cut out the tracing and the dart. Shift some of the dart control to the wrist to widen it (Fig. 87a). Trace the sleeve.

2. Extend the elbow dart across the width of the sleeve (Fig. 87b). Fold it out. Fasten temporarily.

3. Draw a line dividing the sleeve in half from cap to elbow, from elbow to wrist (Fig. 87b).

4. Fold each side of the sleeve so the underarm seam touches the center line at the armhole and the wrist (Fig. 87c). Fasten with Scotch tape.

5. Locate new seam lines in the underarm section—1 inch in from the fold at the armhole, ¾ inch at the elbow, and ½ inch at the wrist (Fig. 87c). Notch the seam lines. The underarm section is generally one-third of the total width of the sleeve. Adjust the above measurements accordingly.

6. Cut away the underarm section. Unfold the elbow dart to ¼ inch (not all of its control). Completely unfold the dart in the upper sleeve (Fig. 87d). As you can see, some of the dart control has been shifted to the sleeve seam, making it a control seam. Mark an area 2 to 3 inches at the elbow of the upper sleeve to be eased into the corresponding area of the under sleeve.

7. Correct the seam lines with slightly curved lines. The grain line is the center line of each sleeve section (Fig. 87e).

8. Complete the pattern.

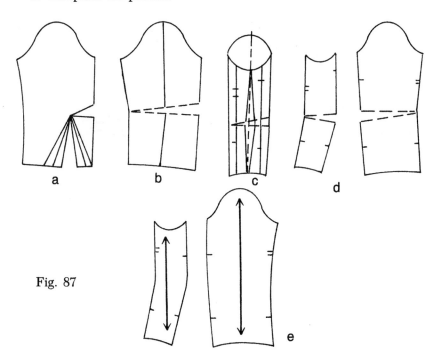

Fig. 87

Fig. 88

THE VERSATILE YOKE

The yoke is a wonderful design device. Its seaming may conceal the dart control (Fig. 88a). Where there is no control it may simply divide a bodice or skirt into interesting areas (Fig. 88b). Often, it provides a smooth, trim area in contrast to fullness in an adjoining area (Fig. 88c). It is a common device for separating a highly decorative area from a very plain one (Fig. 88d).

Fig. 89

When a yoke appears in a lower bodice, it produces a fitted midriff (Fig. 89a). A hip yoke in skirt or pants provides smooth fit (Fig. 89b and 89c).

There are partial yokes (Fig. 89d), yokes in one with panels (Fig. 89e), and yokes in one with sleeves (Fig. 89f). And, this has not begun to exhaust the endless possibilities or indicate the great versatility of the yoke.

SOME SUGGESTIONS FOR DESIGNING YOKES

Remember that an equal division of an area is not nearly as interesting as an unequal division.

Use lines appropriate for the fabric. A solid-color fabric may have straight or curved lines. Use straight lines for stripes, checks, or plaids.

Relate the shape of the yoke to the shape of other style lines in the garment.

FOR DESIGN PURPOSES ONLY—
Yokes That Do Not Involve Dart Control

On the appropriate sloper, draw the style line, place notch marks, establish the grain, cut apart.

When there is no control in the yoke seam, the entire amount of dart control may be used decoratively below the yoke.

As Gathers (Fig. 90a)

1. Draw the yoke style line on the bodice-front sloper. Notch the style line. Cut the yoke from the lower bodice.

2. On the lower bodice draw slash lines from the dart point to the yoke and from the dart point to the waistline.

3. Slash all slash lines. Divide the control for gathers between the waistline and the yoke style line.

4. Complete the pattern.

As Multiple Darts (Fig. 90b)

1. Draw the yoke style line on the bodice-front sloper. Mark notches.

2. Draw the position of the darts. Connect them with the dart point.

3. Cut the yoke away.

4. Slash the dart lines to the dart point. Shift the control to the new darts, dividing it equally between them. Draw new dart legs.

5. Complete the pattern.

a   b

Fig. 90

YOKES THAT DO INVOLVE DART CONTROL

A Skirt Yoke

1. Trace the skirt-front sloper. Cut out the tracing and the dart.

2. Draw the style line of the yoke and notch it. Extend the waistline dart to the yoke style line (Fig. 91a).

3. Cut the yoke away from the lower skirt. Close the extended dart (Fig. 91b). Note that the dart control appears in the seam that joins the yoke with the lower skirt.

4. Correct the waistline with a smooth curved line. Correct the seam line of the hip yoke (Fig. 91b).

5. Complete the pattern.

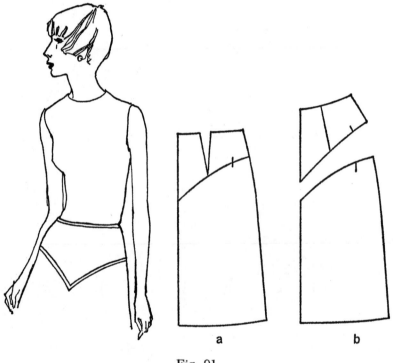

a   b

Fig. 91

A Midriff Yoke

Variations of the midriff yoke are understandably popular. They are a great way to emphasize a slim midriff and small waist while retaining the shaping of the upper bodice.

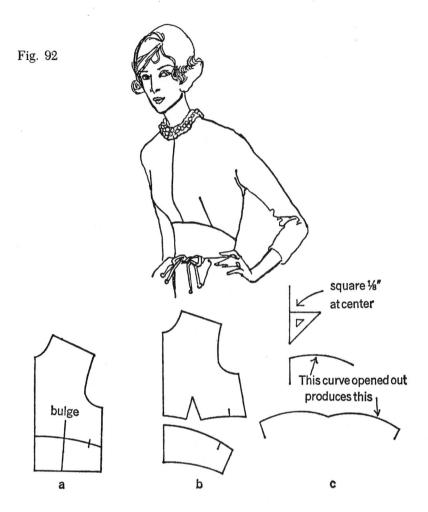

Fig. 92

square ⅛″
at center

This curve opened out
produces this

bulge

a   b   c

1. On a bulging-block bodice with the bulge away from you, draw the yoke style line* and notch it (Fig. 92a).

2. Cut away the yoke. Open the remaining dart control on the bodice (Fig. 92b). This may be used as one dart, multiple darts, pleats, or gathers. Note that the dart control has been split three ways: as a bodice dart, in the control seam, and on the yoke side seam.

3. Complete the pattern.

---

* Whenever drawing a curved style line from the center-front or center-back position, first square a short line (⅛ inch) at the center line. This assures a smooth, continuous curve. If you do not do this, you may discover a point or dip at center when the material is opened out (Fig. 92c).

Call attention to *your* beautiful midriff. Bare it by simply cutting away the midriff yoke from the upper bodice. (Fig. 93).

Fig. 93

A YOKE THAT DOESN'T QUITE MAKE IT—A PARTIAL YOKE

Here is a yoke that is cut only part way from the rest of the bodice. The pattern is all in one piece.

Shift the waistline dart control (Fig. 94a) entirely (Fig. 94b) or in part (Fig. 94c) to the partial yoke line. It looks best when used as soft pleats or gathers.

Since there is practically no seam allowance at the point where the slashing stops, you must provide a facing for this area. (A 1-inch patch of very sheer material in a matching color is best.) When the facing is stitched, turned to the underside, and pressed to position, it becomes the seam allowance.

Fig. 94

STITCH AND REJOIN—DESIGN POSSIBILITIES

If you have to stitch two or more sections of a garment together to form a complete unit, why not make decorative use of the parts and the seaming that joins them?

Use every trick in the bag: color, texture, grain, topstitching, decorative applications, insertions of lace or edgings, pipings to insert in the seam, bandings to apply over the seam, insertions of belts, pockets, welts. In fact, use anything your unleashed fancy and ingenuity can devise. The sky's the limit! See Fig. 95.

Fig. 95

Fig. 96

REPEAT PERFORMANCE—SIMILAR SEAMS

In design, a degree of repetition makes for harmony. The eye is pleased to see a line it has met before. (Too much repetition can become monotonous. Plan just enough.)

In Fig. 96 each of the designs features a pair or trio of similar seam lines. One of the seams is a control seam. The other (or others) has been added for emphasis. It is purely decorative. Can you tell which carries the dart control? Yes, it is the one that comes closest to the apex of the bust.

In Fig. 96a the dart control appears in the lower seam, leaving the band intact.

In Fig. 96b the inset band is developed in the same way.

In Fig. 96c it is the upper seam that is the control seam.

In Fig. 96d the horizontal center seam of the jacket carries part of the dart control. The rest remains as unstitched control at the waistline for the boxy design.

In Figs. 96a, 96b, and 96c the shape of the inset band is interesting by itself. Topstitching would give even more importance to its lines. Or the band could be a contrasting color or texture or both. The dresses would be very effective if the three sections were in gradations of the same color (for example, a warm beige, apricot, and orange) or in contrasting colors (for example, red, white, and blue).

TO MAKE THE PATTERNS FOR FIG. 96

It is easier to work each of these designs on the bulging block. Where necessary, elongate or shorten the waistline dart so it touches the style line of the band. (Fig. 97).

1. On the bulging block, with the bulge away from you, draw the style lines. Make them parallel. Notch them.

2. Cut the sections apart.

3. Shift all or part of the waistline dart control to the appropriate seam. Establish the grain line in each section.

4. Trace the pattern, correcting seam lines as necessary. Add seam allowances. Label each section.

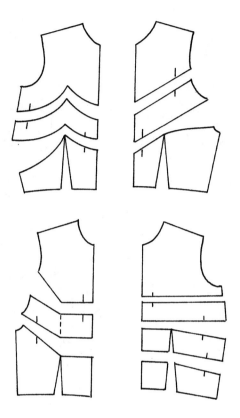

Fig. 97

Fig.

FASHION-IN-THE-ROUND

Though the exercises in this chapter limited the number of divisions of dart control (after all, we were only taking our first baby steps in pattern design), in truth, the number is limitless. Any number will do to create fashion-in-the-round. Be guided by the elements of good design.

What a superbly fitting and slimming dress is the Jean Patou in Fig. 98a. See how many ways the total control has been divided in the vertical seaming.

If you think multiple dart tucks are fuddy-duddy, just study the fascinating midriff of this Pierre Cardin design (Fig. 98b).

Notice how ingeniously the ribbon stripe of the material has been used for the shaping with multiple control seams (Fig. 98c).

These are but a tiny sampling of the infinite design possibilities of control seaming. Do they whet your appetite?

PATTERN WISE

So now you know all the ins and outs of dart control from top to bottom and all the way around. Each new design is a puzzle to be worked out. That's the fun and challenge of patternmaking. It's ever different with each passing season and changing fashion. But the principles of dart control remain the same.

When it comes to dart control in design—you're now on your own!

Chapter 6

The Fullness Thereof

Perhaps the biggest fashion change in recent years has been based on the needs of today's active woman. Whether at work (as so many are), at home, or at play, her new freedom calls for attractive clothes that move with graceful ease while she performs the varied activities of each day. (Evening clothes are another matter.) That means that most clothes require more ease and more fullness than that contained in the basic sloper, however cleverly its dart control is manipulated to give the illusion of relaxed fit (Fig. 99).

There are two types of additional fullness: circular and balanced. The fullness can be gathered, shirred, smocked, or laid in pleats or folds; it can be tucked or held in place with elastic threaded through a casing.

Fig. 99

a

b

Fig. 100

In *circular fullness* (Fig. 100a), there is a change in one edge only. The other maintains the original measurement. (This is the fullness of a flared or circle skirt.)

In *balanced fullness* (Fig. 100b), there is equal change on both edges. (This is the fullness of a dirndl or knife-pleated skirt.)

Wherever found—in blouses, skirts, pants, sleeves, jackets, coats, capes, collars, cuffs, peplums and the like—the methods of producing fullness in patterns are the same.

SLASH AND SPREAD FOR CIRCULAR FULLNESS

1. On paper of sufficient size for the completed pattern draw a rectangle and divide it into equal parts (Fig. 101a). The more circular the design, the more parts you will need to establish the outside style line of the pattern (Fig. 101b).

2. Slash each of the dividing lines *to* one edge but not through it. Start the slashing at the edge you want to make full. (The slash must go clear across the pattern to the opposite side. Only then will the pattern lie flat. A partial slash when spread produces bulging and straining.)

3. While maintaining the measurement of one edge, spread the other to the desired fullness, making sure to leave equal spaces between the strips (Fig. 101c). In circularity, the fullness spreads open like a fan. If spread sufficiently, a complete circle is obtained (Fig. 101d).

4. Using the strips as a guide, draw the new (full) edge with a curved line.

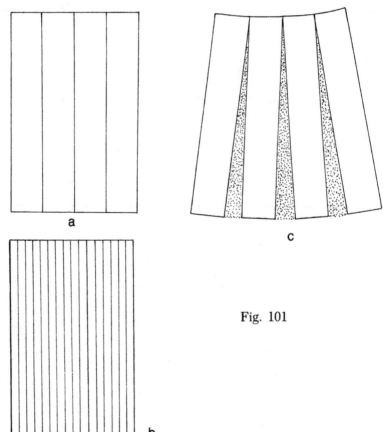

a

b

c

Fig. 101

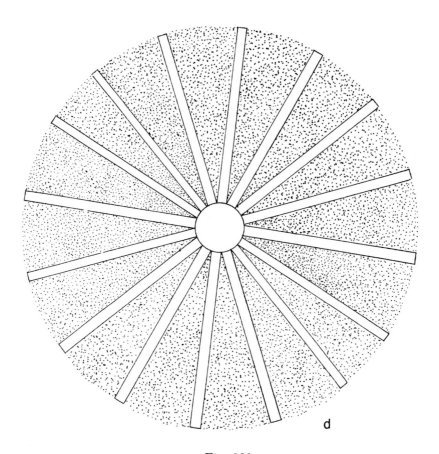

d

Fig. 101

SLASH AND SPREAD FOR BALANCED FULLNESS

1. On paper of sufficient size draw a rectangle and divide it into equal parts.

2. Draw a horizontal guideline at right angles to one side (Fig. 102a). This is necessary so that you will know how to line up the strips after they have been cut apart and separated. When shaped pattern strips are involved it is also a good plan to number them so that you will know in what order to put them together again (see Fig. 120a & b).

3. Slash all slash lines.

4. On another sheet of paper of sufficient size (considering the projected fullness), draw a horizontal guideline.

5. Place the strips of paper in the correct order, matching the guidelines, and spread to the desired fullness (Fig. 102b). The guideline acts as a skewer on which all the little strips are speared in position. Make certain that the spaces between the strips are equal at both top and bottom.

6. Trace the outline (across the open spaces), correcting any lines as necessary.

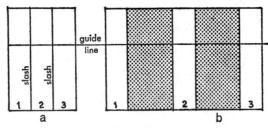

Fig. 102

How much you spread the sections for any type of fullness—circular or balanced—depends on the design and the fabric you plan to use. You may have to do some experimenting before you decide just what the fullness should be.

Unless the fabric to be used is extremely wide or the size of the pattern extremely small, the material will likely need to be *pieced for extra width or length*. The piecing must look like an extension of the fabric. The added piece must be cut on the same grain. If there is a decorative weave or print, it is desirable that the motifs match. The piecing must be placed in such position that it will be lost in the folds of a full section (Fig. 103a) or in the depths of a pleat or tuck where it will not show (Fig. 103b).

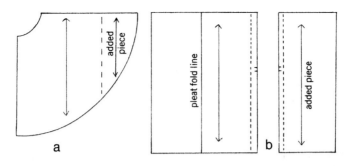

Fig. 103

PATTERNS WITH CIRCULAR FULLNESS

At a Bodice Waistline

1. Start with the bodice-front pattern that has unstitched dart control at the waistline. Use the fullness provided by the dart control as a base whenever possible (Fig. 104a).

2. Draw slash lines parallel to the center front (Fig. 104a).

3. Slash and spread to the desired fullness. Start the slashing at the waistline. Add half the amount of the spread at the center front so the fullness is continuous across the entire bodice (Fig. 104b). This line becomes the new center front.

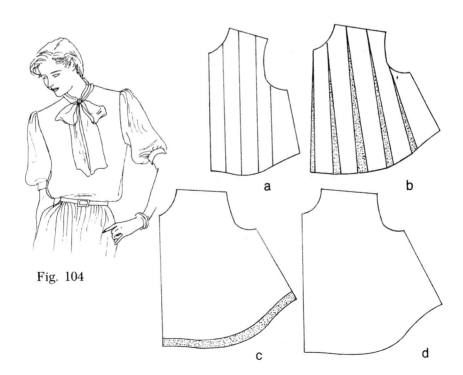

Fig. 104

4. Trace the pattern. Unless you want a taut look to your design, *add length for blousiness* along the entire waistline (Fig. 104c). Designs with width fullness generally require added length as well.

5. Trace the pattern (Fig. 104d) and complete it.

At the Hem of a Skirt

1. Trace the skirt-front or skirt-back sloper. Fold out the dart or darts from waistline to hem. Trace the new pattern (Fig. 105a).

2. Divide the skirt pattern into equal parts at waistline and hem. Draw slash lines (Fig. 105b).

3. Slash each slash line starting at the hem and ending at the waistline.

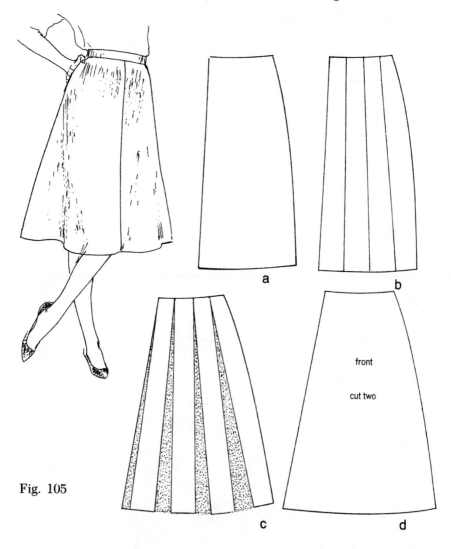

Fig. 105

a

b

front

cut two

c

d

Spread the hem to the desired fullness. Add half the amount of the spread at the center front or back for continuous fullness (Fig. 105c).

4. Trace the pattern (Fig. 105d) and complete it.

At the Hem of Pants

Work out the pattern for the pants in the same way as for the skirt. Add half the amount of spread at the side and inseams. See Fig. 106.

Fig. 106

FASHION COMES FULL CIRCLE

Now you know the theory of adding fullness to the sweep of a skirt. For practical purposes all you need to know is the waist measurement and the length.

HOW TO MAKE THE PATTERN
FOR A CIRCLE SKIRT

1. Draw a rectangle (*half* the front-waistline measurement by the length of the skirt).

2. Divide it into equal parts—at least six, preferably more.

3. Slash and spread the strips for circularity against a right angle so that the center front and the side seam are on straight grain (vertical and horizontal) while the areas between them are on the bias (Fig. 107).

4. Trace the pattern, correcting the angularity of waistline and hemline with curved lines. The center front is generally placed on a fold of fabric. When the skirt front is opened out it will be half a circle.

5. Complete the pattern. Cut two for a complete circle.

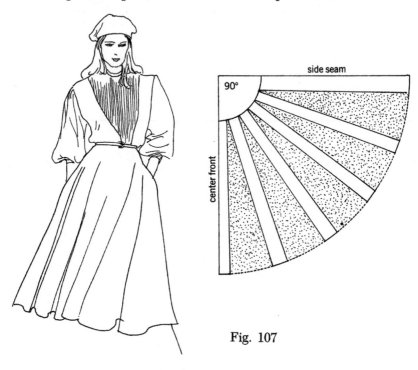

Fig. 107

FOR A DOUBLE-CIRCLE SKIRT

Use a whole circle for the front and a whole circle for the back. To make this pattern you would need to quarter the waistline measurement and proceed as for the circle skirt.

HOW TO MAKE THE PATTERN FOR A SEMICIRCLE SKIRT—Fig. 108

1. Start with a rectangle the sides of which are equal to the *full* front-waistline measurement and the length of the skirt.

2. Divide it into equal parts—at least six, preferably more.

3. On another sheet of paper, draw a right angle.

4. Slash the pattern. Spread the strips for circularity against the right angle so that the side seams will be on straight grain, one vertical, the other horizontal. The center front and back will be on the bias.

5. Trace the pattern, correcting the angularity of waistline and hemline with curved lines.

6. Complete the pattern. Cut two—one front, one back.

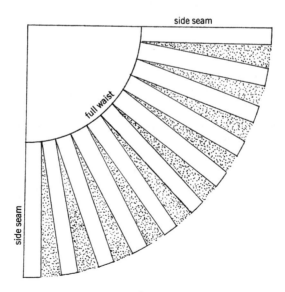

Fig. 108

A NOTE ON WAISTBANDS

The narrower a straight waistband, the better it will hug the waist. Waistbands of 1 inch or 1½ inches work best. When they are wider than this, some shaping is necessary to fit the curve of the waist. Such a waistband is drafted like a midriff yoke or hip yoke. A ¾-inch bias waistband works well.

The length of the waistband is equal to the waist measurement plus ease, plus seam allowances when zippered to the top of the band. When an underlap or overlap is used, add an allowance (about 1½ inches) for the extension.

Trouser waistbands are made in two pieces—a right and a left. Each is as long as the measurement from center back to the front edge of the fly plus seam allowances.

Waistbands are generally cut on the straight of the material. When cut on the bias a correction must be made to allow for the bias-stretch of the material. (See following discussion.)

CORRECTED WAISTLINE MEASUREMENT AND WAISTBAND FOR CIRCULAR SKIRT

A considerable portion of a circular skirt is bias. All bias areas stretch. There is the additional pull on the waistline by the weight of the material. Therefore, in reckoning the length of the waistline, make it 1 inch to 2 inches less than the actual body measurement. How much will depend on the amount of fullness and the heaviness of the fabric.

This corrected measurement also tends to make the skirt fit more smoothly over the hips by lowering the point at which the folds or ripples start.

Stretch the new skirt waistline to fit the skirt band whose measurements are in no way changed unless the band is cut on the bias. In the latter case, the measurement for the bias band would be that of the corrected circular-skirt waistline.

The following patterns show circular fullness. Can you follow the diagrams?

At the Waistline of a Peg-top Skirt (Fig. 109) (or Pants)

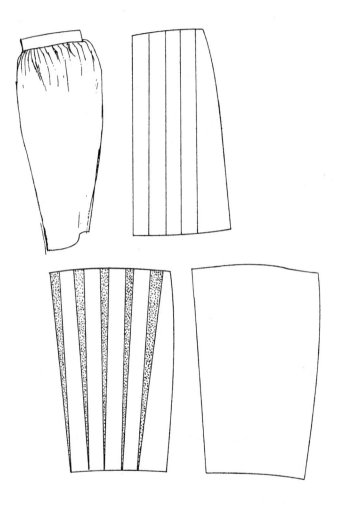

Fig. 109

At a Neckline (Fig. 110)

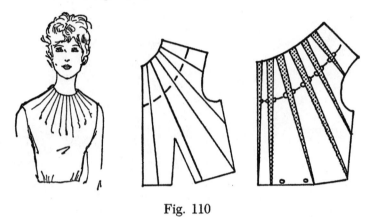

Fig. 110

At the Cap of a Sleeve (Fig. 111)

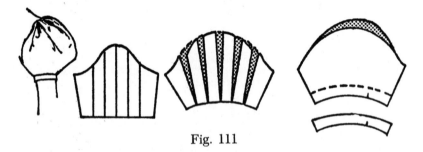

Fig. 111

At a Sleeve Band (Fig. 112)

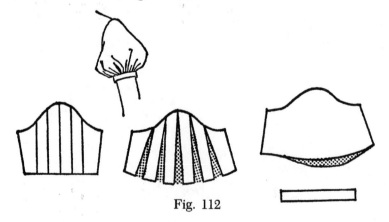

Fig. 112

Below a Bodice Yoke (Fig. 113)

Fig. 113

Below a Hip Yoke (Fig. 114)

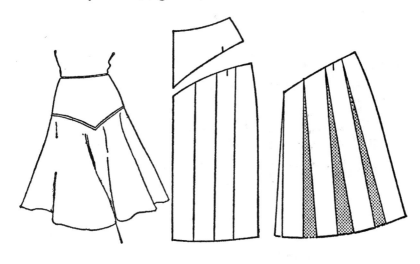

Fig. 114

Above a Midriff (Fig. 115)

Fig. 115

CIRCULARITY VIA GORES AND GODETS

The fit and flare of these designs equals more than the sum of their parts. Each section cut on straight grain accounts for the slim hang. Circularity at the hem provides the graceful swing.

THE MANY-GORED SKIRT

1. Start with the pattern for a flared, semicircle, or circle skirt.

2. Divide the waistline and the hemline into equal parts. Draw slash lines. Notch for easy assembling (Fig. 116a).

3. Cut the sections apart. Fold each gore in half. The center line is the grain line. Make certain that the gores are balanced on each side (Fig. 116b).

There are two ways of deciding the number and size of the gores.

1. Divide the entire waistline and hemline measurement into the de-

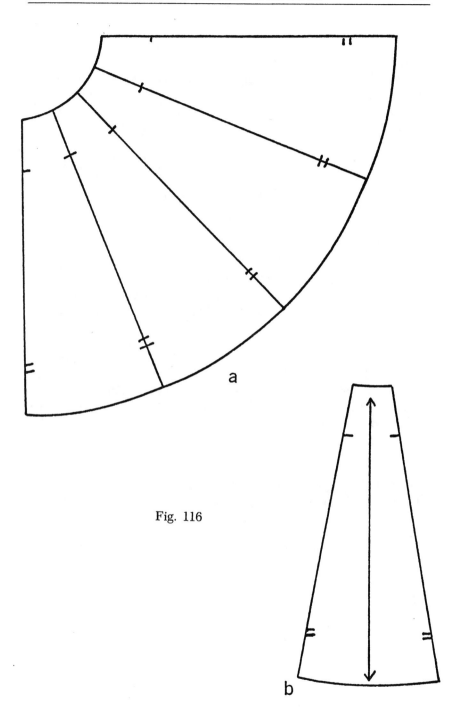

Fig. 116

sired number of gores. This produces a symmetrical skirt with each gore equal to the next both front and back.

2. Divide the front waistline measurement into the desired number of gores. Divide the back waistline measurement into the same number of gores. Each pattern is done separately because the front measurement is larger than the back. The number may be the same but the size is slightly different.

THE TRUMPET SKIRT

Flare added to each gore produces the trumpet skirt.

1. Start with a straight or flared gore, decide where the flare is to begin—at the hips, mid-thigh, knee, mid-calf, or any place between.
2. Draw a line across the gore to indicate the beginning of the flare.

Fig. 117a. Decide how much flare is to be added to each side of the gore at the hem. Be mindful of the fact that a few inches at each side of a many-gored skirt adds up to quite a bit of fullness in the finished skirt. Draw a curved seam line, blending it into the sides of the gores.

Fig. 117b. Divide the gore into thirds lengthwise. Draw the flare line across the gore. Slash and spread above the flare line to the desired fullness. Add fullness below the flare line as illustrated. Draw the side seams, correcting the angularity.

Fig. 117c. Draw the flare line. Divide the gore below it into thirds. Slash and spread for flare. Draw the side seams correcting the angularity.

3. Add seam allowance and notches to each gore. Draw the grain line, which is in the center of each gore.

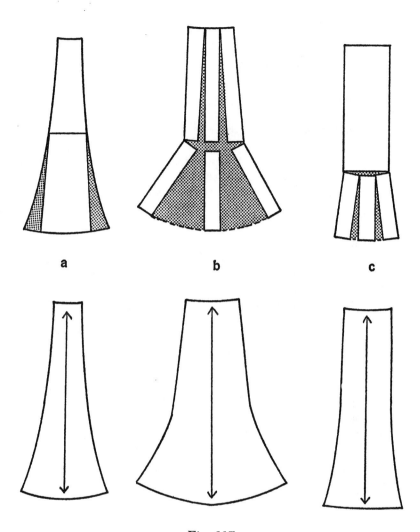

Fig. 117

SEAM OR SLASH FULLNESS: THE GODET

A godet can be added to the edge of a skirt, sleeve, peplum, collar, or any other part of a garment by setting a section of cloth into a seam, dart, slash, or cutout of the garment. It lends flounce, flair, and flip to an otherwise straight style.

The godet is a section of a circle (from the triangular pie shape to semicircle), the radius of which is the length of the godet and the arc of which is the hemline. The top of the godet can be pointed (the usual type) (Fig. 118a), rounded (Fig. 118b), or squared (Fig. 118c). It can be pleated (Fig. 118d). It can contain another godet within its folds (Fig. 118e) or more than one.

The center of the godet is generally on straight grain though it could be bias for design purposes.

Fig. 118

A CURVE THAT COMES TO YOU STRAIGHT

Another way to achieve circularity is by a slash-and-overlap method, the exact reverse of the slash-and-spread procedure. This is a useful method if you know the length of cloth you have to work with.

1. Start with paper of the given length. Divide it into equal parts.
2. Slash each slash line. This time start the slashing at the edge you want to make smaller.
3. While maintaining the larger edge, overlap the other to the desired measurement. Make certain that the amount of the overlap is equal on each of the strips (Fig. 119a).
4. Trace the new lines, correcting the angularity with a curved line.
5. Complete the pattern.

ANOTHER WAY TO GET A CURVE—BY DARTS

A straight length of material is sufficiently *darted* at the edge you want to make smaller will also produce the circularity of Fig. 119b. This is a good method to use when you have a length of fabric that you do not wish to cut—for example, heirloom lace. Or when you do not have enough material for a pattern with circular fullness (which does take more). Or if you are using a border print.

When the darts are stitched only part way into the width, the result is a bell shape. (Curved darts produce beautiful bell shapes.)

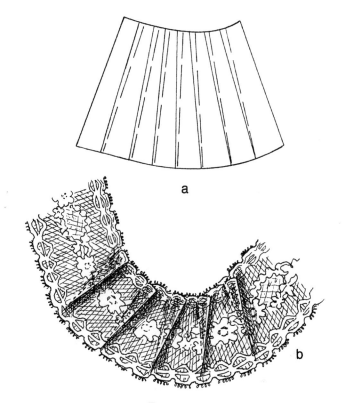

a

b

Fig. 119

BALANCED FULLNESS

For a Bodice

1. Start with the bodice sloper with unstitched dart control at the waistline.

2. Draw slash lines parallel to the center front. Draw a guideline at right angles to it. Number the sections (Fig. 120a).

3. On another sheet of paper draw a guideline of sufficient length for the expanded pattern.

4. Slash and spread for fullness (Fig. 120b):

    a. Spread sections 1, 2, 3, 4 for balanced fullness.

    b. Spread sections 5 and 6 for circular fullness in order to keep the fullness continuous at the waistline without enlarging the armhole.

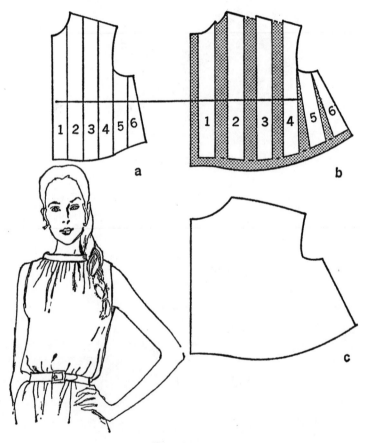

Fig. 120

    c. Add half the amount of the spread at the center front for continuous fullness.

    5. Add length for blousiness (Fig. 120b).

    6. Trace the pattern, correcting all seam lines as necessary with appropriate curves (Fig. 120c).

    7. Complete the pattern.

The amount of added fullness may be anything suitable for the design and material to be used.

The bodice back is done in the same way.

For a Puffed Sleeve (Fig. 121)

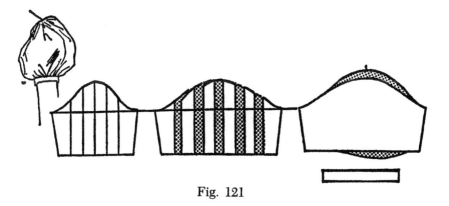

Fig. 121

For Gathers Below a Bodice Yoke (Fig. 122)

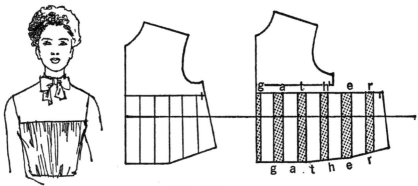

Fig. 122

For a Dirndl Skirt (Fig. 123)

Cut the pattern to the following dimensions: the waist measurement times the amount of desired fullness (twice, three times, and so on) by the length of the skirt. Add the depth of the hem and seam allowances on all outside edges.

Fig. 123

For Balloon Pants (Fig. 124)

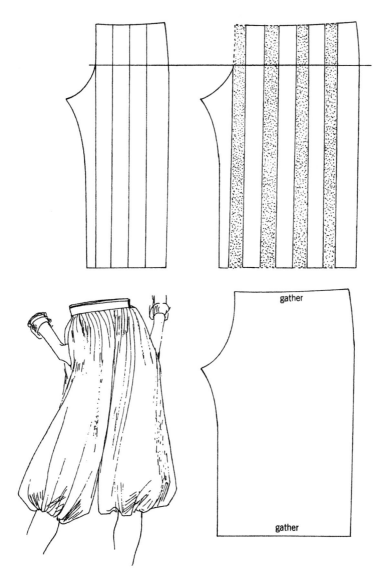

Fig. 124

For a Tiered Skirt (Fig. 125)

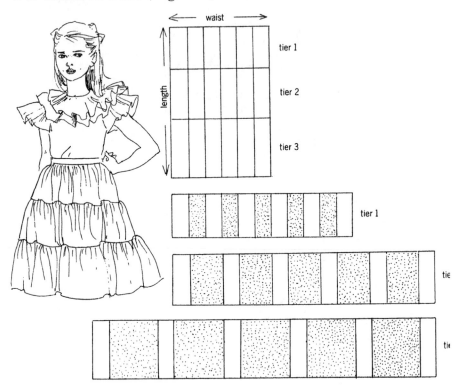

Fig. 125

For Gathers Below a Hip Yoke (Fig. 126)

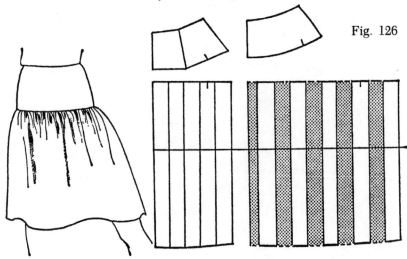

Fig. 126

For a Skirt Flounce (Fig. 127)

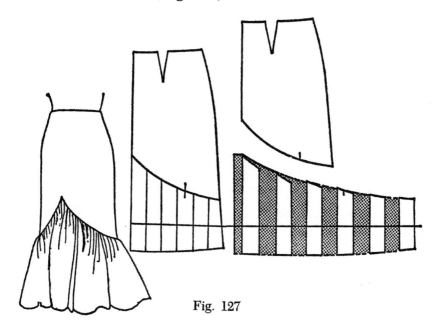

Fig. 127

COMBINATIONS AND PERMUTATIONS

Additional fullness need not be vertical or balanced on an axis (both sides the same). It may be horizontal, diagonal, or asymmetrical. Nor need it be limited to one type of fullness only. It may be balanced as well as circular.

Front Fullness

While balanced on the center front, this design has both horizontal and diagonal circular fullness.

Draft the V-neckline on the hip-length sloper (see pages 191 and 211). Close and Scotch-tape the waistline dart to create a bulging-block pattern. With the bulge away from you, draw the horizontal and diagonal slash lines as illustrated in Fig. 128. Slash and spread to the desired fullness.

Fig. 128

Asymmetric Fullness

Draft the asymmetric neckline on a complete bodice-front sloper. See page 219. Close the waistline darts and Scotch-tape them to create a bulging-block pattern. With the bulge away from you, draw three slash lines from left side seam to the opposite side as illustrated in Fig. 129. Note that the upper slash touches the left dart point, the lower one the right. Slash and spread until the new neckline lies directly on the horizontal grain. In doing so, one takes advantage of the no-ripple, no-stretch straight grain for the surplice line.

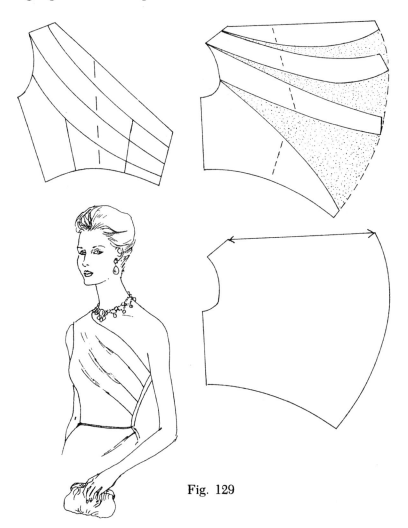

Fig. 129

For a Draped Bodice

Draft the dropped neckline on a hip-length sloper (see pages 190 and 211). Close and Scotch-tape the waistline dart to create a bulging-block pattern. With the bulge away from you, draw the horizontal slash lines as illustrated. Draw a vertical guide line. Slash and spread to the desired fullness. See Fig. 130.

Fig. 130

For Diagonal Drapery

Following the diagram in Fig. 131 and using the above techniques for a draped bodice, create the pattern for this draped bare-shouldered evening dress. Place slash lines in the direction of the drapery.

Fig. 131

STAY THE FULLNESS

Gathered, pleated, or shirred fullness looks best when it is controlled in some way. Otherwise its beauty is lost in a general overall bigness.

Often a stay is used to hold the fullness in place. The stay is a lining cut to the pattern shape before it is slashed and spread. A stay is shaped by darts and control seam.

COMBINATIONS OF BALANCED
AND CIRCULAR FULLNESS

For a Gathered Circle or Semicircle Skirt

First spread the cut-apart strips as for balanced fullness in the amount desired at the waistline. Then spread for circularity against a square (Fig. 132).

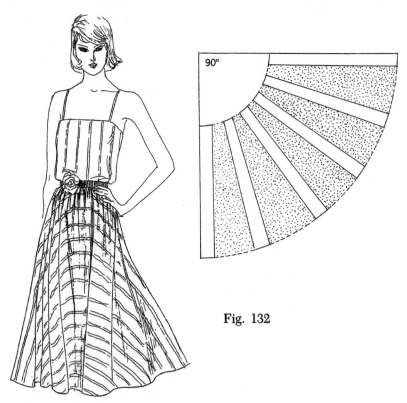

Fig. 132

Pleats for Additional Fullness

Pleats are a way of adding controlled fullness to provide grace of movement as well as design interest. They are folds of fabric made by doubling the material on itself. This forms a section of three thicknesses which are stitched as one along the side which will be attached to another section of the garment.

Pleats may either hang free for their entire length or be stitched part way. They may be made singly, in clusters, or in a series. They may be balanced or flared, pressed or unpressed, stitched or unstitched, shallow or deep. Pleats may be formed and stitched either on the right or on the wrong side of the garment, depending on the garment's design and the type of pleat.

Some fabrics lend themselves better to one type of pleat than to another. Sharp pleats require firm, closely woven fabrics. Unpressed pleats can be done in any fabric but are best in soft fabrics. Knitted fabrics and crease-resistant finishes on fabrics make pleating difficult. Soft fabrics and wash-and-wear fabrics (except of the permanent-press type) won't hold pleats. For such fabrics, edgestitching both front and back folds will ensure that the pleats stay in. Edgestitching also crispens soft edges. Some pleats (accordion, sunburst, or crystal) should be done by commercial pleaters.

It is easier to crease, press, or stitch a pleat if it is cut on the lengthwise grain and if its fullness is balanced top and bottom. Pleats cut on the crosswise grain tend to stand out more stiffly. However, this would have to be the case with most border prints. Part of a flared pleat is always cut off-grain. For this reason a flared pleat is generally a soft fold of fabric. Another method for dealing with flared pleats is to cut each pleat separately on the straight grain (see Fig. 149). By stitching the sections together one can achieve great circularity without throwing off the grain too much in each pleat. This is also a good way to handle striped, plaid, or checked fabric.

MEET THE PLEAT

The following are the most frequently used pleats.

A *side pleat* is fabric folded to one side. The fold may be in either direction (Fig. 133a).

Knife pleats are crisply pressed, even pleats of any size, folded so they all go in one direction (Fig. 133b).

When folds of two equal side pleats meet at the center on the right side, the pleat is called an *inverted pleat* (Fig. 133c).

A *box pleat* is just the reverse of an inverted pleat. The folds turn in opposite directions on the right side and meet at the center on the wrong side (Fig. 133d).

A *kick pleat* is a side or inverted pleat used near the hemline of a narrow skirt to provide walking room (Fig. 133e).

Kilt pleats are large vertical side pleats, each one overlapping half the next one in a one-way series (Fig. 133f).

A *released pleat* is one that is stitched part way on either the right or wrong side, releasing its unpressed fullness below the end of the stitching (Fig. 133g).

Fig. 133

There are also make-believe pleats (simulated pleats)—simply lines pressed or stitched to imitate a pleat but not constructed like one. They are really feats of dressmaking. When used as part of the styling, they must be so indicated on the pattern. *Umbrella pleats* (Fig. 134a) fall in this category. The flared seams or lines, pressed or stitched close to the edge, suggest the rib lines of an umbrella. *Cartridge pleats* are rounded pleats, extending out from the garment rather than lying flat against it as most pleats do. They resemble a cartridge belt (Fig. 134b). They are used strictly for decorative effect.

a

b

Fig. 134

HOW DEEP A PLEAT?

Generally, each pleat takes three times its width: the pleat (as it appears on the surface), the underfold (turn-under), the underlay (return) (Fig. 135a).

Sheer fabrics may have shallow pleats. Heavy fabrics require deep pleats.

It is possible to achieve much greater fullness by making the turn-under and the return much deeper than the pleat itself (Fig. 135b). The

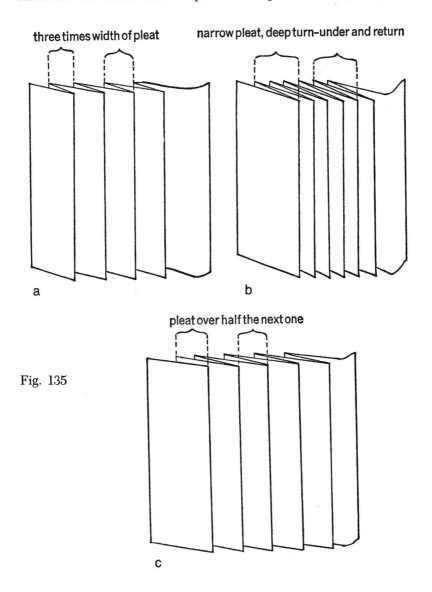

Fig. 135

kilt pleat is an example of this type of pleating: a large pleat overlaps half the next one in a one-way series (Fig. 135c).

A good way to use a vast amount of material so it looks comparatively trim is to gather a pleated length.

TUCKS FOR TRIM

Tucks are a kind of pleat but they are *stitched folds of fabric* used to hold the fullness in place. Tucks may be narrow, quite wide, or any width between. They may be used singly, in clusters, or in a series. The series may be of uniform or graduated width.

Tucks of themselves are a decorative feature of a design but they can be further enhanced with any of an assortment of edgings (Fig. 136a). Just be sure to leave sufficient space between the tucks for the width of the edging.

While generally done on the lengthwise grain of the fabric which is firmer (Fig. 136b), tucks may also be made on the crosswise grain (Fig. 136c) or on the diagonal (Fig. 136d). Nor need they always be straight; they may be slightly curved.

The procedure for developing a pattern for tucks is the same as that for pleats.

Fig. 136

PLEAT MEETS

Pairs of markings are needed for each pleat—one line for the fold of the pleat (fold line), the other for the line to which the fold is brought (placement line). The term "roll line" is used for pleats that will form soft folds; the term "fold line" is used for crisp or edgestitched pleats.

The markings may be either large O's and small o's (Fig. 137a) or solid lines and directional arrows (Fig. 137b). Both may be supported by printed directions: "Bring large O's to meet small o's" or "Pleat . . . band meets."

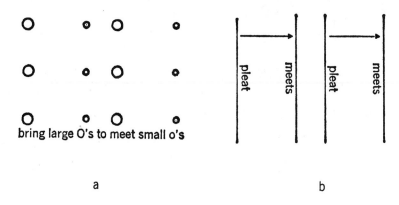

bring large O's to meet small o's

a   b

Fig. 137

PRETTY PLEATS

Pattern for Pleated Skirt

1. Trace the skirt sloper but do not trace the dart. Measure the amount of dart control and make a note of it.

2. Draw slash lines for the pleats parallel to the center front and/or center back. Draw a guide line at right angles to the center line (Fig. 138a). Draw a guide line on another piece of paper large enough for the enlarged pattern.

3. Slash the pleat lines and spread for the depth of each pleat, with the guidelines matching (Fig. 138b).

4. There are several ways in which the skirt dart control can be absorbed in the control seams of the pleats:

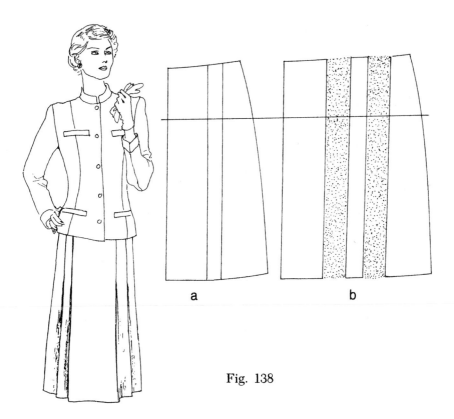

a   b

Fig. 138

Method 1. Take off half the amount of dart control on each of the two pleats *on the placement line.* Correct the angularity with a curved line (Fig. 139a). Bring the straight fold line to the curved placement line for the stitching.

Method 2. Take off half the amount of the dart control on each of the two pleats, dividing it *between the fold line and the placement line* (Fig. 139b). Correct the angularity on both lines which now become curved seam lines.

Method 3. Place all the dart control *on only one of the pleats* leaving the other intact (Fig. 139c).

In each case, the dart control is concealed in the control seams of the pleats. Which method you choose depends on the figure, the fabric, and the design of the garment.

5. Fold each pleat into position. Fasten with pins or Scotch tape. Trace the waistline seam. Unfold the pattern and sketch in the traced lines.

If the pattern is too wide for the fabric or the layout, cut it apart at any convenient place. Just be sure that the joining seam is buried in the depth of the pleat.

6. Mark the fold lines, the placement lines, and end of stitching on each pleat. Add seam allowances, fold of fabric, and grain line.

NOTE: The curved control seams necessitate a cutting away of the underpart of each pleat in order for the skirt to fit trimly in the waist-to-hip area. This is also a good way to eliminate the bulk of the several layers of cloth involved in the forming of the pleats.

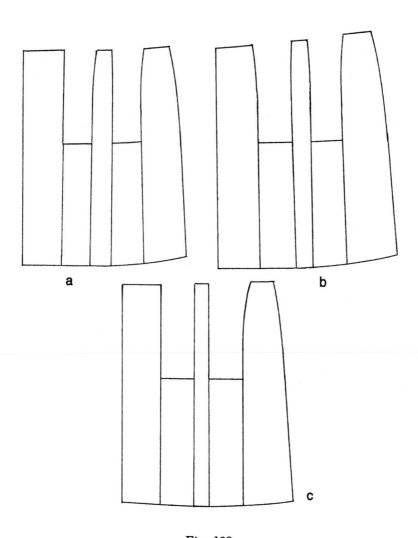

Fig. 139

WAYS OF ELIMINATING BULK
IN A PLEATED GARMENT

When the fullness of a pleat is released below a line of stitching, it is possible to eliminate one of the two thicknesses that comprise the under-part of the pleat above the stitching. The second thickness acts as a stay. With this construction, the pleat hangs well and no outside stitching is required to hold it in place.

Bulk can be eliminated in the pattern (Fig. 140a) or after stitching (Fig. 140b).

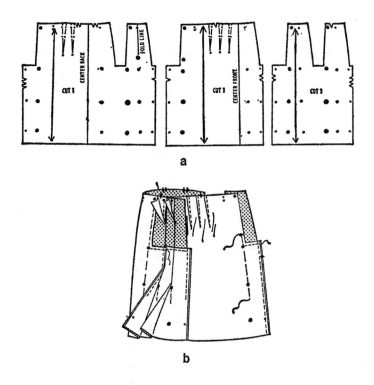

Fig. 140

When both thicknesses of the underpleat are cut away, the pleat must be anchored to the outer fabric by stitching. This is what happens in a kick pleat (Fig. 141).

The pleat may be an inverted pleat (Fig. 141a) or a side pleat (Fig. 141b). The pattern for these designs is made in the same way as for a similar full-length pleat. The only difference is in the length. The kick pleat exists only where the action is needed.

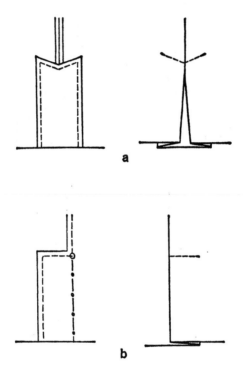

a

b

Fig. 141

Pattern for Bodice with Pleated Shoulders

Whether pleats are planned for the right side (Fig. 142-1) or the wrong side (Fig. 142-2), the pattern is developed in the same way.

1. Trace the bodice sloper with unstitched dart control. (Fig. 142 illustrates the procedure for the front bodice only but the back bodice is treated in the same way.)

2. Draw slash lines for the pleats parallel to the center front and center back. Draw guidelines at right angles to the center lines (Fig. 142a).

3. Draw guidelines for front and back patterns on fresh paper.

4. Slash and spread for the desired fullness of the pleats, guidelines matching (Fig. 142b).

5. Fold the pleats toward the armhole and side seams. Trace the shoulder lines and the waistlines.

6. Open out the pattern and sketch in the traced lines (Fig. 142c). Mark the fold lines, the placement lines, and the end of the stitching on each pleat. Add seam allowances, fold of fabric, and grain lines.

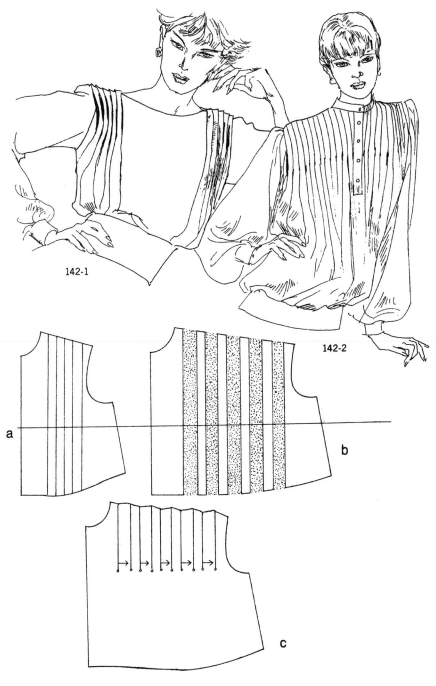

142-1

142-2

a

b

c

Fig. 142

Pattern for a Pleated Sleeve

Can you follow the diagram of Fig. 143? The pattern is developed in the same way as were those for the bodice and skirt.

The pleats may be formed on the right or wrong side; toward the front armhole or back armhole or both.

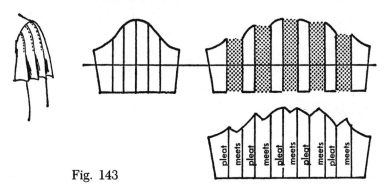

Fig. 143

PLEAT AS YOU PLEASE

When pleats or tucks are used in a series, it is sometimes simpler to make these in the fabric first then cut out the fabric from a simple non-full pattern (for a pin-tucked blouse, for instance). Or as in the case of a pleated plaid skirt, to make it without a pattern.

When striped or plaid material is used, often the pattern markings (when worked out first) do not coincide with or properly use the design of the material. Let the fabric be your guide as to how the pleats should be formed. Decide the dominant color and tonality you wish to feature. (You will get entirely different effects by folding the material into pleats differently.) Decide the length of the garment you want and which dominant color you wish for the lower edge.

Some shaping can be achieved by bringing the straight fold line of a pleat to a placement line on a slight angle, starting with the larger measurement and tapering to the smaller.

The Skirt with Inverted Pleat

This skirt (Fig. 144) is designed so that the turn-under of the pleat is an extension of it while the underlay is a separate piece.

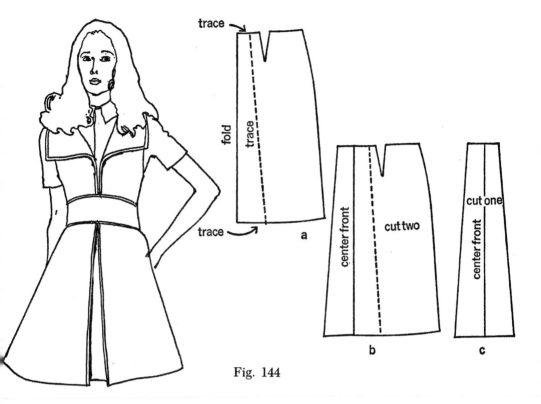

Fig. 144

The Skirt plus Extension

1. On the front- and/or back-skirt sloper, locate the pleat (broken line in illustration). In this pattern the extension tapers toward the waist (Fig. 144a). This gives a deep pleat at the hemline and less material at the waistline. If you wish, make it an even width throughout.

2. Fold the pattern on the center front (or back). Using the tracing wheel, trace the pleat, the waistline, and the hemline.

3. Open out the pattern. Pencil the traced lines (Fig. 144b). Cut two of this pattern.

The Underlay

4. The underlay is equal to the entire pleat as it appears opened out in Step 3, Fig. 144b. Trace the underlay (Fig. 144c). Either place a sheet of tracing paper over the drawing and copy it or place a fresh sheet of paper under the pattern and use the tracing wheel. The center back or front becomes the grain line. Be sure to trace it, too.

5. Complete both parts of the pattern.

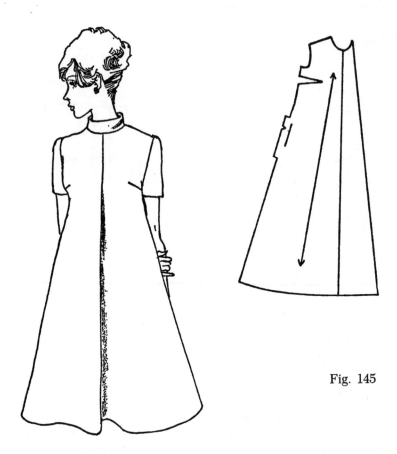

Fig. 145

A Side-Pleated Dress

Here is a dress where the right extension becomes a soft pleat (Fig. 145). The left extension becomes the underlay.

PATTERN FOR PLEAT (OR PLEATS)
BELOW A SHAPED YOKE

1. Trace the bodice or skirt sloper. Draw the style line for the yoke and the position of the pleats (Fig. 146a).

2. Cut away the yoke and close the dart control contained in it. Correct all angularity. Construct the pleat or pleats according to type as in the previous exercises.

3. Open out the pattern. Pencil the traced lines (Fig. 146b). Mark all

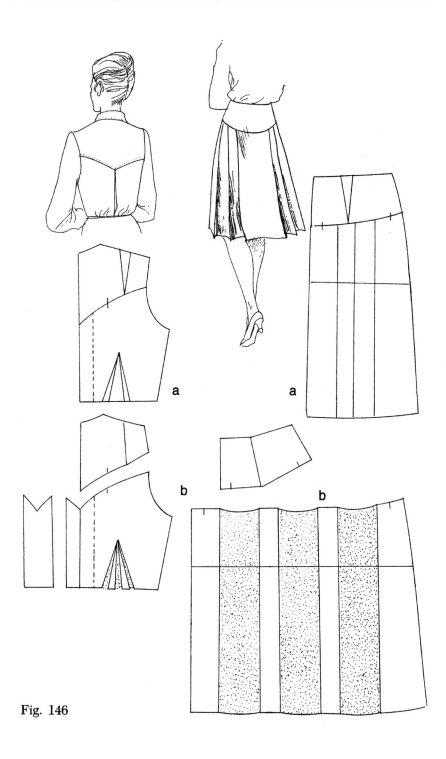

Fig. 146

fold lines and placement lines of pleats and end of stitching where necessary. Add seam allowances, notches, fold of fabric, and grain lines.

PATTERN FOR A FLARED BOX-PLEATED SKIRT

1. Start with the flared-skirt sloper. Draw the flared box pleat centered
on it. Indicate the center of the pleat with a broken line. Number the
sections for easy identification in the construction pattern (Fig. 147a).

2. Cut the sections apart. Spread so there is a complete pleat's width
between them (Fig. 147b).

3. Trace the pattern and complete it. The folds of the box pleat meet at
the broken line on the underside.

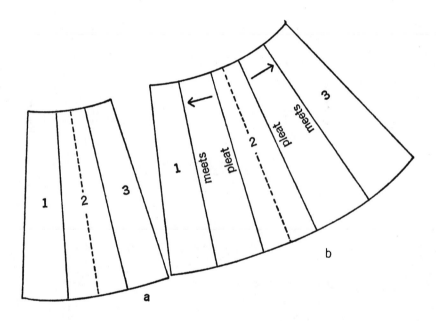

Fig. 147

MORE OF SAME

As full as this box-pleated skirt is, it can be made even fuller by double or triple pleats.

Instead of spreading the sections for one pleat as in Step 3, make the spread for two or three pleats (Fig. 148).

Fig. 148

ALTERNATE METHOD FOR A FLARED BOX-PLEATED SKIRT

The advantage of this pattern is that each pleat and each underlay is cut on the straight grain. You can see how helpful this would be in striped, plaid, or checked fabric. Even solid-color fabric falls beautifully when cut so.

1. Divide the waist measurement into the number of pleats you want— say six, though it could be more.

2. Draw a rectangle that is one sixth of the waist measurement and the full length of the skirt. Mark the position of the hips. Divide the rectangle into thirds lengthwise (Fig. 149a).

3. Slash and spread the strips so the measurement at the hips is one sixth of the hip measurement (Fig. 149b). Proportionate flare at the hem will be automatic.

4. Trace the pattern, correcting the waistline and the hemline. This is the size of the pleat (Fig. 149c). It also becomes the underlay.

5. To Fig. 149c, add half a pleat's width on each side for the underfold (Fig. 149d).

6. Complete the pattern. The center line of each pleat (Fig. 149d) and each underlay (Fig. 149c) is on the straight grain. Cut six pleats and six underlays.

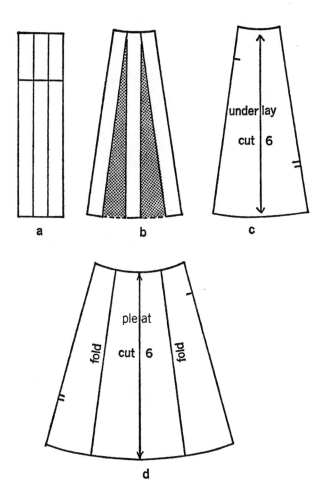

Fig. 149

Fig. 150

IN WHOLE OR IN PART

Wherever the fullness occurs in a design—be it in the skirt, bodice, sleeve, pants, collar, cuff, peplum, jacket, coat, or trim; and in whatever form—circular, balanced, pleated, tucked, gathered—the pattern is developed by the slash-and-spread principle described in this chapter. See Fig. 150.

Chapter 7

A Set of Slopers

Up to this point all of our patterns have been developed from the garment sections that comprise the basic woman's sloper (bodice front and back, skirt front and back, set-in sleeve) because it is easier for beginning patternmakers to see the pattern principles developed in these simple pieces.

Surely you will not want to limit your patternmaking to styles derived from these five pieces. A whole world of design is open to you if you apply the pattern principles you have learned to the set of slopers which follow.

HIP-LENGTH SLOPER

The hip-length sloper can be used for any design that extends below the natural waistline. With some modifications, it becomes the sloper to use for designing blouses, jackets, vests, coats, and full-length dresses.

The following exercises give measurements for a standard medium-size pattern. For individual hip-length slopers, use personal measurements.

FRONT HIP-LENGTH SLOPER (Fig. 151a, 151b, and 151c)

1. Trace the bodice-front sloper. Cut out the tracing and the dart. Trace the skirt-front sloper. Cut out the tracing but *not* the dart.

2. On the skirt sloper, mark the front-hip depth (7 inches) and the side-hip depth (7½ inches). Draw a slightly curved line connecting the two points.

3. Cut away the hip section of the skirt. Line up the skirt and bodice waistline darts. Extend the skirt dart to the hip line and cut it out.

4. Attach the center-front skirt section to the center-front bodice section at the waistline. Attach the side-front skirt section to the side-front bodice section in the same way (Fig. 151a). Don't be surprised to find a

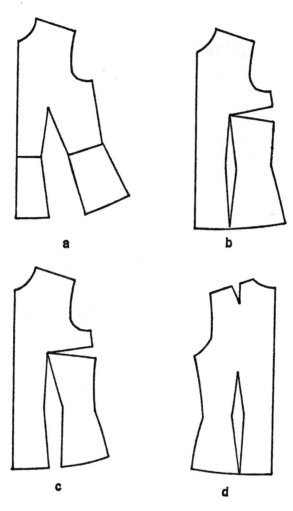

Fig. 151

slightly curved opening at the waistline. This is because bodice and skirt waistlines are opposing curves. (Incidentally, this is where and why a one-piece fitted dress wrinkles.) Ignore the space in this pattern.

5. On the bodice-front sloper, shift some of the waistline dart control to an underarm dart. If the bodice waistline dart is closed to match the skirt dart, the underarm dart must really carry the burden of the shaping (Fig. 151b). If the largest amount of control remains at the waistline, the skirt dart control will end in a dart tuck rather than a dart (Fig. 151c).

6. Correct the angularity at the side waistline with a gentle curve (Fig. 151b and 151c).

a

Fig. 152

b

The amount of dart control shifted depends on the figure requirements or the design to be developed.

A dress with the waistline dart control left unstitched for fullness and an underarm dart that does some shaping (Fig. 152a) would be designed on Fig. 151b.

A dress with shaping in its control seams (Fig. 152b) would be better designed on Fig. 151c.

BACK HIP-LENGTH SLOPER (Fig. 151d)

1. Trace the bodice-back sloper. Cut out the tracing and the waistline dart. Trace the skirt-back sloper. Cut out the tracing but do *not* cut out the dart.

2. On the skirt sloper, mark the back-hip depth (8 inches) and the side-hip depth (7½ inches). Draw a slightly curved line connecting the two points.

3. Cut away the hip section of the skirt. Line up the skirt and bodice waistline darts. Extend the skirt dart to the hip line and cut it out.

4. Attach the center-back skirt section to the center-back bodice section at the waistline. Attach the side-back skirt section to the side-back bodice section in the same way. Make the amount of the skirt dart match that of the bodice dart. If necessary, take the rest of the shaping off the side seam.

5. Correct the angularity at the side waistline with a gentle curve.

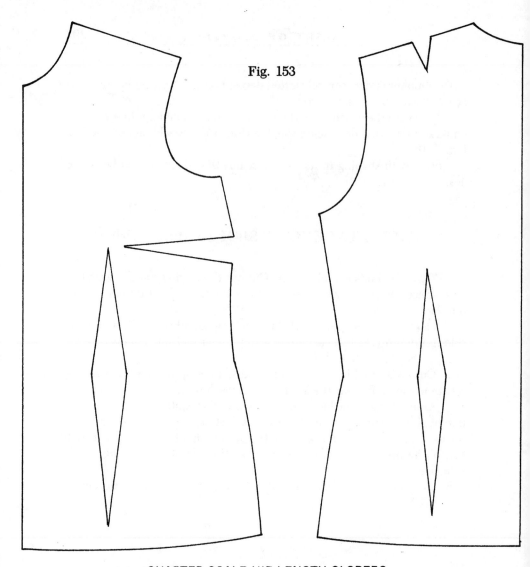

Fig. 153

QUARTER-SCALE HIP-LENGTH SLOPERS

The quarter-scale hip-length slopers in Fig. 153 are provided for your convenience in developing patterns for hip-length garments.

FULL-LENGTH SLOPER

For a full-length sloper, extend the hip-length sloper to full length.

SLOPERS FOR JACKETS AND COATS

The broken lines in Fig. 154 indicate the original hip-length bodice-front sloper. The solid lines show the adjustments which must be made for tailored garments. Fig. 154 shows only the front slopers; similar adjustments are made on the back hip-length slopers.

Fig. 154

HOW TO MAKE THE BASIC-FITTING JACKET SLOPER (Fig. 154b)

1. Start with the hip-length sloper (Fig. 154a).
2. Drop the neckline ⅛ inch.
3. Add ¼-inch ease to the side seams.
4. Broaden the shoulders ½ inch.
5. Lower the armhole ½ inch.

HOW TO MAKE THE BASIC-FITTING COAT SLOPER (Fig. 154c)

1. Start with the hip-length sloper (Fig. 154a).
2. Drop the neckline ¼ inch.
3. Add ½ inch to the side seams.
4. Broaden the shoulders ½ inch.
5. Lower the armhole 1 inch.

Note that in both the jacket and coat patterns, the neckline has been lowered, the shoulders widened, the armhole dropped, and width has been added across the chest, across the back, and at the side seams. Corresponding changes must be made in the jacket and coat sleeves. The sleeve cap is flattened and widened to fit the extended shoulder and the deepened armhole. The underarm seam is lengthened to compensate for the flattened cap. The wrist is widened.

SLEEVE SLOPERS FOR JACKETS AND COATS

HOW TO MAKE THE ONE-PIECE JACKET SLEEVE (Fig. 155)

1. Start with the basic sleeve sloper.
2. Shift some of the elbow dart control to the wrist to widen it as unstitched dart control (Fig. 155a).

Fig. 155b
3. Add ¼ inch to the side seams.
4. Raise the underarm curve ½ inch. (Use the same method as for the sport-shirt sleeve.)
5. Redraw the sleeve cap. Compare the length of the cap with the jacket armhole. Allow 1½ to 2 inches ease.

HOW TO MAKE THE ONE-PIECE COAT SLEEVE (Fig. 155)

Steps 1 and 2 are the same as for the jacket sleeve (Fig. 155).
3. Add ½ inch to the side seams.
4. Raise the underarm curve 1 inch. (Use the same method as for the sport-shirt sleeve.)
5. Redraw the sleeve cap. Compare the length of the new sleeve cap with the coat armhole. Allow 2 to 2½ inches ease.

All of the foregoing slopers—hip-length, jacket, and coat—are for fitted garments. More fullness is added in the usual way for semifitted or loose garments.

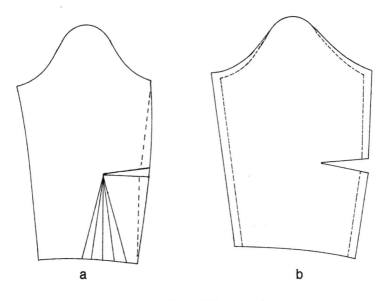

Fig. 155

There is no shoulder-pad allowance in any of the above. Should you wish to use shoulder pads, make the same adjustments for a jacket or coat as for a dress. (See page 379.)

TWO-PIECE JACKET- AND COAT-SLEEVE SLOPERS

These are made in the same way as the two-piece dress sleeve (see page 115). Start with the one-piece jacket- or coat-sleeve sloper.

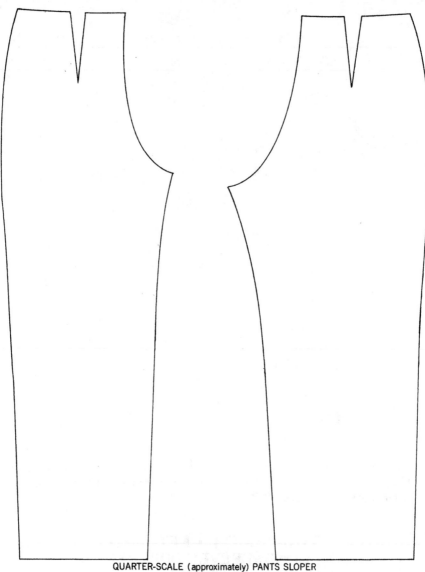

QUARTER-SCALE (approximately) PANTS SLOPER

Fig. 156

PANTS SLOPER (Fig. 156)

To make a pants sloper for a boy, girl, woman, or man, follow the same procedure as for making a basic dress sloper. Select a very simple, trim pants pattern, fitted by darts preferably, though a front pleat is acceptable. Adjust the pattern to personal measurements for length, width, shaping. Test the corrected pattern in muslin or cotton. Transfer the fitted muslin to heavy paper.

SHORTS SLOPER

Straight shorts or trunks are designed on the pants sloper. Pleated shorts are more often designed on the culotte sloper (see below).

1. Trace the front and back pants slopers to the desired distance below the crotch depth. Start with 3 inches on the inseam, 2 inches on the side seam. Join these points with a slightly curved line (Fig. 157a).

2. For a slight flare, add 1 inch to the front and 1 inch to the back at the side seams, tapering to nothing at the hips.

3. For additional flare on the inseam, draw slash lines 2 inches in from the seams (Fig. 157b). Slash and spread 1 inch at the hemline.

4. Draw a grain line at right angles to the hipline. Correct the hemline (Fig. 157c).

5. Complete the pattern.

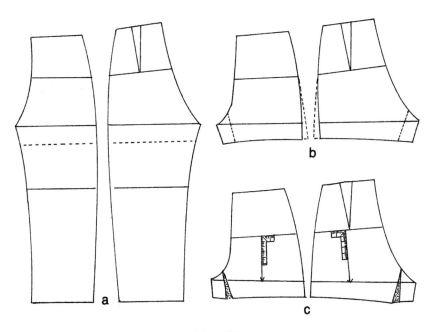

Fig. 157

CULOTTES, OR SPLIT-SKIRT, SLOPER

Culottes have the look of a skirt with the comfort and freedom that pants permit. A basic culotte pattern can be made from the skirt basic pattern plus some of the pants measurements.

Fig. 158

Fig. 158a

AB equals half the front-skirt measurement at the crotch line less 1 inch.

AC equals half the back-skirt measurement at the crotch line plus 1 inch.

DS and ES are slight flares (1 inch) added to the side seams to provide walking room.

BO equals 2 inches from BA on a 45-degree angle as a guide for the front crotch curve.

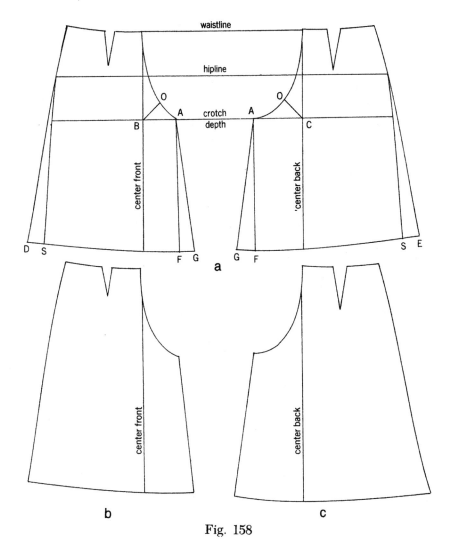

Fig. 158

CO equals 2½ inches from CA on a 45-degree angle as a guide for the back crotch curve.

FG front and back are 1-inch flares. Taper to A.

Trace the culotte front (Fig. 158b). Trace the culotte back (Fig. 158c). Complete the pattern.

Additional fullness, either circular or balanced, and interesting design details make culottes graceful and attractive. A deep inverted pleat (3 to 5 inches on both sides of center) at both center front and back is particularly effective.

CAPE SLOPER

The dart control in this full-length cape sloper can be used for design purposes in the same way any other dart control is.

1. Divide the bodice-front dart control between shoulder and waistline.

Fig. 159a

2. Trace the front- and back-bodice slopers, leaving plenty of room around them.

3. Square a line from the center back to the armhole. Extend it to a distance from the armhole equal to one quarter of its measurement (AB). Do the same with the bodice front (CD).

4. Extend the center back to the length desired for the cape (E).

5. Square a line across from E equal to one quarter of the desired hemline measurement (F). Connect F to B.

6. Extend the center-front line (H). DH equals AE.

7. Square a line across from H to G that equals CD plus the difference between AB and EF. This will assure side seams with similar degrees of angle.

8. Connect G with C.

9. Make BF^1 equal AE. Make CG^1 equal DH. Correct the hemline with a curved line.

10. Extend the shoulder lines and the side seams until they meet. Correct the angularity with a curve for the top of the arm—1 inch over, 1 inch down.

Fig. 159b

11. Trace the pattern and complete it.

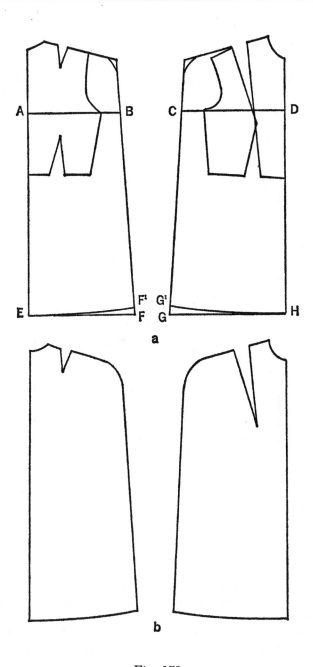

Fig. 159

CHILDREN'S SLOPERS

A child's back is fairly straight with slight bulges. The back sloper re-sembles an adult's except that the darts are smaller (Fig. 160a).

Whereas the greatest bulge in misses' and women's clothing is at the bust, in a child's it is at the waistline. Therefore, the front control dart slides down to the waistline and flops over to the side seam (Fig. 160b).

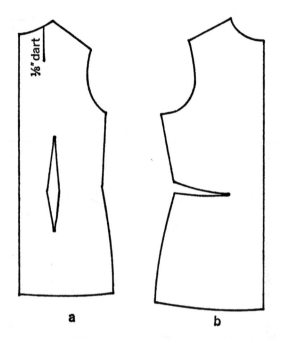

⅜" dart

a   b

Fig. 160

As far as patternmaking is concerned, the position of the control dart makes very little difference since it can be and is shifted to other positions for design purposes.

For instance: it is just as easy to move the control from the waistline to a yoke (Fig. 161a) or to shift it to a seam (Fig. 161b) as it is to move or shift the control from the bust.

a

b

Fig. 161

A NOTE ON MAKING PATTERNS FOR CHILDREN'S CLOTHES

The chief differences between designing for adults and designing for children are largely matters of styling and fitting. While the measurements will be smaller for children than for adults, the proportionate amount of ease should be greater. For comfort, children's clothes must be roomy, particularly at the armholes and the crotch. All-in-one garments such as snowsuits, creepers, or pajamas need a low crotch to provide ample room for sitting (particularly if there are diapers beneath). Necklines should have plenty of ease. Hems should be generous.

Even clothes for little children are designed à la mode. In addition to the aesthetics, however, there must be a degree of practicality. Keep in mind ease of laundering and dressing. (This advice is for sewers who are not mothers of little children; the latter hardly need to be told this.)

PATTERNS WITH A PURPOSE

In addition to a set of slopers, it is a good idea to have a set of staples on hand for instant use. Here are some slopers it would be well to have ready.

Bodice or Hip-Length Slopers

with darts shifted to favorite positions
with favorite control seams
with no darts, for developing décolleté necklines

Sleeveless Dresses and Evening Clothes

with favorite necklines and collars
with unstitched dart control
with princess lines

Sleeve Slopers

for sport shirt with its adjusted bodice
for shirtwaist sleeve
for kimono or cap sleeve

for a two-piece sleeve (dress, jacket or coat)
for a long-sleeve sloper with varying lengths marked off

Pants Sloper

with favorite darts, pleats, or seams
with varying lengths marked off for different styles

Jacket and Coat Slopers

with favorite shaping and degree of fullness

OR any other of your favorite styles.

Slopers that will be used often should be on paper tough enough to stand frequent, hard handling. Use heavy wrapping paper or oaktag. Both are easy to come by. The wrapping paper has the additional merit of being easy to roll for storing.

RESEARCH AND DEVELOPMENT DEPARTMENT—An Aid to Your Own Artistry and Skill

All confirmed sewers have drawerfuls of patterns as well as drawerfuls of fabric awaiting the inspiration and time for attention.

Take out some of the patterns in your collection. Study the designs. Read the descriptive matter on the back of the pattern envelope. Try to work out the pattern, using your so newly acquired knowledge of dart control and additional fullness. When you have done so, examine the ready-made pattern and compare it with yours. See how close your pattern comes to that of the professional patternmaker.

More than likely, the basic structure of the patterns will be the same. Such differences as there are probably will be in the subtleties of line and proportion.

When you have lost your fear of patterns and when you have done enough of them to feel some confidence, you may surprise yourself by the artistry you will come to display.

PART II

STYLING

Chapter 8

Notable Necklines

From turtleneck to waistline plunge, it's a neckline! Whether you are muffled to the ears or bared to the bosom, it's still a neckline. It's important, too. Sitting or standing, moving or at rest, your face and adjacent parts of the anatomy are the center of interest. An attractive or arresting neckline is very much a part of the picture.

A neckline may be round, square, jewel, oval, bateau, V-shaped, keyhole, scooped, asymmetric, high, low, in between. There are endless variations—enough to cover (or uncover) the endless variety of faces, figures, situations, styles, and moods.

The sloper has a "natural" neckline, that is, one that curves around the neck from the hollow between the collarbones in front to the back socket bone. For purposes of pattern construction, no matter how little or how much, any neckline that drops below this line is a dropped neckline; any neckline that rises above this line is a raised neckline.

DROPPED NECKLINES

In general, when a front neckline is low, the back neckline is high; when the front neckline is high, the back may be low. A deep décolletage, both front and back, presents the problem of keeping it in place.

How deeply to drop a neckline depends on current fashion, the beauty of the neck, shoulders, and bosom, the shape of the head, the hairdo, the age of the wearer.

If the design is for your own use, past experience, some study, and a little experimentation should help you decide which style lines and which proportions are most pleasing for you.

General Directions for Making a Pattern for a Dropped Neckline

Since both front and back are involved in a neckline, trace the bodice-front and bodice-back slopers. You may work with each separately or as a unit with shoulders touching. The latter has this advantage: one feels the rhythm of the line from front to back as a whole. In more complicated styling, it is best to develop front and back patterns separately.

1. Decide the front drop, the back drop, and just where the neckline is to appear on the shoulders. This is your great chance to control the drop so it covers your lingerie and shoulder straps.

2. Draw the style line for the neckline.

3. Cut out the slopers. Cut away the pattern at the neckline. Discard what you don't need. Separate the front and back patterns.

It's that simple! No matter what the shape of the neckline, the method for developing the pattern is the same. Now try your hand at the three major types of neckline—V (Fig. 162a), square (Fig. 162b), oval (Fig. 162c).

Hints

For a better-fitting square neckline, square the style line from the shoulder and from the center front.

Don't forget to square a short line at center front and/or center back before drawing a curved style line.

The neckline will look prettier if the curved style line is continuous across the shoulders.

WHAT TO DO ABOUT THE
BACK SHOULDER DART

Often, the back shoulder dart is scooped out along with the neckline. If only a tiny dart is left, you don't need it. The amount of the dart can be taken off the neckline at the shoulder.

If a reasonable amount of dart is left after cutting away the neckline, then this must be retained for the shoulder shaping.

Like any other dart, the shoulder dart may be shifted to another position, say to the back neckline or to a control seam.

The shoulder dart is frequently relocated to the place where shoulder and neckline meet.

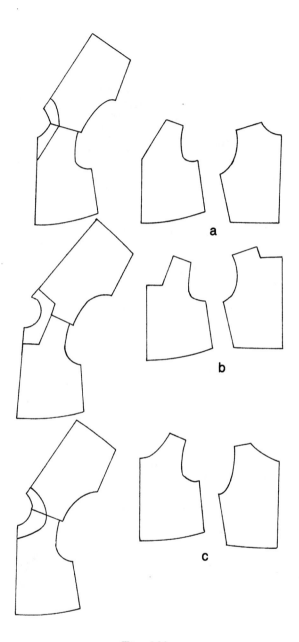

Fig. 162

Fig. 163

VARIATIONS OF CLASSIC TYPES OF NECKLINES

Enormous variety can be obtained by subtle variations in proportion that give your neckline a "new" look. Try your hand at patterns for the necklines in Fig. 163.

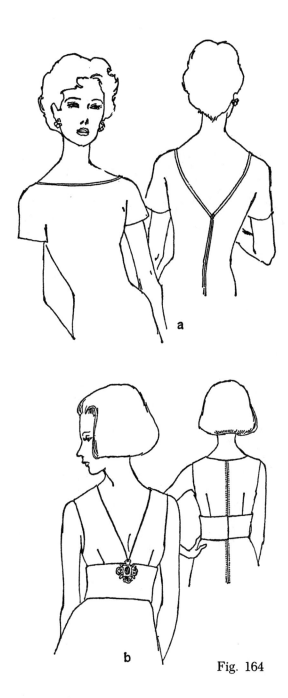

Fig. 164

Coming-and-Going Necklines

Make patterns for these turnabout necklines: high in front, low in back (Fig. 164a); low in front, high in back (Fig. 164b).

Fig. 165

Novelty Necklines

These can be fun to do (Fig. 165).

Dropped Neckline with Additional Fullness

In this design, first work out the pattern for a bodice with cap sleeves. (See page 398.)

1. On the cut-out cap-sleeve bodice-front pattern with cut-out waist-line dart control, draw the style line for the dropped neckline. Draw the style line for the midriff yoke (Fig. 166a). In like manner, develop the pattern for the bodice-back neckline and midriff yoke.

2. Cut away the pattern at the neckline. Cut away the midriff yoke. Use the remaining dart control in the upper bodice in any way you choose—as folds, gathers, or darts. Close the waistline dart control in the midriff yoke (Fig. 166b).

3. In the upper bodice, draw the slash lines for the neckline folds. Locate the position and size of the openings for the ribbon that will hold them in place (Fig. 166b).

4. Slash and spread the neckline for circularity to the desired fullness (Fig. 166c).

5. Trace the pattern (Fig. 166d) and complete it.

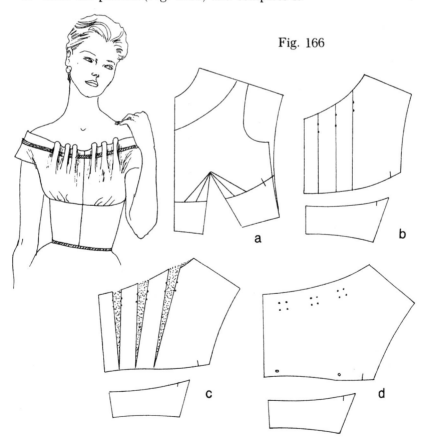

Fig. 166

a

b

c

d

Fig. 167

V-Neck Cross-Over Yoke, a Popular Style

1. Draw the style line for the V neck and the V-shaped yoke on a complete bodice-front sloper. Show the cross-over with a dotted line (Fig. 167a).

2. Cut the yoke away from the bodice. Cut out the neckline (Fig. 167b).

3. Cut out one side of the cross-over yoke. Label the pattern CUT TWO. *Or* trace a second side (Fig. 167c).

4. To prevent stretching of the yoke neckline, place the straight grain parallel to the V-neck edge (Fig. 167c).

5. Complete the pattern.

Fig. 168

ASYMMETRIC NECKLINE

All of the foregoing necklines were of the formal balance variety—exactly the same on both sides. The asymmetric neckline is different on each side. Its beauty is in its informal balance. Its exaggerated and free-form style lines can be quite interesting and rather sophisticated. A few asymmetric necklines are shown in Fig. 168.

In order to work out a pattern for any of these necklines, you will need to use a complete bodice-front (or bodice-back) sloper.

1. Trace the complete bodice-front sloper. Decide where on the shoulders you would like the neckline to appear. Decide the position and the amount of the drop (Fig. 169a).

2. Draw the style line (Fig. 169b).

3. Cut out the tracing. Cut out the neckline (Fig. 169c).

4. Complete the pattern.

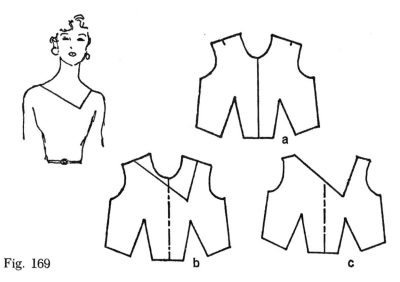

Fig. 169

NECKLINE FINISHES

Not many designs can be outlined in raw edges. Nor can many fabrics take this treatment. The outside edges of most garments need some finish. Since the neckline is a very visible edge, it calls for a particularly decorative or unobtrusive finish.

You could bind the raw edges with bias, braid, or banding, with leather or lace, with ribbon or rickrack, with fur or feathers. All of these are fine finishes—in their fashion. What's more, they do not require a pattern since you can buy or make them by the yard. However, in many instances, the best finish is simply with a facing.

FINISH WITH A FACING

The facing is a second layer of material, generally applied to the underside of the garment so that this in no way detracts from the design or the material of which it is made. The exception is a decorative right-side facing. (See "Facing to the Fore," page 223.)

The facing acts not only as a finish but also as a support. It adds body, sustains the shape, and reinforces the outside edge, which is subject to stress and wear. To strengthen these areas additionally, the garment needs an interfacing too. Current fashions are inclined to dispense with this.

In dressmaking, the interfacing is cut from the same pattern as the facing. In tailored garments, the interfacing is often extended to include some shaping as well.

FACINGS—STRAIGHT OR SHAPED

When the edge to be faced is a *straight* one, the facing is usually an extension of the garment turned back at a fold line to form a hem. Where necessary for purposes of layout, color or texture, it may also be a separate piece cut to the same size and grain, plus seam allowances.

When the edge to be faced is a *shaped* one, the facing must necessarily be a separate piece of fabric cut in the same size, shape, and grain.

The method for *developing a pattern* for a facing, whether straight or shaped, *for any part of a garment* is the same as that illustrated for the necklines in this chapter.

Facing for a Straight Edge

While the facing for a sleeve is illustrated in Fig. 170, the principle would work in the same way for a neckline or part of a neckline.

1. Measure and mark on the pattern the width of the facing—the broken lines in the illustration (Fig. 170a).

2. Fold the pattern on the straight edge to be faced. Using a tracing wheel, trace the facing on all remaining sides.

3. Unfold the pattern and following the marks of the tracing wheel, draw all outer edges (Fig. 170b).

4. Complete the pattern. Make sure to mark the fold line on the pattern.

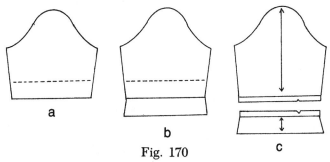

Fig. 170

For a separate facing, cut the pattern away at the original straight edge. Add seam allowances, a grain line (the same as that of the original pattern) and notches at the edges to be joined (Fig. 170c).

Facing for a Shaped Edge

1. From the neckline on both front and back patterns, measure the width of the facing (usually 1½ to 2¼ inches) in a sufficient number of places to ensure that the outer edge of the facing is parallel to the neck edge (Fig. 171a).

2. Draw the facing's outer edge by connecting the markings (Fig. 171b). Locate the grain line (the same as for the garment). Place pairs of similar notches on the garment and the facing edges. Indicate the fold of fabric. Add seam allowances.

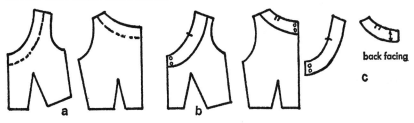

Fig. 171

Make a slight adjustment in the length of the facing, because it should fit the inside rather than the outside of the garment, which has a slightly larger measurement.

For necklines with a small drop, take off ⅛ inch at the shoulder (more, if the fabric is heavy). Or take off ¹⁄₁₆ inch at the shoulder and ¹⁄₁₆ inch at the center front or center back. When the center front, center back, or shoulder are so specially shaped as to call for precision matching with the outer fabric, do this: tuck the pattern or slash and overlap it in some place where it will not affect the style line. This latter method works well when the neckline drop is a deep one.

There is another virtue in this slight adjustment. When the smaller facing is stitched to the now relatively larger outer fabric, there is sufficient material to roll the joining seam to the underside of the garment—out of sight.

Fig. 172

3. Trace the facing onto another sheet of paper (Fig. 171c).
4. Complete the pattern. (Use the same pattern for an interfacing.)

Keep facings simple in shape, particularly in novelty or asymmetric designs. If the pattern includes any seams or darts that enter the edge to be faced, eliminate them by overlapping. The width of the facing is so comparatively narrow that shaping by small seams and darts is unnecessary.

Should the garment be a sleeveless one, it is easy enough to add the armhole facing to the neck facing. Cut the pattern as one (Fig. 172).

When a pattern is too deeply cut out for a narrow facing, a complete lining cut to the bodice pattern is used instead for a finish and reinforcement. See the halter design on page 225.

Now go back and provide the facings for the neckline patterns you have made.

FACING TO THE FORE: RIGHT-SIDE DECORATIVE FACING

Why hide a facing on the underside of a garment when it can become an attractive feature on the outside—perhaps an unusual shape (Fig. 173a) or a contrasting color (Fig. 173b) or a different texture (Fig. 173c)? A right-side hem makes a decorative band at the lower edge of a skirt, sleeve, overblouse, jacket, or the like (Fig. 173d).

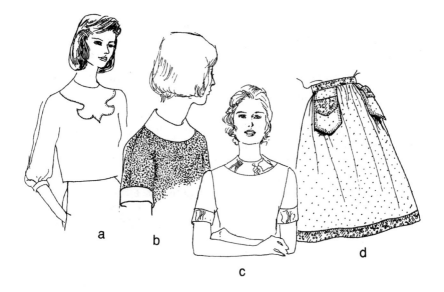

Fig. 173

Since the band or decorative facing is applied to the outside, it must be cut slightly larger than the garment. This adjustment floats it on the surface. It also adds the size necessary for rolling the joining seam to the underside. To make the adjustment, reverse the previous procedure for making the facing smaller.

The interfacing of a decorative band is cut without seam allowance. It is applied to the underside of the band or facing by hand stitching at the seam line.

From this point on, whenever necessary, your patterns should include the facings.

THE BARE-AND-BEAUTIFUL DEPARTMENT

A minimum of coverage can mean a maximum of appeal.

Décolleté, close-fitting, and strapless dresses are designed on the sloper without ease in chest, bust, and waistline areas. Larger darts, curved darts, and darts in more places will help shape the bodice closer to the bust. Control seams do this well. On the other hand, additional fullness provides an easy, draped look.

A BASIC HALTER DESIGN

1. Place the no-ease, cut-out, bodice-front and bodice-back slopers together at the shoulders. Make them touch at the neckline. Fasten with Scotch tape (Fig. 174a).

2. Draw the neckline from center back to center front. The plunge is as deep as you dare bare (Fig. 174a).

3. Draw the lower style line from center back to side front (Fig. 174a). The line may be higher or lower than the sloper underarm.

4. Cut out the neckline. Cut out the halter. Place the remaining back sloper so its center back is parallel to the center front, the waistlines line up, and the slopers touch at the style line (Fig. 174b). Fasten in this position with Scotch tape.

5. Continue the style line from the bodice side seam to the center back in a sweeping line (Fig. 174b).

Front and back patterns may be used as one or be separated at the side seam. Dart control can be used as a dart (or darts) (Fig. 174–1), folds of fabric, or control seam (Fig. 174–2). The center backs of the neck piece may be joined so the halter can be slipped over the head. Or, extensions may be added to the center backs at the neckpiece so they can be tied or buttoned.

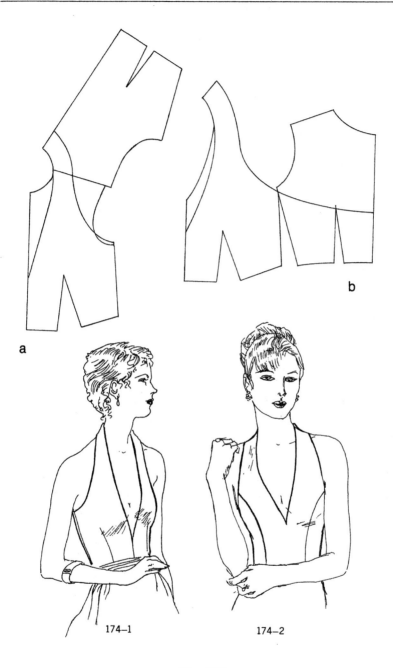

a

b

174–1

174–2

Fig. 174

ONE-SHOULDER DESIGNS

1. Start with the no-ease, cut-out slopers for a complete bodice front and a complete bodice back.

2. Draw the style lines from one shoulder to the opposite side seam (Fig. 175a).

3. Cut away the neckline (Fig. 175b).

4. Complete the pattern.

a   b

Fig. 175

STRAPLESS DRESSES (Fig. 176-1 and Fig. 176-2)

1. Start with the no-ease, cut-out bodice-front and bodice-back slopers. Place them so side seams touch (Fig. 176a).

2. Draw the style line from center front to center back (Fig. 176a). In the sloper, the underarm drops 1½ inches below the armpit for ease. Since the arm is perfectly free in a strapless dress, the drop is not necessary. The underarm style line can be brought up as a continuation of the front and back style lines.

3. Cut away the pattern at the décolletage.

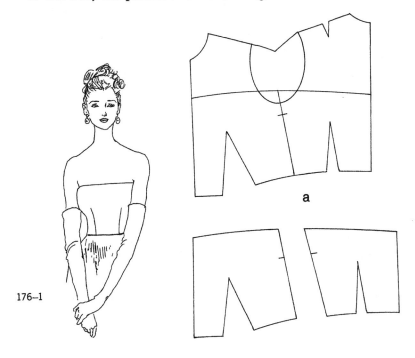

a

176–1

Fig. 176

b

176-2

Fig. 176

Fig. 176–1 is fitted close to the body at the darts and side seams while the control seams of the princess style in Fig. 176–2 do the fitting (Fig. 176b).

If you are a little nervous about how a strapless dress can really stay up, try one of these props.

Fig. 177a. Add shoestring straps that don't hold much but your interest.

Fig. 177b. Instead of two fragile straps, add only one substantial one.

Fig. 177c. A faced yoke and a strapless gown, separated by design, are held together by hardware.

Fig. 177d. This strapless dress is harnessed to a turtleneck collar.

Fig. 177e. Here is a strapless dress suspended from a richly ornamented yoke band hung around the neck.

Fig. 177

FROM A LOW LOW TO A HIGH HIGH

Basic Raised Neckline

The raised neckline must fit not only the shoulders but also part of the neck. Since the neck tapers slightly as it rises from its base, the measurement of the raised neckline is somewhat smaller than is the neckline of the sloper. The curve and size of this portion of the pattern can only be determined by careful fitting. If you are fond of this type of neckline, prepare a personal sloper for the neck area. Here is one way to produce the standard raised neckline.

1. Trace the bodice-front and bodice-back slopers leaving room for the raised necklines.

2. Extend both center front and center back lines 1 inch (or more) (Fig. 178a). Slide the front-bodice sloper along the center-front line to the 1-inch extension and trace the front neckline again in the new position. Do the same with the back neckline (Fig. 178a).

3. Make the new raised neckline equal the neck measurement minus ¼ inch so it fits the smaller neck measurement at that height.

4. For shaping at the neck, draw a curved line from the front raised neckline to the shoulder, blending it into the shoulder line (Fig. 178b).

5. Cut out the front bodice.

6. Place front and back bodices together, shoulders matching. Trace the new front shoulder on the back pattern so the shoulder seams will be identical (Fig. 178c).

7. Complete the pattern including the facing.

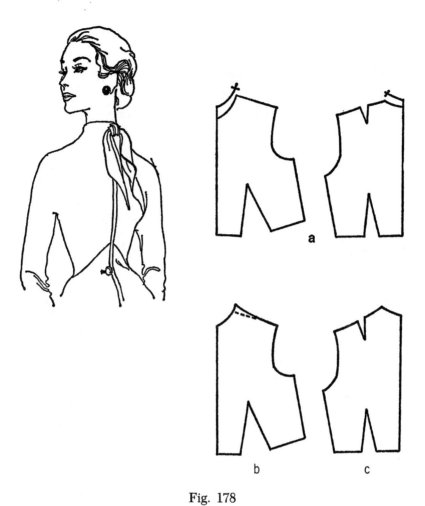

Fig. 178

RAISED NECKLINES WITH STYLE DETAILS

Raised Neckline with Dropped, Shaped Center Front (Fig. 179a) or Center Back (Fig. 179b)

On the raised-neckline pattern, determine the drop in front or back. Connect the drop with the raised neckline (Fig. 179).

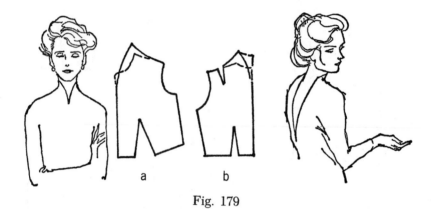

a   b

Fig. 179

Raised Neckline with Front Fullness at a Triangular Design Detail (Fig. 180)

Fig. 180

Raised Stand-away Neckline

1. Trace the front- and back-bodice slopers. Extend the center-front and center-back lines to the amount of the rise.

2. Draw the style line for the neckline and connect it to the shoulder with a curved line (Fig. 181).

3. Complete the pattern.

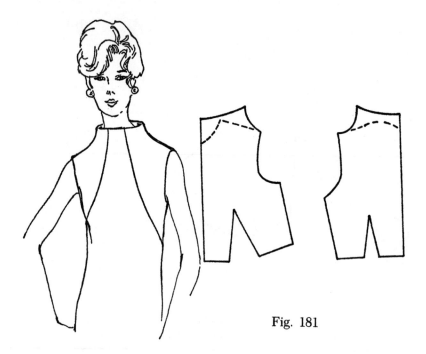

Fig. 181

DRAPERY SOFTENS THE NECKLINE: THE COWL

It's a far cry from a medieval monk's hood, but nevertheless, that's the origin of all those lovely cowl necklines. Like the hood, its characteristic shape is square at the center. Since the cowl is a drape, it is cut on the bias (which drapes best) of some fabric that will fall in soft folds—chiffon, velvet, jersey, crepe, satin.

Patterns for front or back necklines are developed in the same way.

HIGH COWL WITH A SINGLE DRAPE

1. Trace the bodice-front sloper with waistline fullness. Extend the center front 1 inch above the neckline. Take off 1 inch of the shoulder at the neckline. Draw the new neckline from the extension to the drop (Fig. 182a).

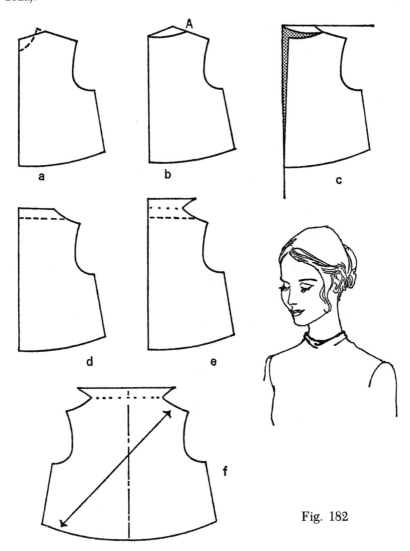

Fig. 182

2. Cut out the sloper with its new neckline, which is now a straight line. Measure down 1 inch on the shoulder from the neckline. Label the point A. Draw a curved slash line from the center-front neckline to A (Fig. 182b).

3. On another sheet of paper draw a square (or use the corner of a sheet of paper). Slash and spread the sloper against the square as illustrated (Fig. 182c). The straight neckline rests along the horizontal line of the square. The waistline center touches the vertical line of the square. The additional fullness of the spread becomes the drape.

4. Trace the pattern leaving enough room for a facing and for the other half of a complete front. Correct the angularity of the shoulder (Fig. 182d).

5. Measure down 1½ inches from the neckline for the facing (the broken line in Fig. 163d). Fold the neckline and trace the facing. Remember to include the center front and the shoulder seam.

6. Open out the pattern and draw in the facing, which is cut in one with the bodice and turned back as a hem (Fig. 182e).

7. *Bias calls for a complete pattern.* Half a pattern on a bias fold may result in inaccuracies in cutting. Fold the pattern at center front and trace the other half (Fig. 182f).

8. Complete the pattern.

COWL ON A DROPPED NECKLINE

1. Use the sloper with unstitched dart control at the waistline. Drop the neckline 1 to 2 inches at center front. From this point, draw a curved line to the shoulder in a wide sweep. Cut out the neckline (Fig. 183a).

2. Starting 1½ to 2 inches below the neckline at center front draw a slash line to the shoulder (Fig. 183a).

3. Slash and spread the pattern against a square (Fig. 183b). The neckline touches the horizontal line of the square at the shoulder. The upper line of the slash touches the vertical line of the square as does the waistline center.

4. Trace the pattern, leaving enough room to complete it. Correct the shoulder seam and the waistline (Fig. 183c).

5. Construct the facing in the same way as for Figs. 182d and 182e (Fig. 183d).

6. Trace the second half of the pattern as in Fig. 182f (Fig. 183e).

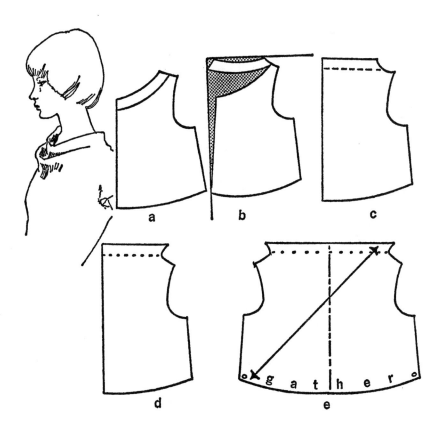

Fig. 183

DRAPES ON A DEEP NECKLINE

1. Drop the neckline on the bodice-front (for Fig. 184–1) or bodice-back (for Fig. 184–2) sloper with unstitched dart control at the waistline. Make it not quite as deep a drop as you wish it to be in the finished pattern. Some length will be added by the construction. Cut out the neckline.

2. Draw several slash lines from the center front (or back) to those points on the shoulder and armhole from which you would like the folds to drape. Each slash line becomes a drape. Plan as many slashes as you would like drapes (Fig. 184a).

3. Slash each drape line. Spread the pattern against a square. Make the neckline rest on the horizontal line of the square. The center front of the lower bodice rests at the waistline on the vertical line of the square. Place the middle sections between the upper and lower sections (Fig. 184b).

4. Trace the pattern. Correct the shoulder seam and the waistline. Construct the facing (Fig. 184c).

5. Trace the other half of the pattern (Fig. 184d) and complete it.

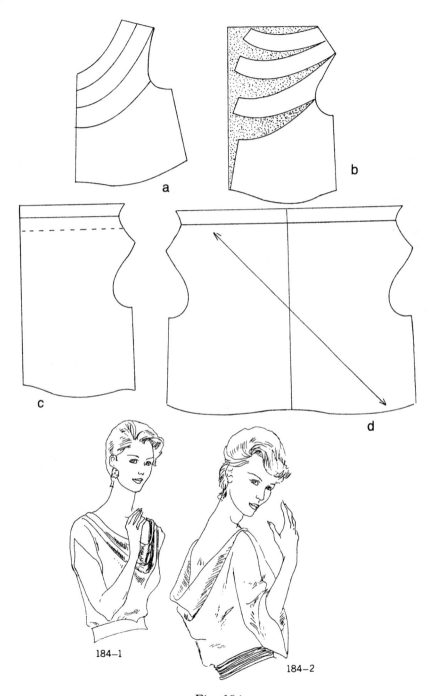

a

b

c

d

184–1

184–2

Fig. 184

COWL YOKE

A cowl yoke has the advantage of being cut separately from the bodice. While the cowl is cut on the bias, the rest of the bodice can be cut on the straight of goods. This produces a fitted bodice with drapes only in the yoke. It's a great neckline for a suit blouse.

1. On the bodice-front sloper, draw the style line for the yoke. Notch the style line (Fig. 185a).
2. Cut away the yoke from the rest of the bodice (Fig. 185b).
3. Draw drape lines on the yoke (Fig. 185c).
4. Slash and spread the pattern against a square (Fig. 185d).
5. Trace the new yoke pattern, correcting the shoulder line.
6. Construct the facing (Fig. 185e).
7. Trace the other half of the yoke pattern (Fig. 185f). The cut-away lower half of the bodice completes the pattern.

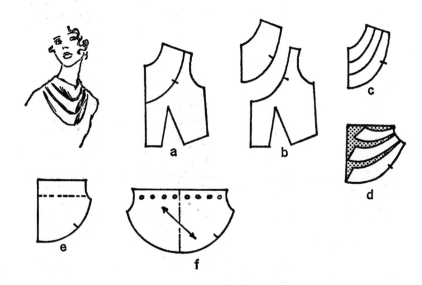

Fig. 185

FOR DEEPER, FULLER FOLDS

As with other necklines, the cowl too may have fullness added via pleats or soft folds to make the drapes deeper and fuller.

1. On the bodice front (or back) with unstitched fullness at the waistline, drop the neckline as desired. Draw drape lines. Draw a guideline parallel to the shoulder seam (Fig. 186a).

2. Draw the guideline on another sheet of paper. Slash and spread the pattern for balanced fullness along the drape line (Fig. 186b).

3. Draw a square (B) starting at the shoulder (C) and ending at the center-front waistline (A) (Fig. 186c). The new center front is AB.

4. Trace the pattern and the folds. Correct the waistline. Construct the facing (Fig. 186d).

5. Trace the other half of the pattern (Fig. 186e) and complete it.

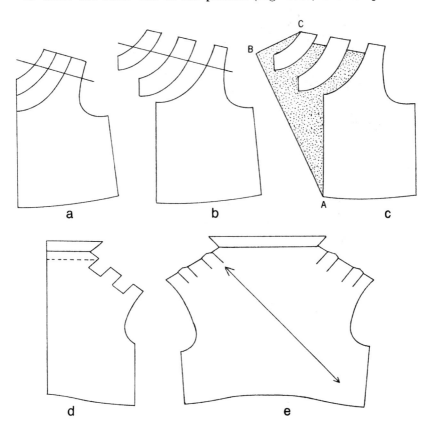

Fig. 186

OTHER COWLS

Cowls need not be limited to front or back necklines. They may appear on skirts, pants, and sleeves as well. Made of firm or stiff material, the drapes become dramatic as shown in Fig. 187.

Fig. 187

SKIRT OR PANTS WITH DEEP COWL DRAPES AT THE SIDES

1. Trace the front and back slopers of skirts or pants. Move the dart control to the side seams. Straighten them and eliminate the flare at the hems.

2. Place the front and back slopers together at the side seams. Draw drape lines (Fig. 188a). Label sections 1 and 2.

3. Draw a horizontal line on a fresh sheet of paper large enough to take the full pattern.

4. Slash and spread the pattern against the straight line (Fig. 188b). The side seams of front and back touch at the hemline.

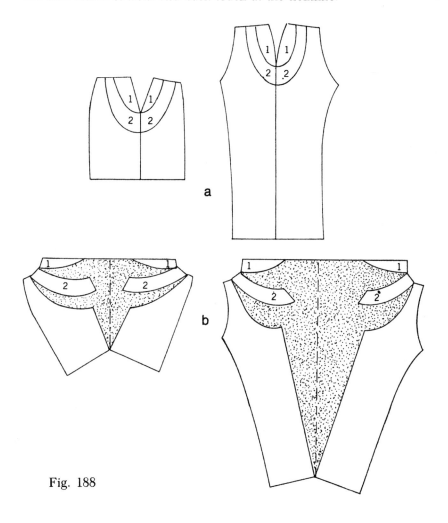

Fig. 188

Section 1 lies against the horizontal line.

Section 2 is placed midway between section 1 and the rest of the pattern.

5. Trace the entire outside line of the pattern. Correct the angularity at the hemline and the waistline. Plan the facing (broken line) (Fig. 188c).

6. Trace the entire pattern and the facing (Fig. 188d).

7. Complete the pattern.

NOTE: There will be seams at the center front and center back but none at the sides. Fold line AB at center (C); stitch. Attach a covered weight at C to bring the folds into place.

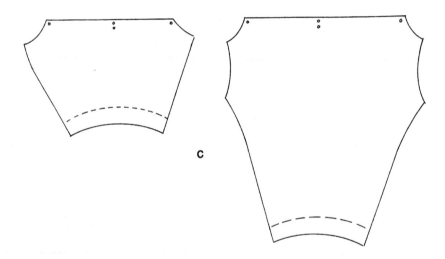

c

Fig. 188

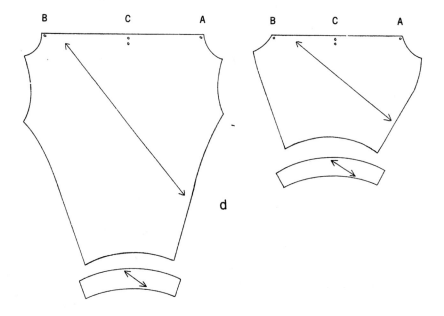

Fig. 188

COWL ON THE SLEEVE

This is constructed in the same manner as for the skirt or pants.

1. Use a short-sleeve or long-sleeve sloper. Divide the sleeve in half lengthwise. Draw the drape lines. Label sections 1, 2, and 3 (Fig. 189a).

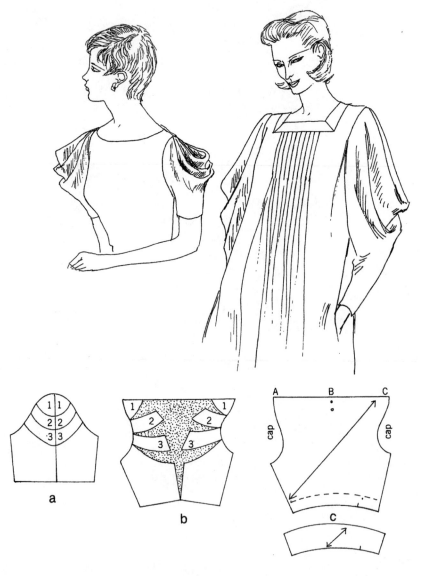

Fig. 189

2. Draw a horizontal straight line on paper large enough for the pattern.

3. Slash the center line and the drape lines.

4. Spread sections 1, 2, and 3 as illustrated (Fig. 189b). The hem of the sleeve remains closed at the hem center.

Section 1 lies against the straight line.

Sections 2 and 3 are placed so all spaces between sections are equal.

5. Trace the outside line of the pattern correcting the hemline with a curved line (Fig. 189c).

6. Construct the facing and trace it (Fig. 189c).

7. Complete the pattern.

NOTE: There will be an underarm seam and a seam at line ACB. Fold AB at C and stitch. Attach a covered weight at C.

COWL DRAPERY HELD IN PLACE

For holding the drapery in place use spot weights, dressmakers' weights—small disks that come in ⅝-inch to 1½-inch diameters. For uniform weighting, use weighted tapes (¼-inch enclosed flat lead weights).

As with other designs with additional fullness, a lining stay is desirable for keeping the fullness of cowl draping in its rightful place. Cut the stay from the basic-fitting sloper. Tack the drapes to this undercover control at strategic points.

A little experimentation will undoubtedly be needed to achieve the effect you have in mind, but the result is so immediate and so beautiful that your new clothes will probably burgeon with cowl drapes.

Be it ever so simple, a neckline can be notable.

Chapter 9

Easy Access

We have worked out some mightily interesting designs to this point but they all have one unfortunate feature in common—no way of getting into them. It's somewhat like designing a house without a door. It's true that some of the fuller designs could be slipped over the head but that may prove a gymnastic feat for the wearer or a peril for the wearer's new hairdo and makeup. For most garments some easier access is imperative—particularly if the garment is a fitted one.

We have seen before how designers make decorative use of structural necessity. This is especially true of closings. If a closing there must be, it may as well be beautiful. Though the simpler, less gadgety closings are always chic, there are times when your imagination can run free.

What are the choices? A garment may be single-breasted, double-breasted, asymmetric, or surplice. It may be fastened with rope or rare buttons, with hardware or hooks and eyes, with braid, buckles, or bows. It may sport exquisitely made buttonholes or be held together by unseen snaps. It may be zipped shut in a very matter-of-fact manner. The closing can be straight, diagonal, or shaped; very simple or very intricate. Whatever the closing, it is so essential and so prominent a part of the design that it requires special thought in planning. Often, the closing can "make" an otherwise unassuming design.

DECISION, DECISION

You cannot make a pattern and then decide how to fasten the garment. *The pattern depends on the kind of closing you choose.* You must make a decision about the type of closing and the fastening first and *then* the pattern.

Should you plan to use a *zippered closing,* decide whether it is to be long, short, or in between; whether it will be in front, at the side, or in back; whether it will be in a construction seam, in a dart, in a slash, or under a pleat; whether it is to be brazenly exposed or completely hidden in a seam that belies its existence.

When you plan to use a *buttoned closing,* decide how many buttons you want, what size they will be, and where they are to be placed. Decide whether they will be placed singly, in a series, or in groups. Decide whether the buttonholes are to be horizontal, vertical, or at an angle.

If a *novelty fastening* is your choice, decide where and how it is to be used.

ZIPPERED CLOSING

No need to sing the praises of the zipper for a closing. It is the easiest to account for in a pattern, the simplest to sew, and the easiest to use in a garment.

Generally, a seam allowance is sufficient for the installation of a zipper. To make very sure there is enough width to accommodate it, make the placket seam a little wider—¾ to ⅞ inch instead of the more usual ½ or ⅝ inch.

When a zipper is set into a slash in the material rather than into a seam, a facing piece is necessary.

The neatest zippered closing is that with an *invisible zipper in a construction seam.* This is simple and quick to install on the underside of a seam line. Since no stitching is visible from the right side, there is nothing to distract the eye. This makes it possible to use any decorative style line for the zipper installation (Fig. 190).

The two standard types of zippered closing are the lapped (regulation) and the centered (slot seam).

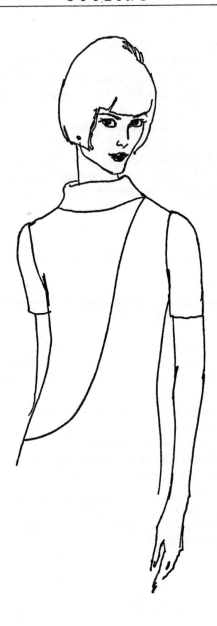

Fig. 190

In the *lapped closing* (Fig. 191a), the zipper is hidden in a lapped seam. The overlap may be to the right or the left depending on which is easier for the wearer to use. Generally, an overlap to the right is easier for right-handed people, an overlap to the left for the left-handed. Only one line of stitching is visible.

There is this, too: Women's clothing usually laps right over left, men's clothing left over right.

In the *centered closing* (Fig. 191b), the zipper is concealed by two folds of material which are centered over the zipper. There are two lines of visible stitching, one on each side of the seam line.

Both types of zippered closing are acceptable whatever the location of the zipper. Which to use depends on the design and the fabric. Use a centered type when a symmetrical appearance is consistent with the design. It makes a trimmer opening for heavy and pile fabrics; faced, slashed, or wrist openings; openings concealed in box or inverted pleats. Use a lapped closing for a fly front and when the design is "dressy" and the fabric delicate or looped or the kind that may catch in the teeth of the zipper when it is closed.

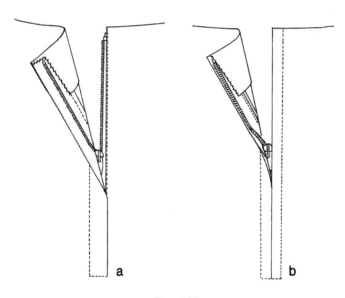

Fig. 191

The *separating zipper* is a favorite form of closing for casual jackets. Its installation can be that of the exposed zipper, with lapped (Fig. 192a) or centered construction (Fig. 192b).

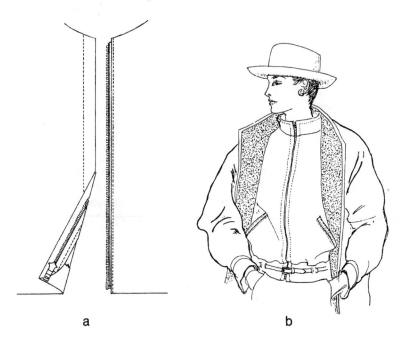

a   b

Fig. 192

While other zippers hide beneath a fold of fabric, the *exposed zipper* bravely bares its teeth—color, texture, and all (Fig. 193). Some zippers are designed especially for this purpose.

The pattern for the exposed zipper is the same as for other zipper types. How it is installed is a dressmaking choice.

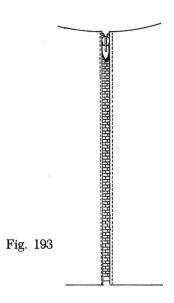

Fig. 193

BUTTONED CLOSING

You could buckle it, bolt it, tie it, zipper it, lace it, or chain it, but chances are you will choose the time-honored buttoned closing for most of your clothes.

Bound machine- or hand-worked buttonholes require a slash in the fashion fabric, hazardous in some materials and a terrifying thought to many sewers. The loop-and-button closing is a welcome alternative. So is the in-seam buttonhole that takes advantage of any appropriately placed seam.

Buttonhole-and-Button Closing

When planning the buttonhole-and-button closing, consider the fabric of your design.

Making buttonholes in loosely woven or ravelly material is risky. Making them in knits or stretchy cloth is chancy. Bound buttonholes in transparent material reveal all the inner workings. Jeweled or rough-surfaced buttons often damage the material as they are passed through a buttonhole or may, in turn, be damaged by it.

You may fake a buttoned closing by sewing a button to the right side of the garment with or without a snap directly beneath the button on the underside of a worked but uncut buttonhole. Decorative rather than functional buttons do have their place in design.

BUTTONHOLE PLACEMENT

When a garment is buttoned, its two sides must overlap each other for a secure closing. The overlap is an extension of the material beyond the closing line toward the outer edge. There is a rule which governs its width. It is this: *the extension equals the width of the button to be used* (Fig. 194a). When the garment is buttoned, there should be half a button's width between the rim of the button and the finished edge of the garment (Fig. 194b). In addition to a good overlap, this bit of mathematics assures a proper setting for a beautiful button.

You may use a slightly smaller button in the same space but rarely a larger one. When an outsize button is used, the extension must equal at the very least half a button's width plus ½ inch (Fig. 194c).

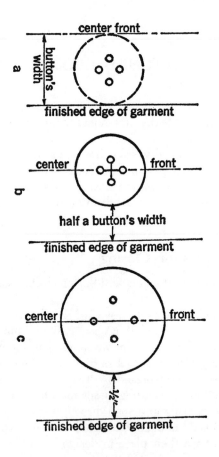

Fig. 194

In a garment that is buttoned to the neckline, the first button is placed a button's width from the finished edge of the neckline (Fig. 195a). When a garment has a lapel, the first button is located at the break of the collar (Fig. 195b). In a fitted garment, buttons should be so placed that the garment does not pop open at the bust or gap at the waist (Fig. 195c). In an unfitted or semifitted garment, the buttons may be widely spaced. Such designs look better when the garment is held closed between the buttons with snaps covered to match in color (Fig. 195d).

If a belt is used at the waistline, place the buttons sufficiently above and below so they don't interfere with the belt (Fig. 195e). Do not place a button in the hem or too close to the hem for comfort or for appearance.

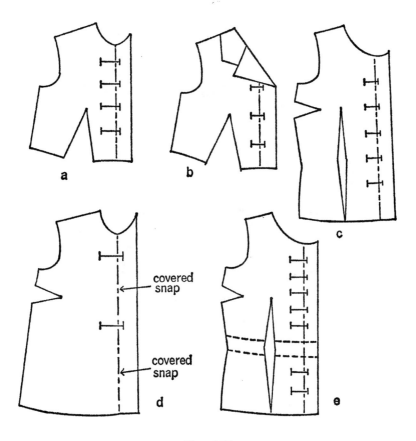

Fig. 195

Technically, button sizes are measured in "lines"—forty lines to an inch. (A forty-line button is a one-inch button.) Fig. 196 is a button gauge in actual size. It will help you determine the correct size of button required.

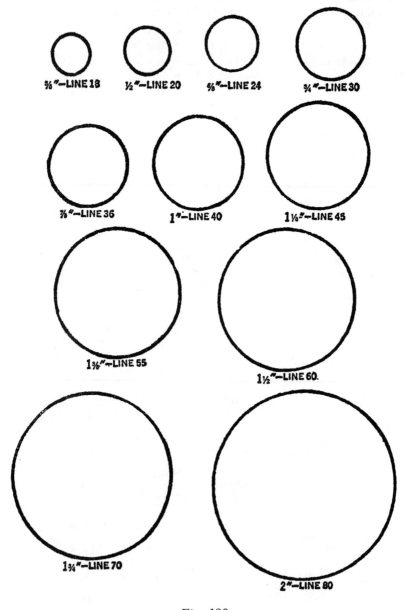

Fig. 196

BUTTONHOLE SIZE AND MARKING

To ensure an exact closing on the designated line, it is necessary to make an allowance for the thickness of the shank or stem of the button. The standard amount for this correction is ⅛ inch. Therefore the button-hole begins not at the closing line where you would expect it to begin but ⅛ inch beyond the closing line toward the outer edge of the garment in a horizontal buttonhole (Fig. 197a) and ⅛ inch toward the upper edge of a garment in a vertical buttonhole (Fig. 197b). The ⅛ inch also allows for the tendency of a garment to pull away from a horizontal closing and down from a vertical closing.

For small buttons, buttonholes are not usually placed closer than ½ inch from a closing edge.

The opening of the buttonhole extends inward from the placement line for horizontal buttonholes and downward from the placement line for vertical buttonholes for the length of the buttonhole.

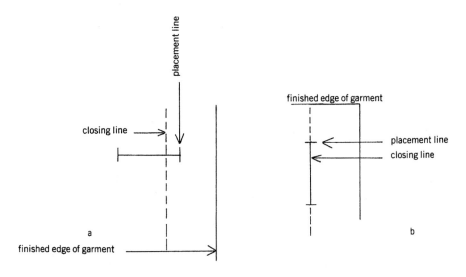

Fig. 197

Buttonhole size depends on the size and type of button.

A buttonhole for a comparatively flat button is equal to the diameter of the button plus ⅛ inch ease (Fig. 198a). For a thick or bumpy button, the length of the buttonhole is equal to the button's width plus its thickness (height). An easy way to determine buttonhole length is to wrap a strip of narrow paper around the button at its widest part (Fig. 198b). (A very narrow tape measure would be even better.) Half the measurement is the correct size for the buttonhole.

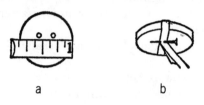

a   b

Fig. 198

When in doubt as to the proper length, make a test slash. Keep in mind that buttonholes tend to work up smaller than the designated length. Don't skimp on the buttonhole length. On the other hand, don't exaggerate the length; you wouldn't want a large opening with insufficient button to fill it. Aside from being unsightly, the button wouldn't stay buttoned.

Buttonholes work best when made on the horizontal or crosswise grain of the material. This is the direction of the stress on them. Buttonholes on an angle are very pretty but present a problem in the cutting and making; bias buttonholes tend to ripple. However, in a bias garment, bias buttonholes really place them on straight grain, which is fine. When a diagonal style line is involved, the buttonholes may be placed at right angles either to the closing line or to the center front or back. This is purely a matter of design of the garment.

In a narrow band (as for instance in a shirt or shirtwaist closing), the buttonholes must be made vertically in order to fit the space.

On your pattern draw the closing line, the placement line, and the position and length of the buttonholes.

Right or Left?

The color of bootees—pink or blue—is not the only way of telling which are the girls' and which are the boys'. Little (and big) girls' clothes button right over left; little (and big) boys' clothes the opposite way. Both front and back. Want a surprise design element? Try lapping a woman's garment left over right to dramatize a style line (Fig. 199a). An interesting counterpoint can be achieved by an alternate right and left overlapping (Fig. 199b).

a

b

Fig. 199

CLOSING OVERLAP

The construction of the pattern for a closing overlap is the same wherever it is located on the garment—front, back, bodice, skirt, sleeve, jacket, coat, collar, cuffs, pockets, button-in lining, and so on (Fig. 200).

The overlap may be only enough to accommodate a single row of buttons, a generous overlap, a diagonal overlap, an asymmetrical closing, or any decorative variations of the above.

Necklines are designed on the sloper *before* the overlap; *collars* are designed *after*.

General Procedure for All Overlaps

1. On the *complete* front and/or back sloper or the particular pattern part, draw the closing and overlap lines.

2. Cut away the excess pattern.

3. Indicate the type and location of fastening.

4. Complete the pattern by adding grain line, notches, and seam allowances.

Facings for Overlap Closings

Facings for overlap closings can be made in one of two ways—either all in one with the overlap or seamed at its edge.

An *all-in-one facing* is used when the overlap line is straight (either vertical or horizontal), the material wide enough for the layout, and a fold of cloth is desired rather than a seam. There is no particular virtue in having a seam. The seam does not make the garment hold or hang better. In fact, if you eliminate the joining seam, you may eliminate a stitching or matching problem.

A *separate facing* is used when the overlap line is diagonal or shaped, when the material is not wide enough for the layout, or if the layout is more economical by use of a separate pattern section.

Fig. 200

PROCEDURE FOR DEVELOPING
THE PATTERN FOR THE FACING

1. On the pattern with the overlap, draw the outer line of the facing. You may make the facing any suitable width. Just be sure to make it wide enough to completely cover any buttonholes plus a little more.

2. For a facing all in one with the overlap, fold the pattern on the overlap line and trace the entire facing. Unfold the pattern and pencil in the facing.

3. For a separate facing, place another sheet of paper under or over the pattern and trace the entire facing and the grain line.

4. Add seam allowances and notches to match those of the garment.

HOW THIS GENERAL PROCEDURE WORKS ON
THE FOLLOWING TYPES OF CLOSINGS

SINGLE-BREASTED CLOSING

1. On a complete front or back sloper, mark the center-front (or center-back) closing line. Show the position and size of the buttons. Draw the overlap line a button's width away from the closing line (Fig. 201a).

2. Cut away the excess pattern. Trace the new pattern with the closing extension on fresh paper.

3. Trace the closing line and the position and size of all buttonholes. Establish the grain line (Fig. 201b).

4. Add seam allowances and notches.

Fig. 201

Make the Pattern for the Facing

1. On the bodice pattern with the closing extension (overlap), measure 1½ inches over on the shoulder from the neckline. On the waistline, measure over 2½ to 3 inches from the center front (or any other suitable width, keeping in mind the width of the buttonholes). Connect the two points with a slightly curved line (Fig. 202a).

2. On the skirt pattern, measure over the same amount at the waistline as for the bodice. Carry this width down the length of the skirt to the hem (Fig. 202a).

3. For an all-in-one facing, fold the pattern on the overlap line and trace neckline, shoulder, outer edge, and waistline of the bodice; trace the waistline, outer edge of the facing, and the hemline of the skirt. Unfold the pattern and sketch in the facing (Fig. 202b). Add seam allowances.

4. For a separate facing, place another sheet of paper under or over the bodice and/or the skirt pattern and trace the entire facing, grain line, and notches (Fig. 202c). Add seam allowances.

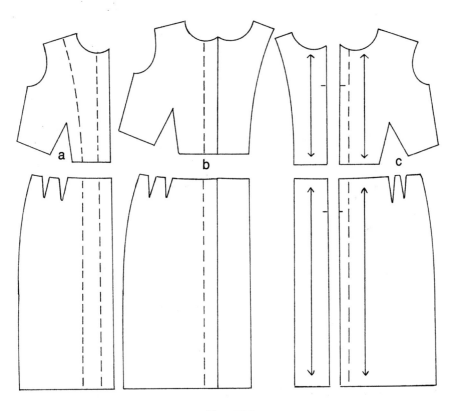

Fig. 202

DOUBLE-BREASTED CLOSING

For the design illustrated in Fig. 203, start with the hip-length sloper and extend it to full length.

1. On the complete front pattern, mark the center-front closing line. Draw the overlap line (Fig. 203a).

2. Cut away the excess pattern (Fig. 203b). Cut two identical fronts. This deep overlap is characteristic of a double-breasted garment.

3. Locate the line for the buttonhole and button placement a button's width *in* from the edge (the overlap line) (Fig. 203b). The buttonholes are squared off the center (closing) line.

For the placement of the second row of buttons on the other side of the center-front line, fold the pattern on center front and trace the button positions (Fig. 203b).

4. Locate the facing in the same way as for the single-breasted garment but make it wide enough to include the second row of buttons plus a little extra (Fig. 203c).

5. Trace the facing as a separate section (Fig. 203d). The double-breasted garment plus facing is usually too wide for an economical layout on most fabric widths.

6. Complete the pattern.

To construct the collar for this design, see page 336, Fig. 254.

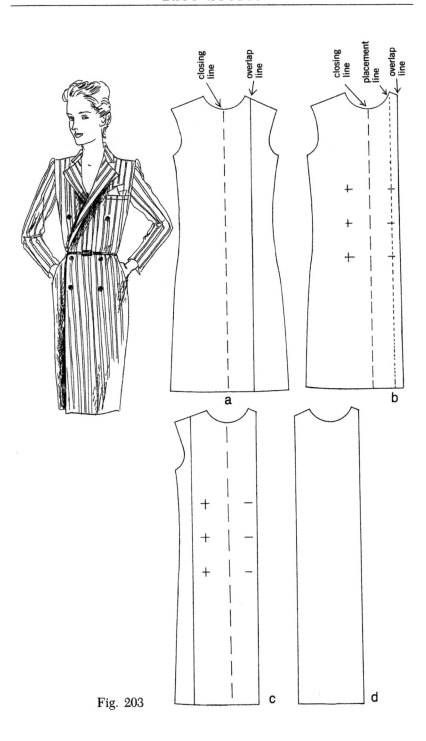

Fig. 203

BUTTONED ON A BAND OR UNDER IT

On a Band

In some designs, the overlap closing is incorporated in a band centered over the closing line. Buttonholes are placed vertically on the closing line. There is a button's width (at least) on either side of the buttonhole. Buttons are sewn to the closing line of the other front.

The band may be as plain as in a shirt or shirtwaist (Fig. 204–1) or gussied up with a ruffle, lace, or edging (Fig. 204–2).

1. On a complete front, draw the band. Mark the closing line and the location of the buttonholes (Fig. 204a).

2. Cut away the excess pattern (Fig. 204b).

3. Cut the band away from the rest of the front (Fig. 204c).

4. Establish the grain in the front and band. Add seam allowances and notches.

Right and left fronts may be identical or the left front may be designed without the band.

Face the band only or cut a standard facing for the front.

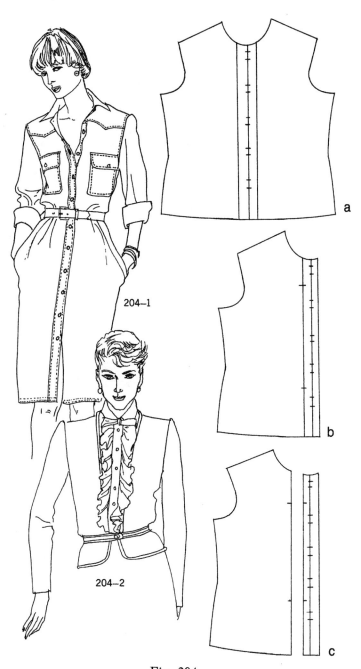

204—1

204—2

a

b

c

Fig. 204

Under a Band

The *fly front* frequently used in sportswear has a right-front (or left-front) overlap which conceals a strip of buttonholes.

1. Make the front pattern with the overlap extension in one with the self-facing to be turned back as an underfold (Fig. 205a). Mark the fold line, the closing line, and the topstitching line by which the understrip is attached to the front. Add seam allowances.

2. Make a separate understrip (fly) pattern slightly narrower than the underfold to ensure that the fly is concealed. Double it for a self-facing. Mark the fold line, the closing line, and the buttonholes (Fig. 205b).

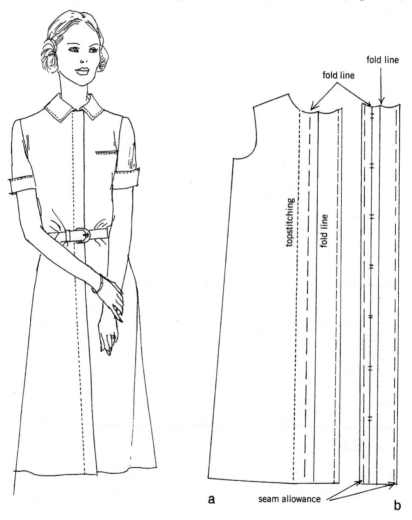

Fig. 205

3. Add seam allowances.

4. Mark the button positions on the other front.

Should you wish a one-piece fly pattern, Scotch-tape the fly strip to the front self-facing.

SINGLE-BREASTED GARMENT
WITH DEEP OVERLAP

It is possible for a single-breasted garment to have a deep overlap, too. One way is to make the closing extension much wider than the diameter of the button would indicate (Fig. 206a).

Another way is to preserve the formula for the extension on the right front but design the left front with a much deeper extension (Fig. 206b). This has the advantage of preserving a single-breasted appearance while providing a deep overlap. It's a good way to solve the winter-coat overlap problem.

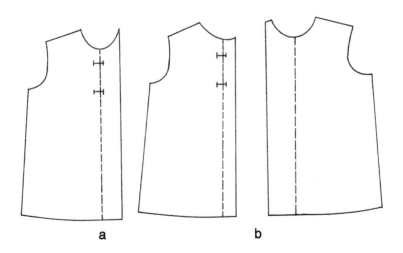

a   b

Fig. 206

A RIGHT SIDE THAT DOESN'T KNOW
WHAT THE LEFT SIDE IS DOING

A design need not be asymmetric for right and left extensions to be different. For example, a single-breasted design with a scalloped extension on the right front need only have a standard left front (Fig. 207).

The left front does not have to duplicate the right. It will not be seen. It has nothing whatever to do with the fit of the garment. To make both sides alike would entail a great deal of unnecessary work.

1. On a complete-front dress-length pattern, draw the style line for the right front, the closing line at center front, and the overlap line of the left front (broken line). Locate the buttons and buttonholes (Fig. 207a).

2. Trace the right and left fronts. Draw the facings on each pattern (Fig. 207b). Trace them (Fig. 207c).

3. Complete the pattern.

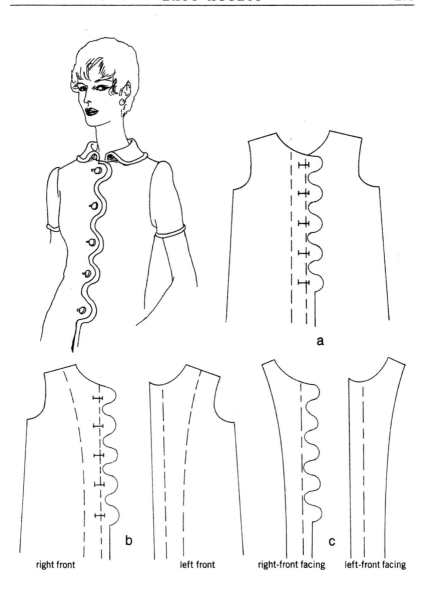

right front   left front   right-front facing   left-front facing

Fig. 207

THE SURPLICE CLOSING

The easy-to-get-into surplice garment overlaps diagonally either front or back. It may be buttoned (Fig. 208a) or wrapped (Fig. 208b). A cut-away surplice style can be quite intriguing (Fig. 208c).

Though asymmetric in design, both sides are cut identically. The pattern is developed as for a double-breasted closing.

a   b   c

Fig. 208

Because only one row of buttons is used in Fig. 209, this design too appears asymmetric. However, its structure also is that of a double-breasted closing.

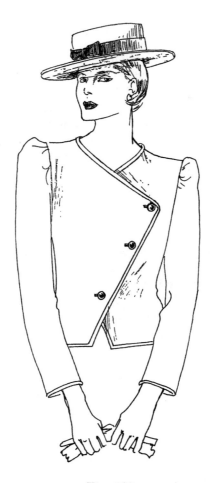

Fig. 209

ASYMMETRIC CLOSING

In a true asymmetric design, each side of the closing is different.

Fig. 210a

1. Start with a complete bodice-front pattern. (This design has waist-line fullness and a dropped neckline.)

2. Draw the asymmetric style line (right overlap line) and the closing line a button's width away from it. Locate the position of the buttons and buttonholes which are at right angles to the center front.

3. With a broken line, draw the left-front overlap line a button's width away from the closing line toward the right front.

4. Establish the grain in the left front parallel to the center front which is on straight grain.

5. Mark the center front.

Fig. 210b

6. Trace the complete right-front bodice from the right overlap line to the right side seam. Trace the complete left-front bodice from the left overlap line to the left side seam.

7. Draw the facing on each pattern parallel to the neckline and the overlap line. It should be deep enough to accommodate the buttonholes plus a little extra.

8. Notch the pattern on the overlap lines on both sides. Trace the grain lines.

Fig. 210c

9. Trace the right-front bodice, center front, grain line, closing line, notches, and buttonholes. Trace the left-front bodice in the same way. Trace the facings, center front, grain line, and notches.

10. Complete the pattern.

left-front overlap line   closing line

right-front overlap line

a

b

c

right front   left front   right-front facing   left-front facing

Fig. 210

ASYMMETRIC DESIGNS WITH DEEP OVERLAPS

There is very little overlap in the previous design. Some designs call for a greater overlap; for instance, the coat dress in Fig. 211.

Fig. 211a

1. Start with the hip-length sloper. Extend it to dress length. Use the dart control as illustrated: fullness under a yoke, unstitched control at the waistline.

2. On the complete front pattern, draw the center-front line, the style (overlap) line of the closing, and the closing line a button's width away. Locate the position of the buttonholes at right angles to the closing line.

Fig. 211b

3. Trace the complete right-front pattern. Trace the center-front line, the closing line, and the buttonholes. Trace the complete left-front pattern to the center-front line. Trace the closing line and the position of the buttons. Trace the grain lines.

4. Draw the facings on each pattern in the same way as for the asymmetric closing of Fig. 210. Trace the grain line. Mark notches.

Fig. 211c

5. Trace the left-front and right-front patterns with all markings. Trace the facings with all markings.

6. Complete the pattern.

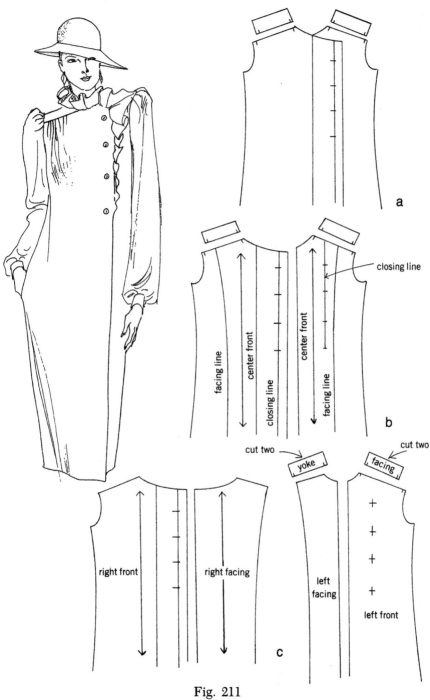

closing line

facing line

center front

closing line

center front

facing line

a

b

cut two

yoke

cut two

facing

right front

right facing

left
facing

left front

c

Fig. 211

OVERLAP BONUS—THE WRAP GARMENT

A deep overlap closing produces the design for the wrap dress (Fig. 212a), the wrap skirt (Fig. 212b), and the wrap sleeve (Fig. 212c).

In a wrap garment, left and right sides may be either identical as in Figs. 213a and 213c or different as in Fig. 213b.

Fig. 212

To Construct the Patterns in Fig. 213

1. Start with the complete-front skirt sloper with waistline fullness for Figs. 213a and 213b. Start with the complete short-sleeve sloper with cap fullness for Fig. 213c. Draw the center (closing) line.

2. Draw the style (overlap) line.

Fig. 213a

3. Cut away the excess pattern.
4. Cut two identical patterns.

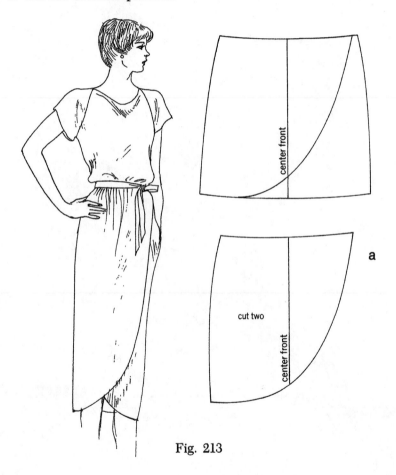

Fig. 213

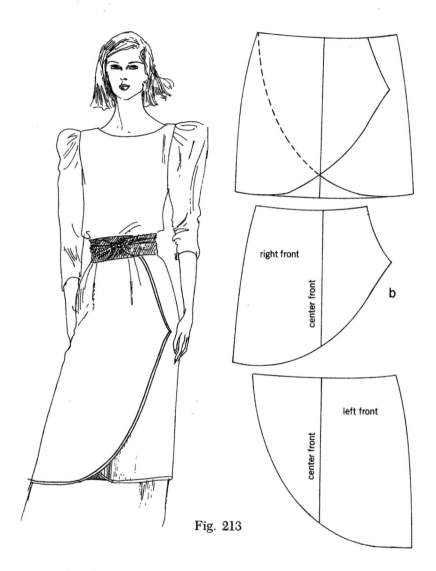

Fig. 213

Fig. 213b

3. Trace the right-front pattern.

4. Use the complete-front pattern (for a best overlap) or trim away a slight amount along the right-front edge.

Fig. 213

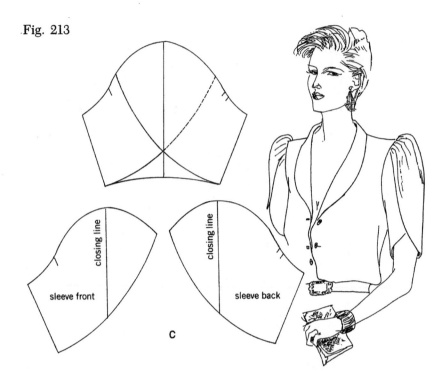

c

Fig. 213c

5. Trace the front sleeve; trace the back sleeve. While right- and left-sleeve style lines are identical, the sleeve caps are different.

For All Patterns

6. Mark the center (closing) line which becomes the straight grain.
7. Complete the patterns.

A wrap dress is developed in the same way using the extended hip-length sloper as a base.

IN-SEAM BUTTONHOLE

The in-seam buttonhole is a delightfully easy way out of the buttonhole bother. A seam line is left unstitched at intervals to provide openings for the buttons. Any seam can be used for this purpose if properly positioned.

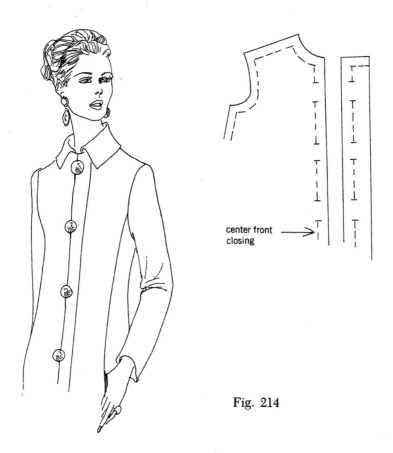

center front
closing

Fig. 214

Mark the buttonhole openings on the pattern. Leave similar openings in any facings or linings.

In Fig. 214, the rule for the width of the extension holds (a button's width) even though it appears as a band in this design.

LOOP-AND-BUTTON CLOSING

This is a decorative alternative to the more usual buttonhole-and-button closing. It is particularly practical when cutting into fabric is hazardous or would disrupt the continuity of the fabric design.

In this closing, both loops and buttons are stitched to the closing line. There is no overlap except that made by the loops themselves. There may be (Fig. 215a) or may not be (Fig. 215b) an underlap.

Fig. 215

a

b

When there is an underlap, make the button side with a closing extension as for a single-breasted closing. On the loop side, simply add seam allowance to the closing line. Make a facing to match each side.

Button loops are inserted in the seam that joins facing to garment in a planned sequence which should be indicated on the pattern.

Fig. 216

The pattern for a garment with *decorative frogs* (Fig. 216) is developed in the same way with or without an overlap. The frogs are centered over the closing with the loop on the right half and the button on the left half. Should you wish, you might include a diagram for the formation of the frog you have in mind.

WITHOUT BENEFIT OF OVERLAP

There are always contradictions in design. Take the designs in Fig. 217, for instance. They lace, loop, and link on center front without benefit of

Fig. 217

extensions (also without benefit of a complete closing if you want it that way). All that is needed on the pattern of such designs is the locations of the eyelets, loops, or buttonholes.

PLACKET OPENING

A placket is a finished opening in fitted or semifitted styles for convenience in putting them on. There are a number of finishes suitable for a placket opening depending on the type of garment, the design, the fabric, and the location of the opening. Since there are so many placket possibilities, the placket is often more the concern of the dressmaker than the patternmaker. The opening only is indicated on the pattern and the choice of construction left to the sewer. When the placket becomes part of the design (as in the tailored placket below), then it does concern the patternmaker.

Plackets may be made in the opening left in a seam, added to a seam, or set in a slash or dart. (See also Chapter 14, "Sleeve Finishes.")

TAILORED PLACKET (FRENCH PLACKET, SHIRT PLACKET)

The tailored placket is the familiar opening of tailored shirts, blouses, dresses, sleeves (Fig. 218). It is a strong as well as decorative finish.

In the tailored placket, a band and its facing, cut as one piece, is attached to each side of the opening so that one band overlaps the other.

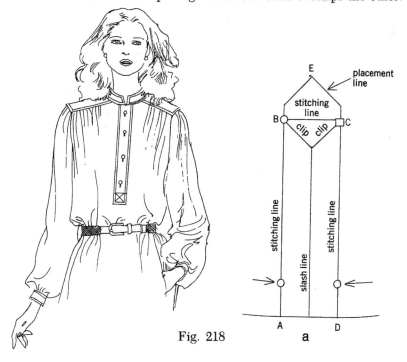

Fig. 218

The underlap is generally a plain band while the overlap, frequently top-stitched, has either a plain or shaped end.

The underlap and overlap may be made in two pieces (Fig. 219) or in one piece (Fig. 220). Either is acceptable wherever the placket is located. When the placket is at a neckline, it often includes a combination neckline and placket facing (Fig. 221).

TWO-PIECE TAILORED PLACKET

1. On the pattern piece involved, draw the placket band (overlap) as it will appear in the finished garment. Show the placement lines, the stitching lines, the slash line midway between the stitching lines, diagonal clips to B and C, and points to be matched, □ and ○ (Fig. 219a).

2. Trace the underlap ABCD and points □ and ○.

3. Fold on line CD and trace the band again. Open out the pattern and pencil in the lines. Add seam allowances and grain line (Fig. 219b).

4. Trace the overlap ABECD. Trace the stitching line BC and points □ and ○.

5. Fold on line AB and trace the shaped band.

6. Open out the pattern and pencil in the lines. Add seam allowances, grain line, and topstitching line when used (Fig. 219c).

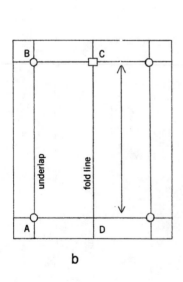

b

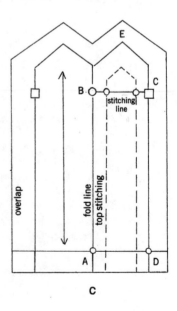

c

Fig. 219

ONE-PIECE TAILORED PLACKET

1. On the pattern piece involved, draw the placket band as it will appear in the finished garment. This shows the placement lines for the placket. Mark points A, B, C, D, and E and the ○, ○, and □. Line BC represents the stitching line that attaches the upper shaped section of the placket to the garment (Fig. 220a).

2. On a fresh piece of paper, trace the placket and stitching line. Within this placket band, locate the underlap construction: the stitching lines HG and CD; the slash line KI midway between HG and CD; and

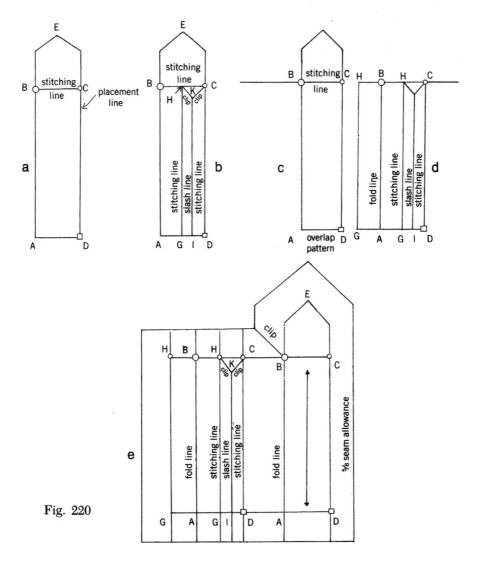

Fig. 220

the clips HK and CK (Fig. 220b). Note the placement of the construction toward one side of the band. It takes up one half its width.

3. *For the overlap:* Trace Fig. 220a. Extend the stitching line BC as a guide line for the positioning of the underlap pattern (Fig. 220c).

4. *For the underlap:* Trace the underlap construction of Fig. 220b on a separate piece of paper. Fold the underlap pattern on line AB and trace BH, HG, and GA. Open out the pattern and pencil in the lines BH, GH, and AG (Fig. 220d). Line AB becomes the fold line for the lip of the underlap.

5. *To join the overlap and underlap patterns:* Place and trace or tape the underlap pattern so its upper edge lies along the extended line in Fig. 220c and line CD is away from the overlap line AB a distance equal to the width of the overlap. This area—CBAD—becomes the overlap facing. The placket folds to position on line BA.

Trace the completed pattern. Add seam allowances on all outside edges. Indicate a clip in the seam allowance to point B. Add a grain line in the overlap section (Fig. 220e).

TAILORED NECKLINE PLACKET WITH FACING

Fig. 221a

On the complete-front pattern, draw the placket overlap band as it will appear in the finished garment. Label points ABCDE. Show stitching lines (one of which—FG—is the center-front closing line), the slash line, and diagonal clips from slash line to points D and F. Mark the placement line and the points which need matching □ and ○. When used, indicate the button positions on the center-front closing line. Draw the facing with broken lines.

Fig. 221b (underlap)

Trace the left facing and the placket band minus the triangle at its base. Mark points ABCD. Fold the band on BC and trace it once more. Open out the pattern and pencil in the traced lines. Now the left underlap band and facing are in one piece. Mark the center-front closing line and position the buttons when used. Add seam allowances, grain lines and points that need matching.

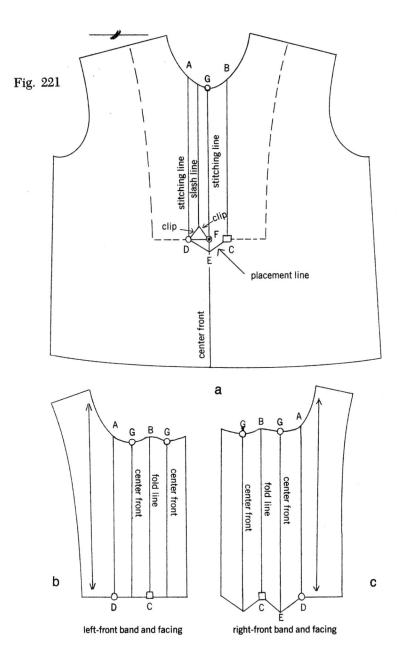

Fig. 221

left-front band and facing

right-front band and facing

Fig. 221c (overlap)

Trace the right facing and the shaped band ABCED. Fold the pattern on line BC and trace the entire shaped band ABCED again. Open out the pattern and pencil in the traced lines. Show the center-front closing line, the buttonholes, points that need matching. Add seam allowances, the grain line, and topstitching lines when used.

TABS ARE NOT TRIFLES

Tabs added to an ordinary edge can turn it into a distinctive one (Fig. 222). They may be added to any outside line of a pattern—a closing, the shoulder, the neckline, the waistline, a sleeve, a construction seam, a yoke seam, a pocket, a collar, a cuff—just about anywhere there is an edge that could benefit in interest by the addition of a tab.

How it's done:

1. Draw a tab of some interesting shape and cut it out. If you work more freely with scissors in hand, cut the tab directly. Make it curved, pointed, square, round, triangular, free-form, or whatever shape you want. Keep straight the side that will be attached to the garment's edge.

2. Scotch-tape the tab to the pattern.

3. Trace the pattern, complete with tab extension.

4. Plan a shaped facing for the shaped edge.

Fig. 222

BUTTONS, BOWS, BUCKLES, AND BANDS

A Closing Needs a Fastening (Fig. 223)

Have you ever built a dress around some very special buttons? Have you ever sighed with relief at the thought that you could skip the buttonholes and fasten your dress modishly with buckles or bows? Have you ever been tempted to use that bizarre-looking chain your Aunt Hepzibah willed you (so fashionable now)? Have you ever been lured by outsized hooks and eyes or intricate frogs? Of course you have! Everyone who sews has a collection of such choice items tucked away somewhere waiting for just the right project to come along. No need to wait any longer. Now, you can design one.

Fig. 223

Chapter 10

The Pocket Picture

Practical or pretty . . . used sparingly or in droves . . . so tiny you can't get more than a finger in them . . . so large they weigh you down . . . just-right-for-use ones . . . just-for-fun ones . . . in unlikely places . . . and baffling sizes . . . and surprising shapes. From the standpoint of design there are no limits to size, shape, and placement of pockets in women's clothing.

(Pockets in men's clothes are more functional. Actually, there are no such things as male and female pockets. Pockets are pockets when it comes to style and type. However, because of their considerable use in men's clothing, pockets are made of sturdier stuff and sturdier construction.)

Many garments are so simply cut that they offer considerable leeway in the choice of pocket design. In fact, pockets become the chief design detail.

There are *pockets applied to the surface* like the patch pocket. Also applied to the surface are the fake flaps and welts that simulate pockets.

There are *pockets stitched into a construction seam* like the in-seam pocket *or into a style line* like the front-hip pocket.

There are *pockets set into a slash* of the material like the bound pocket, the self-welt, and the stand pocket.

There are *pockets* that have elements of all these constructions—*part applied, part set in a seam or slash,* like the welt pocket or flap pocket.

FOR-REAL POCKETS

If the pocket is there for a purpose, it should be so placed and so sized that you can get a hand into it. A safe rule to follow for pocket size is this: a horizontal or diagonal opening should be as wide as the fullest part of the hand plus 1 inch; a pocket which opens vertically should be as wide as the fullest part of the hand plus 2 inches. (The hand must make a double motion to get into the pocket.) Place the pocket where it can be reached easily.

PATTERN PROCEDURE FOR POCKETS

pockets

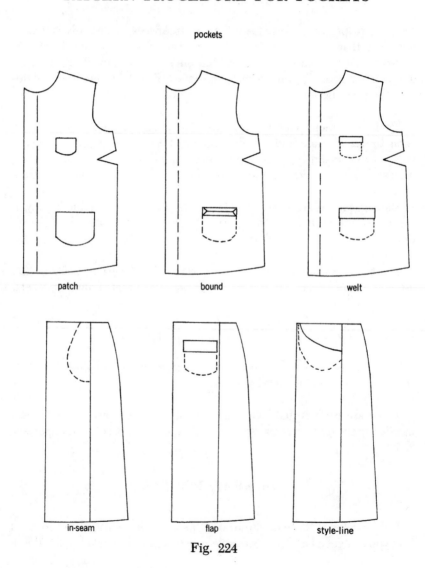

| patch | bound | welt |

| in-seam | flap | style-line |

Fig. 224

You may want to experiment with paper cutouts or scraps of fabric until you get just the right size, shape, placement, and number of pockets. Just remember to keep the lines of the pockets in harmony with the lines of the garment design.

1. Draw the pocket on the pattern showing its size and position. Use solid lines to show what will appear on the surface of the garment. Use broken lines for the part that will not be seen (Fig. 224).

2. Trace off all parts that are applied to the right side.

3. Trace off all parts that appear on the underside.

4. Make the pattern for the under pocket, the upper pocket, and any necessary facings or linings. The *under pocket* is closest to the body (under the hand); the *upper pocket* is closest to the outer fabric (over the hand).

5. Complete the pattern.

POCKET APPLIED TO THE RIGHT SIDE OF THE GARMENT: THE PATCH POCKET (Fig. 225)

1. Draw the pocket on the pattern. Work out the appropriate size, shape, and proportion.

For design interest you may do anything to the patch pocket that you have learned to do with the bodice and the skirt. Divide the area into interesting shapes, add fullness, and a tab or a flap, add a band, button it, trim it, topstitch it, use the grain as part of the design. (See Fig. 225)

2. Trace the pocket. Develop the pattern for any of the above details.

3. For a straight pocket edge, add the hem (in proportion to the size of the pocket). For a shaped pocket edge, add a shaped facing.

Patch pockets topstitched in from the edge need facings slightly deeper than the distance of the topstitching from the edge.

For a lined pocket, make a lining pattern ⅛ inch smaller than the pocket. This is the allowance for rolling the seam to the underside. For heavier fabrics the amount may have to be increased.

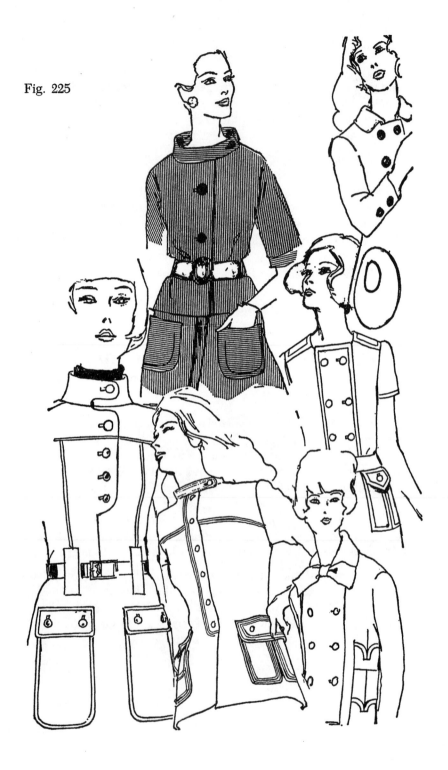

Fig. 225

POCKET SET INTO A CONSTRUCTION SEAM:
THE IN-SEAM POCKET

The in-seam pocket may be concealed (Fig. 226a) or dramatized with topstitching (Fig. 226b) or by sheer size (Fig. 226c). It consists of an under

a

b

c

Fig. 226

pocket and an upper pocket, straight or shaped, stitched together and into the construction seam.

There are three types of in-seam pockets. In the *all-in-one in-seam pocket,* both pocket and garment are cut as one piece (Fig. 227a). A *separate in-seam pocket* is joined to the garment at the seam line of the pocket opening (Fig. 227b). An *extension in-seam pocket* consists of a separate pocket piece joined to garment-plus-extension (Fig. 227c).

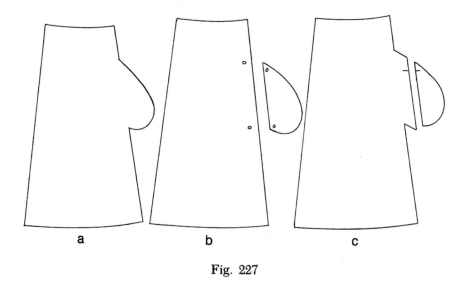

a   b   c

Fig. 227

1. For the all-in-one in-seam pocket: Scotch-tape the pocket pattern to the garment pattern seam line at the pocket opening. Trace garment and pocket pattern as one piece.

2. For a separate in-seam pocket: Add seam allowances to garment and pocket patterns. Mark the pocket opening on the garment and points at which pocket and garment join.

3. For an extension in-seam pocket: Add an extension to the garment pattern at the pocket opening. Make it deep enough to conceal the pocket material. Make the pocket pattern correspondingly smaller.

POCKET SET INTO A STYLE LINE: THE FRONT-HIP POCKET

In this design, the under pocket is an extension of the side-front section. The upper pocket is included in the facing which is attached to the front section. The hip dart appears in the side-front section only. When the dart is stitched, the undarted front stands away from the side section.

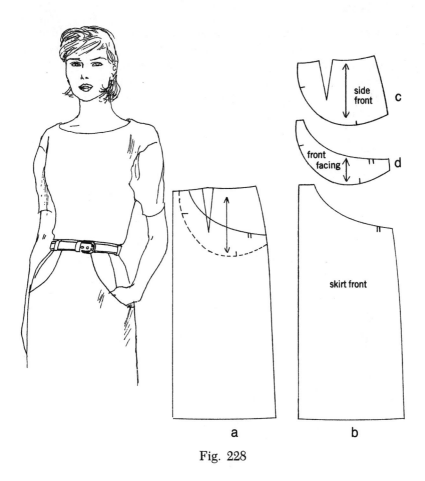

Fig. 228

1. Trace the skirt- or pants-front sloper. Draw the style line for the pocket. Draw the pocket itself with broken lines (Fig. 228a).

2. Trace the front section (Fig. 228b). Trace the side-front section including the extension for the under pocket (Fig. 228c). Trace the front pocket facing (that portion of Fig. 228a between the style line and the broken line) to be used as the upper pocket (Fig. 228d).

POCKET IN A SLASH: THE BOUND POCKET

Classic Variety

The classic-variety bound pocket is an oversize bound buttonhole to which the pocket is attached on the underside (Fig. 229a). Since the under pocket is often exposed, make it of outer fabric or lining material faced with outer fabric.

If you do not want the under pocket ever to show try a zippered pocket for a sporty look (Fig. 229b).

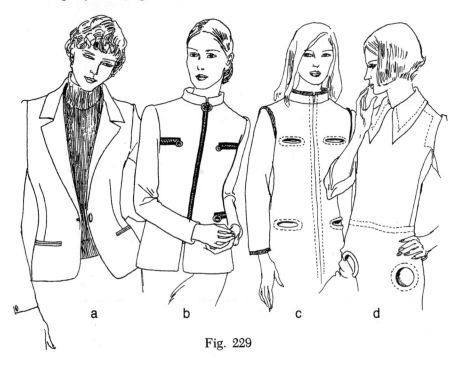

Fig. 229

Contemporary Variety

The French designer Pierre Cardin has designed some wonderful new bound pockets that bear no resemblance to the classic variety except that they're bound, too (Fig. 229c). The slash becomes a cutout, the binding large and welted. Obviously this pocket requires an under pocket of outer fabric.

Cardin's porthole pocket (Fig. 229d) is faced and topstitched rather than bound. What an exciting feature on a simple dress!

POCKET PART APPLIED, PART SET IN A SLASH OR SEAM: THE WELT AND THE FLAP POCKETS

Welt Pocket

The welt pocket has it both ways. The welt is applied to the surface *and* set in a slash (Fig. 230a) or seam (Fig. 230b).

1. Draw the welt as it will appear on the right side of the garment. Draw the pocket as it will appear on the underside.

2. Trace the welt. A straight-edge welt can be doubled on a fold. For a shaped welt, cut two, adding ⅛ inch (or more) to the upper welt as an allowance for rolling the seam to the underside.

3. Trace the pockets. For a one-piece pocket, cut twice the length of one pocket pattern plus an allowance for the depth of the opening. For a two-piece pocket, cut two pockets, one of which has the allowance for the depth of the pocket added to it.

4. Complete the pattern. The grain is generally that of the rest of the garment.

The position of the welt must be shown on the garment pattern.

a   b

Fig. 230

Flap Pocket

To hide the opening of a pocket and enhance its appearance, a flap may be placed over the opening of any kind of pocket—patch (Fig. 231a), in-seam (Fig. 231b), or bound (Fig. 231c).

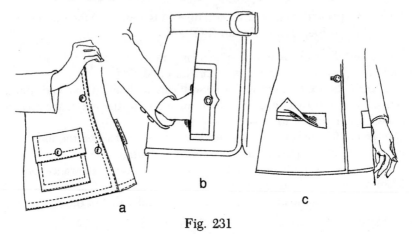

Fig. 231

1. Decide where and what type of pocket you will use under the flap—bound, in-seam, or patch. Construct the pattern for it.

2. Draw the flap as it will appear on the right side of the garment over the pocket opening. Trace the flap.

3. A straight-edged flap can be doubled on a fold. A shaped flap will require two pieces. Generally, flaps are cut on the same grain as the rest of the garment. Add seam allowances.

FAKE FLAPS AND FAKE WELTS

From the standpoint of design, these do as well as the real thing. Plan and develop the pattern for them in the same way as for real flaps and welts. Just omit the pockets.

ALL POCKETS

Be sure to indicate the position of the pocket on the garment pattern.

Whether you really mean to use them or have them just for show, pockets add their pleasing personalities to the total design.

Chapter 11

Collar Capers

A collarless neckline, be it ever so interesting, is difficult to wear. It calls for a firm chin, a smooth and slender neck, and a good set to the shoulders—all attributes of the young and the beautiful. This, alas, leaves so many of us out. Give us, please, a soft bow, a gay scarf, and, at the very least, a flattering collar.

Fortunately there are many collars to choose from—little ones and big ones, tailored ones and frilly ones, dramatic ones and modest ones—something for everybody.

There are more considerations than fashion and style preference. Consider lines that are flattering to the shape of the face. Reserve a nice balance between the collar and the rest of the silhouette. How does one's new hairdo take to the lines of the collar? If the collar is to be worn under a jacket or a coat, choose one that will accommodate to that.

COLLAR TYPES

You may know them by their more familiar names—Peter Pan, sailor, turtleneck, and so on. However, for purposes of pattern construction, it is important to identify the collar type regardless of descriptive name.

There are three basic types of collars with some variations within each.

A *flat collar* is almost identical to the shape and length of the garment neckline and shoulders though it has a slight roll.

A *rolled collar* rises from the neck seam and turns down to create a rolled edge around the neck.

A *standing collar* extends up from the garment neckline in either a soft or stiff manner.

TERMS USED IN COLLAR CONSTRUCTION

A collar has parts and each part has a name (Fig. 232).

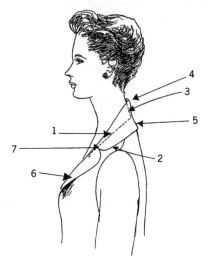

Fig. 232

1. The *neckline.* This is the part of the collar that fits around the neck. Usually, the neckline of the collar is stitched to the neckline of the garment.

2. The *style line.* This is the outer edge of the collar. As with any other style line, this may be anything the designer wishes it to be. The style line always finds that part of the shoulders that equals it in measurement, pushing the rest into a stand. As the style line shortens, the stand increases. As the style line lengthens, the stand decreases.

3. The *stand.* The stand is the amount the collar rises from the neckline to the roll line.

4. The *roll line.* The roll line is the line along which the collar turns down (when it does).

5. The *fall.* The fall is the depth of the collar from the roll line to the style line. The fall must be deep enough to hide the neckline seam.

6. The *break.* The break is the point at which a collar turns back to form a lapel.

7. The *gorge line.* This is the horizontal seam on a jacket or coat that joins collar and lapels. It extends from the crease line of the lapel to the end of the collar.

COLLARS, CURVES, AND STANDS

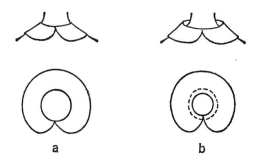

Fig. 233

Any collar that conforms to the shape and length of the neckline lies flat (Fig. 233a). This may be very little better than a collarless neckline. A collar looks prettier when there is even a slight roll. To do this, the neckline of the collar must be shortened. As the collar is stretched to fit the unshortened neckline of the garment, it is pushed into a soft roll.

In the patterns which follow in this chapter, the shortening is accomplished by raising the neckline ⅛ inch (Fig. 233b). (The broken line is the original neckline. The solid line is the raised and shortened neckline.)

When the neckline of a collar curves in a direction opposite to the curve of the neck (or of the garment neckline), its style line pushes the collar into a stand (Fig. 234a).

The shallower the opposing curves, the lower the stand (Fig. 234b). The deeper the opposing neckline curves, the higher the stand (Fig. 234c).

When a collar neckline is more curved than the neckline of the garment, it will ripple (Fig. 234d).

In a standing collar the neckline is the exact length of the garment neckline (Fig. 234e).

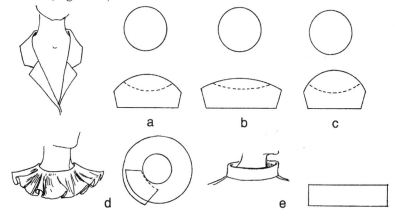

Fig. 234

BEFORE YOU BEGIN YOUR COLLAR DESIGNING

Since a collar fits around the entire neckline, use both front and back slopers to develop the pattern. For most collar patterns it is enough to trace only the upper portion of the slopers—center front, neckline, shoulders, center back, and part of the armhole.

The neckline of the bodice must be established before you begin to draft the collar. If it is to be raised or lowered, this is done first. When there is a closing extension, this, too, is constructed before the collar is designed. Close-fitting collars will fit with a little more ease if the neckline is dropped ½ inch at center front before the new neckline is drafted.

Analyze the collar for type—flat, rolled, or standing—since each type of collar is constructed in its own characteristic way.

Collars are generally faced and interfaced. Both facing and interfacing are cut on the same grain as the collar.

The upper collar should be at least ⅛ inch larger on all edges except the neck edge, as an allowance for rolling the joining seam to the underside. The heavier the cloth, the more the allowance.

Bodice-front and bodice-back slopers are placed so that they meet at the neckline. Shoulders open, touch, or overlap as the directions call for. As positioned, the back shoulder will extend slightly beyond the front armhole when there is a shoulder dart. Unless otherwise directed, ignore the dart in designing the collar.

YOU CAN'T BEAT A BAND COLLAR

A surprising number of interesting collars can be made simply from a band of cloth or lace (Fig. 235). Cut a rectangular pattern in the desired length and width on straight or bias grain. Straight grain stands better, bias grain drapes better. The ends of the band may meet, overlap, button, tie, or loop. It may double back against itself as in a turtleneck collar or fold back at the ends as in the wing collar. A long band may be gathered into a flounce (or several flounces), be pleated, or laid in soft folds. There is no end to the possibilities.

Fig. 235

THE BAND BECOMES . . .

A Fan-shaped Frame

The fan-shaped collar (Elizabethan, Medici) is too dramatic and impractical for ordinary wear but quite impressive for formal gowns, wedding gowns, or hostess gowns. The style must be made of material that will stand or must be stiffened in some way to make it stand.

1. Establish the neckline.

2. Cut a rectangle of paper to the desired length from front to center back and the width of the collar at its widest point.

3. The frame may be achieved in three ways, depending on the material at one's disposal and whether you start with the outer edge or with the neck measurement.

    a. Draw several slash lines. Slash and spread (Fig. 236a).

    b. Draw several slash lines. Slash and overlap (Fig. 236b).

    c. Dart the band to fit the neckline (Fig. 236c). If you use lace that you would not like to cut, use this method. If the lace is bordered, the end may be mitered to preserve the edge completely around the collar (Fig. 236d).

4. Trace the pattern. Correct any angularity. Draw any style line.

5. Complete the pattern.

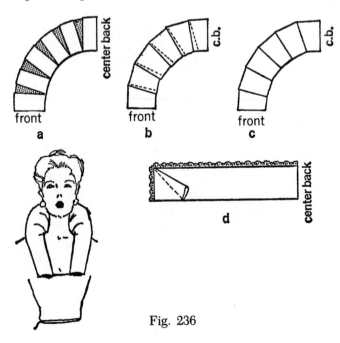

Fig. 236

The Collar of a Coat

When darts are stitched only part way up a band, the collar will stand in a line with the dart points along which the collar rolls (Fig. 237a). This is a great way of handling the excess fullness at the inner neckline of a coat collar. See also page 345.

For that neck-muffling collar, so great on a winter coat, dart both inner and outer neck edges, the latter not quite so much as the former (Fig. 237b). The band encircles the face and doubles back on itself.

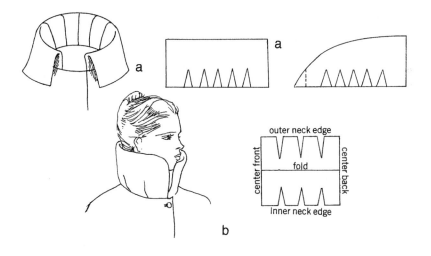

Fig. 237

A BIAS FOLD BECOMES A COLLAR

The collars in Fig. 238 are all made of bias strips of material, cut to the correct length and width and folded lengthwise. The raw edges are attached to the neckline of the garment, the folded edge is out. Because of its bias cut, the outer edges can be manipulated to fit well wherever the band falls on the body (provided it is not too deep).

It is possible to do a little shaping by steam pressing before the collar is attached. Stretch the outer (folded) edge and ease the inner (raw) edge, taking care to press with the grain.

Fig. 238

FLAT COLLARS

Collars that lie flat around the neck may go from tiny ones of 1 inch or so to the bigness of a cape collar. Though in the flat-collar category, the collars do have a slight soft roll.

The flat collar may be one-piece with a front or back opening (Fig. 239–1) or in two sections, a right and a left. It may or may not be faced.

Fig. 239

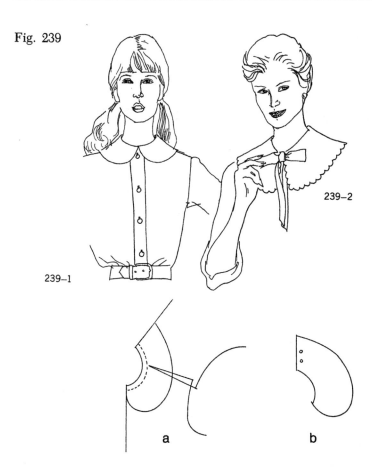

239–2

239–1

a   b

When it is not faced, it has some decorative edge (Fig. 239–2).

1. Trace the neck and shoulder areas of the bodice-front and bodice-back slopers in such position that the shoulder seams touch at the neckline and overlap ½ inch at the armhole (Fig. 239a).

2. Establish the neckline. If the entire neckline is dropped, do this now. Raise the established neckline by ⅛ inch. Both the shortening of the neckline by raising it and the shortening of the outer edge by overlapping the slopers at the shoulders produce the soft roll. Aside from improving appearance, the roll has the additional merit of hiding the seam that joins collar to garment.

3. From the neckline, measure down in a number of places the width of the collar. Draw the style line (Fig. 239a).

4. Trace the pattern (Fig. 239b) and complete it.

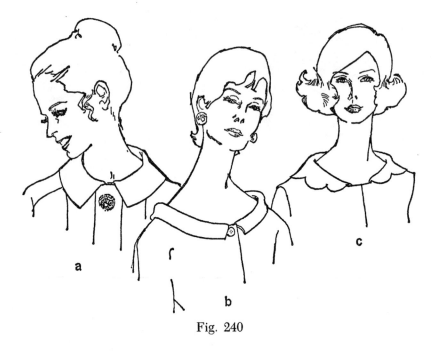

Fig. 240

Fig. 240a. The flat collar on a slightly lowered neckline.

Fig. 240b. The flat collar on a much lowered neckline.

Fig. 240c. A flat collar that doesn't meet at center front. In designing a collar like this make sure that the separation of the collar ends looks purposeful and not as if it were an accident of inadequate sewing.

The *sailor collar* is still another dropped-neckline collar. The pattern for it is a variation of the flat-collar pattern.

1. Trace the neck and shoulder areas of the front- and back-bodice slopers as for the flat collar.

2. Drop the front neckline to a V shape. (The real middy was full enough and the V-neckline low enough to slip the head through without need of any further opening. A bib filler-in covered the too-low V.) (Fig. 241a).

3. Raise the neckline by ⅛ inch at the back only. Taper the raised neckline to the front neckline (Fig. 241a).

4. Square a line from the center back at the desired depth of the back

Fig. 241

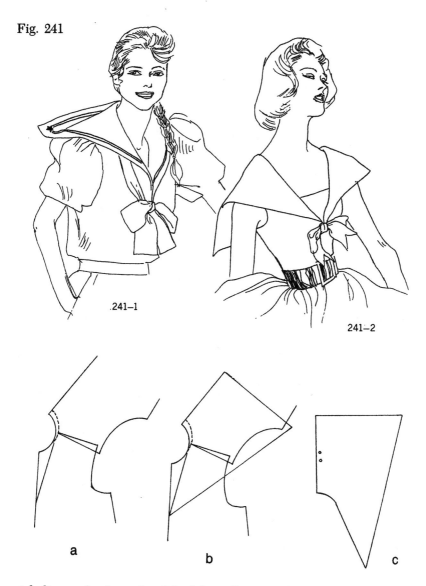

241–1

241–2

a

b

c

style line to the desired width of the collar. Connect the back-collar style line with the V at center front (Fig. 241b).

5. Trace the collar (Fig. 241c) and complete it.

There is tremendous fashion appeal to this collar (Fig. 241–1). In some form or another it seems perennially popular. Fig. 241–2 shows the sailor collar on a neckline dropped at back as well as at front.

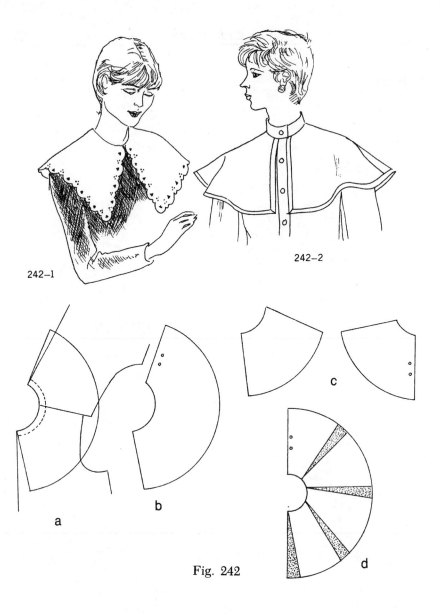

242-1

242-2

a

b

c

d

Fig. 242

The *cape collars*—graceful, flattering, dramatic—also fall in the flat-collar category. Fig. 242-1 shows a cape collar that lies rather close to the body. The cape collar in Fig. 242-1 has more flare.

1. Trace the neck and shoulder area of the front- and back-bodice slopers, shoulder seams touching and meeting at the neckline (Fig. 242a).

2. Lower the neckline for style when necessary but raise it ⅛ inch to shorten it for a soft roll after the neckline has been established (Fig. 242a).

3. From the neckline, measure down in a number of places the depth of the collar. This becomes the style line (Fig. 242a).

4. Extend the collar ¼ inch at the center-back style line for ease. Taper to the center-back neckline (Fig 242a). (In the trial muslin fitting, you may find that it is necessary to slash and spread slightly at the normal shoulder line, too, for a better fit.)

5. Trace the collar (Fig. 242b).

If the shoulders slope more than usual, use a shaped shoulder seam for better fit (Fig. 242c).

If a more flared collar is desired, slash and spread for circularity (Fig. 242d).

6. Complete the pattern.

The ultimate in a flared cape collar is the *circular cape collar.*

1. Draw a straight line. Arrange the front- and back-bodice slopers so that the center front and center back lie along the line (Fig. 243a). The shoulder seams touch at the neckline. Trace the slopers in this position.

2. Establish the new neckline. Raise it ⅛ inch.

3. Draw the style line below the shoulders (Fig. 243a).

4. Trace the pattern (Fig. 243b) and complete it.

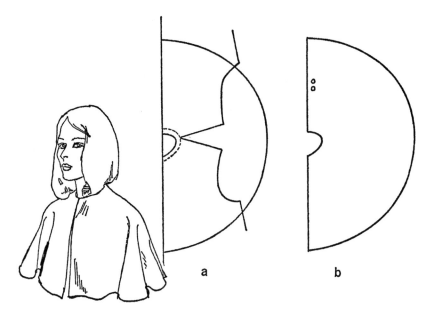

a   b

Fig. 243

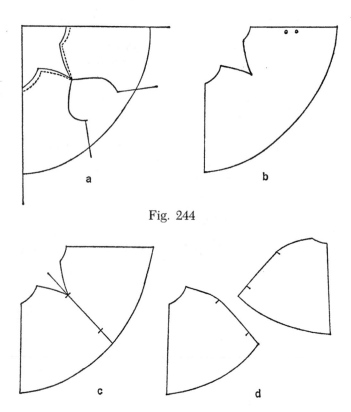

Fig. 244

A *fitted cape collar* can be shaped by a dart (Fig. 244b) or a control seam (Fig. 244d).

1. Draw a right angle. Make its sides sufficiently long to accommodate the length of the collar (Fig. 244a).

2. Trace the bodice-back sloper. Eliminate the back-shoulder dart by folding it out to the waistline (Fig. 244a).

3. Trace the bodice-front and bodice-back slopers so that the shoulders touch at the armhole and are spread open at the neckline creating a dart. The center front lies along the vertical line, the center back along the horizontal line (Fig. 244a).

4. Establish the neckline. Raise it ⅛ inch.

5. From the neckline, measure down the depth of the collar in a sufficient number of places to provide the style line (Fig. 244a).

6. Correct the dart that forms at the shoulders with curved dart legs (Fig. 244a). The collar will fit the shoulder better with a curved dart than with a straight one.

7. For the *cape collar shaped by the shoulder dart,* trace the center front, front neckline, shoulder dart, back neckline, center back, and style line (Fig. 244b).

For the *cape collar shaped by a control seam,* draw a straight line through the center of the dart and continue it to the style line (Fig. 244c). Notch the seam. Cut out the collar. Cut it apart on the seam line (Fig. 244d).

8. *Both collars:* Complete the pattern.

Fig. 245

Now, use your new-found skills in developing the flat collar designs in
Fig. 245.

ROLLED COLLARS

The rolled collar is one with a pronounced roll which divides it into a stand and fall. The roll may go around the entire collar as in the shirt collar or at the back only (half-roll) as in the notched collar, the shawl collar, and the one we have termed "roll-fitted" (see page 324).

The under and upper layers of the rolled collar are generally cut separately on the straight grain or the bias. When the design is a stand-away rolled collar, the entire collar is cut on the bias with the upper collar and undercollar in one piece.

Convertible Shirt Collars

In this convertible shirt collar, the stand and fall are cut all in one. See also "Collars on a Stand," page 342, where stand and fall are cut in two pieces.

Fig. 246a

1. Trace the neck and shoulder area of the bodice-front sloper. Drop the neckline at center front ½ inch. Draw the new neckline. Label center-front A and shoulder B.

2. Connect A and B with a straight line. Extend it so the line equals the neckline measurement from center front to center back. Label the end of the line C.

3. Fold the pattern on line ABC.

4. Trace the neckline curve AB. Unfold the paper and draw the traced neckline. Notch it.

Fig. 246b

5. From C, square a line up, equal in length to the stand of the collar (1 inch to 1½ inches). Label the end of the line D.

6. For *fall of collar:* From C, square a line down, equal in length to the stand of the collar plus ½ inch. Label the end of the line E.

7. From D, square a 2-inch line toward the center front. Label the point F.

8. From E, square a 2-inch line toward the center front. Label the point G.

9. From F, draw a line to the highest point of the neckline tracing.

For less stand at center front, draw a line from D to B and continue the neckline curve from B to A (Fig. 246c).

10. Draw the style line from the center front A all the way around to G (Fig. 246b).

11. Trace the collar and the roll line ABC (Fig. 246d).

12. Draw two slash lines evenly spaced (Fig. 246d).

13. Slash and spread ⅛ inch (Fig. 246e).

14. Trace the new pattern. Trace the roll line (Fig. 246f).

15. Complete the pattern.

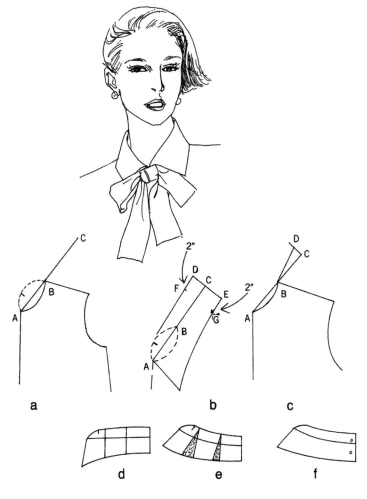

Fig. 246

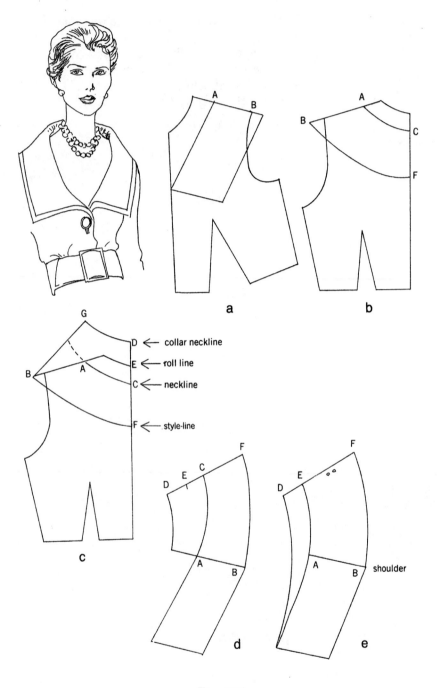

a

b

G
D ← collar neckline
E ← roll line
A
C ← neckline
B

F ← style-line

c

F
D E C
A
B

d

F
E
D
A
B shoulder

e

Fig. 247

ROLL-FITTED COLLARS

This flattering collar has a medium roll at the back and fits flat at the front. (In a sense, the sailor collar did this very thing, but to so slight a degree that it fell in the flat-collar category.)

1. Trace the bodice-front sloper and establish the neckline. Draw the style line for the front collar. Label points A and B at the shoulder (Fig. 247a).

2. Trace the bodice-back sloper but do not trace the shoulder dart. Establish the new back neckline AC. Draw the collar style line BF. Points A and B correspond to the bodice front (Fig. 247b).

3. To create the stand (Fig. 247c): From C measure up a distance equal to twice the desired stand of the collar. Label point D. Mark point E halfway between C and D. This marks the position of the roll line. From D, draw a new slightly straightened neckline equal to the back neckline AC and label the end of the line G. Connect G and B with a straight line. Extend the neckline AC to line BG.

4. Cut out the front collar. Cut out the back collar. Join front and back collars at the shoulders, matching B's. The back collar will extend beyond the front collar at the neckline because of the stand (Fig. 247d).

5. Draw the neckline from center back D to center front, blending the curved back neckline into the straight front neckline at the shoulder (Fig. 247e).

6. Draw the roll line from center back E to the center front, blending the curved back roll line into the straight front roll line at the shoulder through A (Fig. 247e).

7. Draw the style line from center back F to the front style line, blending the curved back style line into the straight front style line at the shoulder B (Fig. 247e).

8. Complete the pattern.

In this design the fall is quite deep so there would hardly be a problem in relation to the neck seam. Remember for any future roll collars that the very least the fall can measure is the stand plus ½ inch to cover the neckline seam.

Using this same method, make the patterns for the designs in Fig. 248.

Fig. 248

TAILORED COLLARS

There are two collars associated with tailored garments.

In the *shawl collar* (Fig. 249a), the entire collar is part of the garment front. It rolls back to position from the first button. The seam that joins the right and left collars is at the center back. No seaming is visible from the front.

In the *notched collar* (Fig. 249b), part of the front rolls back to form lapels. A separate collar is set on the lapel a little distance in from its end. However high or low on the garment this joining seam may be, it is visible from the front.

In a tailored notched collar, the notch is automatically created by the setback on the gorge line. In the shawl collar, a notch may be created by a cutout on the style line (Fig. 249c).

a   b   c

Fig. 249

SHAWL COLLARS

The shawl collar may be drafted in one of two ways depending on whether the design calls for a high closing, as in most dressmaker styles, or a lower closing, as in man-tailored styles.

Shawl Collar on a Single-breasted Dressmaker Style

1. Trace the bodice-front sloper. Label point A at the shoulder. Add a closing extension (Fig. 250a).

2. Square a line from A to half the back-neck measurement. Label point B (Fig. 250a).

3. From B, measure over ¼ to ½ inch to correct the angle of the collar. Label point C. Draw a line from C to A (Fig. 250a). CA is the back neckline now.

4. From C, square a line up equal to the entire width of the collar— that is, stand, fall, and ½ inch to cover the neckline seam. Label point D (Fig. 250b).

5. Connect D to the front extension with a curved line (Fig. 250b).

6. Draw the facing on the pattern (Fig. 250b) and trace it (Fig. 250c). Since it is the facing that becomes the upper collar, add at least ⅛ inch to the style line as an allowance for rolling the seam to the underside.

7. Test the collar in muslin. Should more ease be needed on the style line for better fit, extend the shoulder line to the style line and use it for slashing. Slash and spread ⅛ inch (or more) (Fig. 250d). Make the same change in the facing.

8. Complete the pattern.

Fig. 250

Shawl Collar on a Double-breasted Dressmaker Style

The shawl collar on a double-breasted bodice is drafted in the same way with the following exceptions:

1. The extension is double-breasted (Fig. 251a).

2. From the shoulder line to the center back, the collar is slashed and spread for additional ease (Fig. 251b).

Fig. 251c shows the double-breasted shawl collar and its facing.

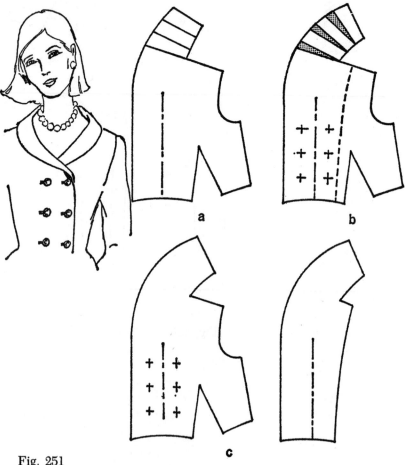

Fig. 251

Shawl Collar on a Single-breasted Man-tailored Garment

Because of its deeper neckline and generally heavier material, this shawl collar is drafted as follows.

Fig. 252

Fig. 252a

1. Trace the appropriate front sloper. Lower the neckline for style. Shift some of the front-waistline dart control to the center front. This lengthens the roll line from the break of the collar to the center back. It makes the collar fit with a little more ease. The amount of control that is shifted varies from about ¼ inch if the break is above the bustline, to ¾ inch at the bustline, to 1 inch or more if the break is at or close to the waistline.

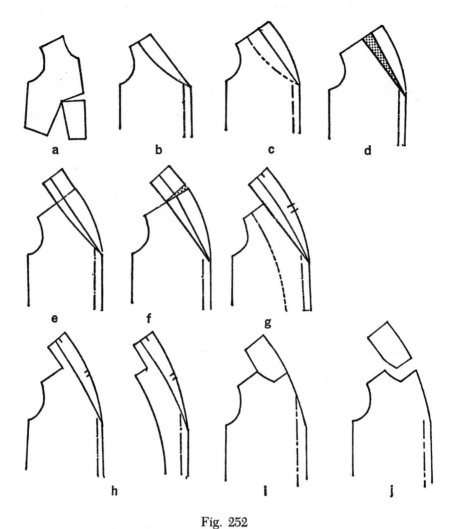

Fig. 252

Fig. 252b

2. Draw the opening extension, the V-neckline to the break, and the collar style line just as you wish them to appear in the finished garment.

3. Cut out the pattern. Discard what's not needed.

4. Trace the pattern.

Fig. 252c

5. Fold on the neckline and trace the collar. Unfold and draw the collar. (It will look as if the collar were flipped up on a cold day.)

Fig. 252d

6. Slash the neckline from shoulder to break. Spread to the amount you plan for the stand of the collar. Trace the pattern. The upper line of the stand becomes the roll line.

Fig. 252e

7. Extend the neckline and the roll line to half the back neck measurement less ¼ inch. (In the sewing, the collar is stretched to fit the neckline for a better roll.)

8. Connect the neckline and the roll line with a straight line. Extend it to the amount of the fall of the collar plus at least ½-inch allowance for the turnover.

9. Draw the back style line to meet the front style line. Blend the lines.

Fig. 252f

10. Extend the shoulder line through the collar. Slash and spread ½ inch so the angle formed by the collar and shoulders is less than a right angle.

Fig. 252g

11. Locate the facing and trace it. Since it is the facing that will become the upper collar, add at least ¼ inch to the style line as an allowance for rolling the seam to the underside.

Fig. 252h

12. Trace the jacket (or coat) pattern.
13. Complete the patterns.

Fig. 252i

In many of the newer shawl collar designs, the undercollar is applied as a separate collar in the same way in which the set-on notched collar is. It gives the tailor a little more control in fitting than the all-in-one shawl collar.

On Fig. 252i, draw a curved line from the shoulder to the roll line following the curve of the original neckline, then a straight line from the roll line to the style line.

Fig. 252j

The finished pattern will show the jacket (or coat pattern) with the undercollar cut away, the separate undercollar to be cut on the bias, and the facing cut all in one with the collar.

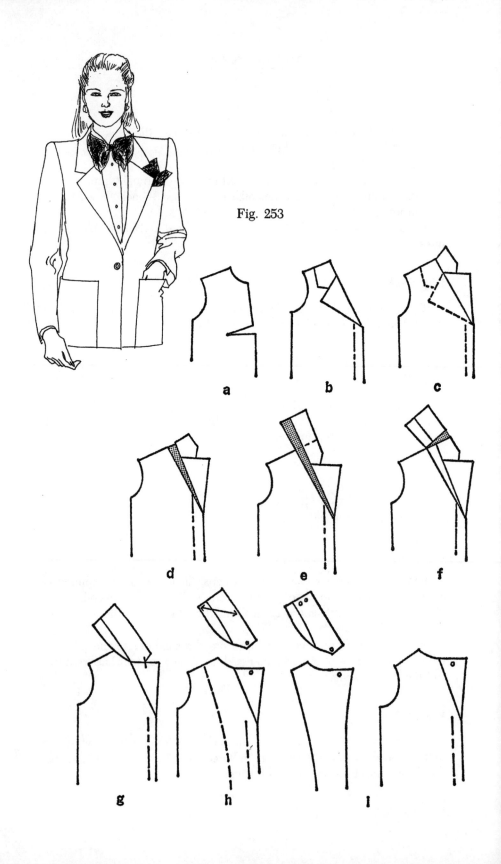

Fig. 253

a

b

c

d

e

f

g

h

i

For a *double-breasted man-tailored shawl collar*, slash and spread the collar from the shoulder to the center back for additional ease. See Fig. 251.

NOTCHED COLLAR FOR A DRESSMAKER STYLE

This collar is drafted like the convertible shirt collar or like the man-tailored notched collar.

Notched Collar for a Single-breasted Man-tailored Garment

Steps 1 to 10 in Figs. 253a to 253f are exactly the same as for the shawl collar (Figs. 252a to 252f).

11. Connect the neckline of the back collar and the gorge (neck) line of the front collar with a curved line (Fig. 253g).

12. Cut the collar away from the rest of the pattern (Fig. 253h).

13. Correct the angularity of any lines.

14. Draw the facing (Fig. 253h) and trace it (Fig. 253i). Add ¼ inch on the outside edges of the facing lapel as an allowance for rolling the seam to the underside. Trace the jacket (or coat) pattern (Fig. 253i). Trace the collar and add ¼-inch allowance on all outside edges for rolling the seam to the underside. Trace the undercollar to be cut on the bias.

15. Complete the pattern.

In the notched collar for a double-breasted man-tailored garment (Fig. 254), it may be necessary to slash and spread the collar from the gorge line to the center back in several places and spread for additional ease. See Fig. 251.

Fig. 254

STANDING COLLARS

Like other collar types, there is considerable variety in standing collars. There are two types of these collars—those stiffened to stand like a band or Chinese collar and those soft enough to fold over like the turtleneck or roll-over collar. The basis of these collars is a straight or shaped band.

The *stiff standing collar* can be either rectangular or curved in design. Because both neckline and style line are the same length, a straight rectangular band collar stands away from the neck unless it is cut on the bias and pressed into a curved shape. Because its style line is shorter than its neckline, a curved band fits closer to the neck which tapers slightly as it rises from its base. Both types are generally cut on the straight grain though curved collars are sometimes cut on the bias.

The *soft standing collar* is generally rectangular in shape and cut on the bias for an easy fit around the neck.

A rectangular collar can be cut so collar and facing are either in one piece or in two pieces—a separate collar and facing. The curved standing collar must, of necessity, be cut in two pieces.

For all types of standing collars, use fabric firm enough to stand. Or stiffen them with interfacing and/or stitching.

Fig. 255

PATTERN FOR A STRAIGHT-BAND STANDING COLLAR (ALL TYPES)

1. Establish the garment neckline. See Fig. 255.
2. Draw the pattern for a rectangular band equal to the length of the garment neckline by the desired width. If the collar is of the fold-over variety, allow sufficient width for the lengthwise fold.
3. Add grain, seam allowances and notches.
4. Complete the pattern.

The *funnel collar* (Fig. 256) is a variation of the straight-standing band collar.

1. Make the pattern for a straight-standing band collar.
2. Slash the pattern and spread the style line to the desired fullness.
3. Complete the pattern.

Fig. 256

SHAPED-BAND STANDING COLLARS

The Chinese collar is the most familiar example of the shaped-band standing collar. It may be constructed in one of two ways.

Method 1—with a separate facing

1. Cut a strip of paper to the length of the neckline from center front to center back. Make it the desired width (generally 1 inch to 1½ inches) (Fig. 257a).

2. Draw several slash lines. Make them a slightly longer distance from center front and center back than the width of the spaces between the slash lines. This helps the collar fit better at front and back.

3. Slash from the outer edge to the neckline. Overlap the slashed edges until the outer edge fits the neck measurement at comparable height with a bit of ease (Fig. 257b).

4. Trace the pattern, correcting the angularity (Fig. 257c).

5. Draw the center-front style line (Fig. 257d).

6. Make the upper collar slightly larger than the facing on all but the neck edge to allow for the seam roll.

7. Complete the pattern.

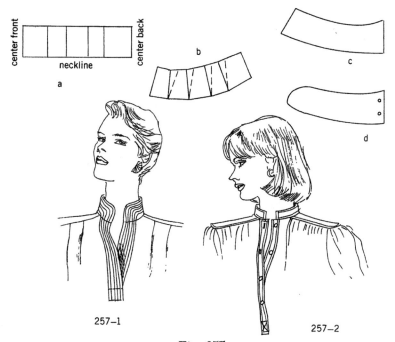

Fig. 257

The slight shaping of this standing collar prevents it from poking out at back and overlapping at the front edges. The Chinese collar developed by Method II takes care of these matters in a different way.

Method II—a double collar on a lengthwise fold

1. Trace the neck and shoulder area of the bodice-front sloper.
2. Measure the neckline from the center front A to the shoulder B. Draw a straight line of equal length starting at B and ending at C (Fig. 258a).

Fig. 258b

3. Square a line from C equal to the stand of the collar. Label the end of the line D.
4. Square a line from D to E equal to the length of the neckline from the center front to the center back.
5. Square a line from E to F equal to the stand of the collar plus ¼ to ⅜ inch. This deepened stand at the center back sets the point from which the neckline shaping begins.
6. Square a line from F to the shoulder at G.
7. Connect G with C.

Fig. 258c

8. Trace the collar.
9. Measure over ½ inch from D to H. Draw a line from H to C. This shortens the upper edge of the collar for fit and prevents the center front edges from overlapping. HC may be the center-front style line or become the guide for a curved style line.

Fig. 258d

10. Trace the new collar, correcting all angularity.

11. Fold the collar on line HE and trace. Unfold and draw the collar facing in one with the collar.

12. Complete the pattern.

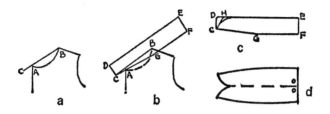

Fig. 258

Which of the two methods one chooses for making a pattern for a shaped standing collar depends on the preferred style and the amount of available material. The curved shape of Fig. 257–1 requires a little more material than the collar of Fig. 257–2, which can utilize a single straight strip of material on a fold for the entire double collar.

There is this difference, too: There are not too many style variations possible with Method I collar. When the ends of Method II collar are extended, they may button or tie in a bow or be folded over like a cravat.

COLLARS ON A STAND

The standing-band collar becomes the basis for a series of interesting collars—from a shirt collar to a coat collar. It consists of a separate band (the stand) and a style collar joined by a seam at the upper edge of the band (Fig. 259).

Fig. 259

Standing Band

Construct the stand like the straight-band standing collar (Fig. 255) or the shaped-band standing collar (Fig. 257). Add a front extension for buttoning or tieing where necessary.

Collar

1. Trace the standing band. Over it, draw the collar as it will appear (neckline, center front, style line, center back). Notch the neckline (Fig. 260a).

2. Trace the collar and cut it out (Fig. 260b).

3. Draw two slash lines evenly spaced (Fig. 260b).

4. Slash and spread about ⅛ inch (Fig. 260c).

5. Trace the collar and the standing band (Fig. 260d).

6. Complete the pattern.

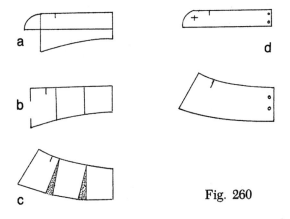

Fig. 260

Variations

A ruffle of self-fabric or lace added to the upper edge of the standing band produces a soft, flattering neck treatment (Figs. 261a and 261b).

Since coat fabrics are generally bulky and heavy, excess fullness forms at the inner neckline of the collar. One way to get around this (if the design permits) is to design the collar with separate stand. Just be sure to add more length for the turnover and rollbacks (Fig. 261c).

a

b

c

Fig. 261

ASYMMETRIC COLLARS

You may want to add an asymmetric collar on your asymmetric closing (Figs. 262, 263, 264, 265) or an asymmetric collar on a symmetrical closing (Fig. 266).

Like other collars, the asymmetric collar may be flat (Fig. 262), rolled (Fig. 263), standing (Fig. 264), on a stand (Fig. 265), or roll-fitted (Fig. 266).

In each case, start with a complete front sloper to develop the pattern. In some instances, a complete back sloper will also be necessary.

Asymmetric Flat Collar

1. Join the neck and shoulder areas of the complete bodice-front and bodice-back slopers at the right shoulder. Establish the dropped neckline and the style line of the collar. Raise the neckline (Fig. 262a).

2. Trace the collar (Fig. 262b) and complete the pattern.

For a deeper roll: Draw slash lines around the collar. Slash and overlap at the style line (Fig. 262c). Add width to the collar to compensate for the newly created stand (Fig. 262d).

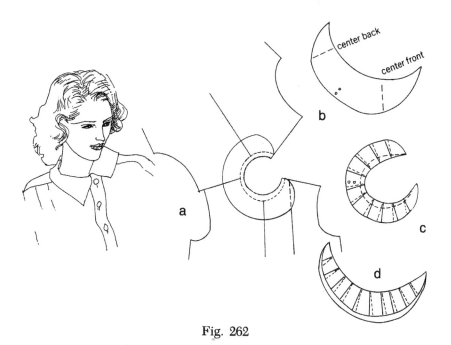

Fig. 262

Asymmetric Rolled Collar

The pattern for Fig. 263 is developed like any rolled collar (see page 322). However, left and right sides are constructed individually: the left side from the center back to center front; the right side from center back to right-front extension.

Fig. 263

Asymmetric Standing Collar

Fig. 264-1

1. Draw a band equal to the entire back-neck (shoulder to shoulder) measurement by the width of the collar (Fig. 264a).

2. Draw a band equal to the right-front neckline (including the extension) by the width of the collar (Fig. 264b).

3. Draw a band equal to the left-front neckline (including the extension) by the width of the collar (Fig. 264b).

4. Join the bands at the shoulder lines (Fig. 264c).

5. Trace and complete the pattern.

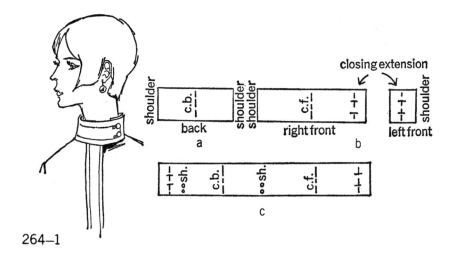

Fig. 264

Fig. 264-2

This pattern is developed in the same way as the one above except that the front and back bands meet at the closing without any extensions. In this design, additional fullness is added to the upper collar only. The un-full undercollar, cut in one with it, acts as a stay. The entire collar is cut on the bias to achieve the drape.

264–2

Fig. 264

Asymmetric Collar on a Stand

Make the pattern for the stand shown in Fig. 265 in the same way as the asymmetric standing collar in Fig. 264-1.

Make the pattern for the collar in the same way as the flat collar in Fig. 262.

Fig. 265

Asymmetric Collar on a Symmetrical Closing

The pattern for the collar shown in Fig. 266 is developed in the same way as that of the notched collar for a single-breasted man-tailored garment (page 334). However, left and right sides will each have to be developed individually.

Fig. 266

Fig. 267

STRUCTURAL DESIGN VS. ADDED DECORATION

With collars, as with any other part of a garment, there arises the question as to whether the lines of the collar alone are interesting enough to carry the design or whether the assistance of trimming is needed—or wanted. This is something you will have to consider with your artist's eye.

Should you decide on trimming, there is plenty to choose from: lace, ruffling, pleating, beading, embroidery, appliqué, edging, cording, piping, and many others (see Fig. 267).

CHOOSE YOUR COLLAR

The most difficult thing about drafting a collar is deciding which type it is—flat, rolled, on a stand, standing, or roll-fitted. Some are pretty obvious; others need studying.

If you are copying a picture or an actual garment, or if you are developing one of your own designs, analyze it for neckline shape, stand, roll, seaming, and style line. This will enable you to classify it as to type. Once you've done this, the rest is easy. Simply find the directions for that particular type of collar and follow them.

TEST ALL COLLARS IN FABRIC

You really cannot tell how a collar will fit just by looking at half a flat pattern. Not only does one need a whole collar, one also needs the drapability of fabric to test the design.

Cut the undercollar of muslin or some other interfacing material. Overlap any center-back seam. *Lap the seam line of the collar over the seam line of the neckline.* Only in this way can you get a reasonable idea of how the collar fits and looks. Check the length of the collar, the stand, the fall, and the roll line. Make sure the neckline seam is covered by the fall of the collar. Make any needed adjustments and transfer them to both upper and undercollar patterns.

COLLARS GALORE

A thousand and one ways to design collars! Keep a scrapbook of interesting ones. You may find yourself using the ideas. Some collar types are timeless. Only the proportions and style lines change.

Chapter 12

The Set-in Sleeve Scene

There are no new principles in this chapter. There are merely the old ones used in new ways and applied to the sleeve.

The dart control may be shifted or concealed in a control seam. It may be converted into gathers or multiple darts. Fullness may be added—balanced, circular, or inserted into a seam. The sleeve may have a cowl or an opening extension. And so on . . .

SET-IN SLEEVE TYPES

While more difficult to handle in sewing than the sleeve cut in one with the bodice, the set-in sleeve has certain built-in advantages. The sleeve follows the natural "hang" of the arm while retaining freedom of movement—all this without bulk or underarm wrinkling. This is something one cannot claim for the kimono or dolman sleeve.

While the cap may be the same, the set-in sleeve can be cut in one or two pieces. Occasionally, more.

The *one-piece sleeve,* shaped at the elbow with darts or gathers, is the one most frequently used for dresses, blouses, and dressmaker-type jackets and coats. Usually the sleeve seam is an underarm one (Fig. 268a). Sometimes the underarm section is cut in one with the overarm section and the sleeve is seamed at the back (Fig. 268b).

The *two-piece sleeve* is the one usually found in tailored garments. Instead of darts or gathers, its shaping is in its seams, providing a more natural arm shape than the one-piece sleeve (Fig. 268c).

From the standpoint of design, the two-piece sleeve offers more opportunity for style features. See page 378.

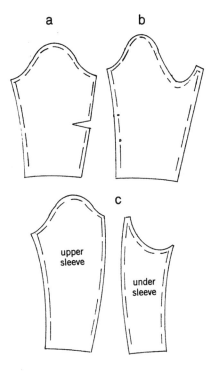

Fig. 268

ANATOMY OF A SLEEVE

Sleeves come in pairs. Lay the bodice front, bodice back, and sleeve side by side on a flat surface. Place the front of the sleeve toward the front bodice, the back of the sleeve toward the back bodice.

That portion of the sleeve above the horizontal line in Fig. 269 is the *sleeve cap*. The vertical broken line separates the cap into front and back. The front cap is drafted to fit the front armhole, the back cap to fit the back armhole. Note that the division produces a shorter, deeper front armhole curve than the back armhole, which has a longer, shallower curve. This is because the arm movement is forward, requiring an allowance in size and shape for the expanding shoulder muscle.

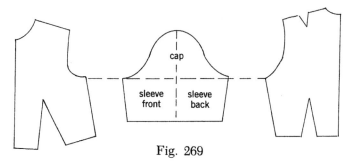

Fig. 269

Fronts and backs are not reversible. There is a right sleeve and a left sleeve. Notches on the pattern tell which it is (Fig. 270).

If you are ever in doubt as to which is front and which is back, fold the sleeve in half lengthwise. The front cap is the deeper, the back shallower. In a below-elbow-length sleeve, there is another way to tell front from back. The elbow darts, gathers, or easing are always in back.

The armhole and sleeve cap are also divided into *overarm* and *underarm* (Fig. 270).

Notches are placed at those points where the seam lines that arch over the shoulder swing into underarm curves. Change of direction occurs at the points where arm and body meet, both front and back.

The *underarm curves* of both sleeve cap and armhole are identical, therefore easy to match when you are setting the sleeve. In a fitted misses' dress sloper, the armhole generally drops 1½ inches below the arm. The drop in a jacket or coat sloper is more (see page 195). This provides comfort in wearing and room for movement. Many great couturiers set the sleeve higher than this on the underarm. They hold that a high setting provides greater ease of movement and greater trimness to the garment, with no unsightly pulling up of garment when the arm is raised.

(*Sleeveless garments,* too, are generally built up under the arm. Since there is no sleeve to restrict the motion in any way, the underarm curve can be brought up as high as is comfortable. See page 380.)

The *overarm curves* of sleeve and armhole, unlike the underarm curves, do not match in length and shape. The sleeve cap is slightly longer than the armhole and has different curves. The difference in length and shape represents the *cap ease.*

Style changes are usually made on the overarm rather than the underarm. With few notable exceptions, underarm designs are lost to view. Additional fullness on the underarm may interfere with the comfort of the sleeve.

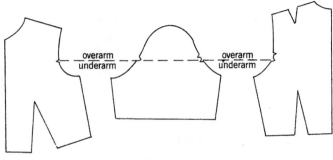

Fig. 270

SLEEVE-CAP EASE

Ease in a sleeve is a must—as necessary as it is in a bodice or skirt or pants, and for the same reasons—comfort and ease of movement.

In a fitted-dress sleeve sloper, the minimum cap ease is 1 to 1½ inches. In fitted jacket and fitted coat sleeves, the minimum cap ease is 1½ to 2 inches. How can you tell if the amount is right? By comparison of sleeve cap with the armhole.

1. Start the comparison at the front underarm seam. Match the underarm curve of the sleeve with the underarm curve of the armhole (Fig. 271a).

2. Using a pin for a pivot, continue to match a tiny section at a time (about ⅛ inch) of sleeve and armhole from the underarm to the shoulder.

3. Mark the point where the garment shoulder appears on the sleeve cap.

4. Do the same for the back. The leftover space between the two marks is the ease (Fig. 271b).

5. Place the shoulder notch of the sleeve cap at the center of the space, dividing the ease equally between front and back (Fig. 271c).

NOTE: The notch should be at the crest of the curve. If it isn't, redraw the curve so that it will be (Fig. 271d). This will assure that the back sleeve cap will fit the back armhole and the front sleeve cap, the front armhole.

Fig. 271

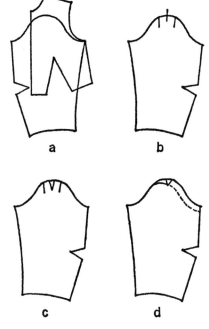

a   b

c   d

If the comparison of sleeve cap and armhole reveals too much or too little ease, make the necessary adjustment. Draw a line across the cap of the sleeve. Draw a line at right angles to this and extend it to the shoulder marking (Fig. 272a). Slash both lines.

To remove ease: Overlap a small amount at the cap. Note that there will also be some overlapping at the horizontal slash line (Fig. 272b). Redraw the cap.

Instead of removing the ease, it can also be converted into a dart (Fig. 272c). In addition to the design possibilities of any dart, this is a fine way to handle the ease in plaids, checks, and stripes that need matching with the bodice.

To add ease: Spread the cap a small amount. Note that this raises the cap at the horizontal slash line (Fig. 272d). Redraw the cap.

Test the new sleeve cap in the armhole.

Some sleeves are best designed on slopers where some or most of the ease has been removed. This would be so when the design calls for a smooth fit at the cap and fullness below. If there is enough fullness in the sleeve itself, the cap does not need the ease. As a bonus, you will find that removing some of the ease is a useful device when working with materials (stiff or firmly woven) that are difficult to set and stitch.

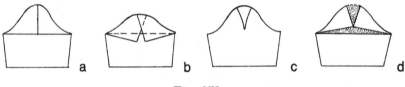

Fig. 272

HOW TO DETERMINE THE GRAIN
OF THE SLEEVE

Most sleeves are designed to hang with the vertical grain. Fold the sleeve in half lengthwise. The fold line is the vertical grain line (Fig. 273a).

Sometimes sleeves are designed on the bias (Fig. 273b). This may be for purposes of design or for fit. Bias gives easy mobility to a set-in sleeve. It "gives" with every arm motion. Expect the hemline of a bias sleeve to "bell" (gracefully) with time. Use the 45-degree triangle to determine the bias.

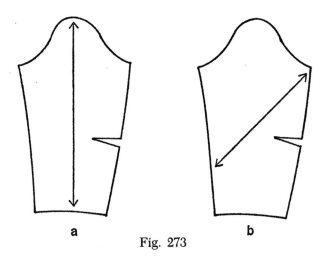

a   b

Fig. 273

THE LONG AND THE SHORT OF IT

In a dress a long sleeve ends at or just below the wrist bone.

A short sleeve is as short as the season, the fashion, and the beauty of the arms of the wearer permit.

Between the long and the short sleeves are many gradations of in-between-length sleeves.

1. Trace the basic sleeve sloper—above the elbow dart for the short sleeve, below the elbow dart for the in-between sleeve.

2. *For a short sleeve,* measure *down* an equal distance from the base of the sleeve cap on both underarm seams. *For an in-between-length sleeve,* measure *up* from the wrist in several places.

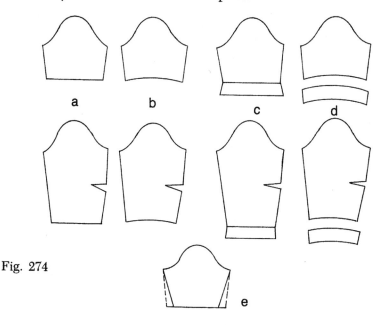

a   b   c   d

Fig. 274

e

3. Draw the lower line of the sleeve. This may be a straight line (Fig. 274a) or a curved line (Fig. 274b).

4. If the lower line is straight, the facing may be turned up as a hem (Fig. 274c). If the lower line is curved, a separate facing must be provided (Fig. 274d).

5. Complete the patterns.

The standard sleeve sloper contains at least 2 inches of ease at the biceps. This may make the short sleeve derived from it too wide to be pretty. Reduce the width at the hemline on the underarm seams. The broken lines of Fig. 274e are the original pattern; the solid lines, the adjusted pattern.

SPORT-SHIRT SLEEVE

Shirts, dresses, and uniforms designed to be used in motion require sleeves which will not pull or ride up while in motion. To provide greater ease in movement, the sleeve cap is flattened and widened and the underarm seam is lengthened. The armhole of the bodice is adjusted to fit.

1. Trace the bodice-front, bodice-back, and sleeve slopers. Use a sleeve sloper with ½ to ¾ inch of the ease removed.

On the Bodice Front and Back

2. Lower the underarm curve about 1 inch. (This may vary with your design or your need.) The lowering starts from the armhole notches. Redraw the underarm curve (Fig. 275a).

On the Sleeve

3. Draw two deep curved lines from the shoulder notch to the underarm seams (Fig. 275b). These become slash lines. Draw two more straight slash lines dividing each new winglike section in half (Fig. 275b).

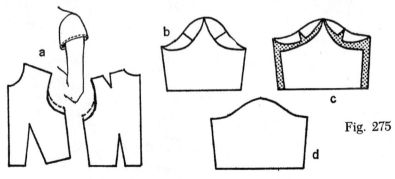

Fig. 275

4. Slash and spread so that the underarm-seam tips are raised and extended about 1 inch (or to match the underarm drop) (Fig. 275c).

5. Widen the sleeve to match (Fig. 275c).

6. Trace the sleeve pattern (Fig. 275d). Compare the new cap length with the front and back armholes. Make any necessary adjustments.

7. Complete the pattern.

The sport-shirt sleeve is designed for action and looks best when in action. When the arm hangs naturally, the sleeve has a tendency to wrinkle under the arm and poke out on the overarm. The vertical grain fits as usual but because of the flattening of the cap, the horizontal grain cannot. It will droop to the front and back. There is nothing you can do about this. Remember that this sleeve is designed for comfort in action rather than beauty at rest.

BASIC SHIRTWAIST SLEEVE PATTERN

1. Trace the full-length sleeve sloper. Cut out the tracing and the dart.

2. Elongate the dart to mid-sleeve. Shift it to the wrist as for gathers (Fig. 276a). Trace the pattern.

3. Draw a line across the cap of the sleeve. Square a line from each end of the cap to the length of the sleeve (Fig. 276b).

4. Draw a curved line at the wrist, making it about 1 inch longer at the deepest part of the wrist curve and blending it into the original wrist line at the underarm seams (Fig. 276b). The additional length provides room for the arm when bent.

This basic shirtwaist sleeve may be gathered into a band and slipped over the hand. Or it may have a placket opening for easy access. See Chapter 14, "Sleeve Finishes."

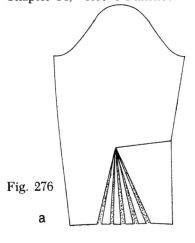
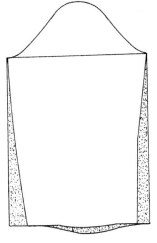

Fig. 276

a   b

ADDITIONAL FULLNESS FOR A SLEEVE

Additional fullness may be added to any sleeve by the slash-and-spread method. The fullness may be circular or balanced.

Additional fullness in width must be accompanied by additional length as well. This may be overall length for general puffiness or in varying amounts.

Make certain that both underarm seam lines are on the same angle. If not, there will be off-grain pulling and puckering when the sleeve is stitched.

FIVE STANDARD SLASH LINES

Generally, fullness is confined to the overarm area of the sleeve.

Fig. 277a

1. Draw a line across the sleeve cap.
2. Draw five slash lines at right angles to it:
   slash line #1 (front)—from the front notch on the cap
   slash line #2 (front midway)—from the front cap midway between the front and shoulder notches
   slash line #3 (shoulder)—from the shoulder notch
   slash line #4 (back midway)—from the back cap midway between the back and shoulder notches
   slash line #5 (back)—from the back notch on the cap

Fig. 277b

When a great deal of circular fullness is to be added, slash lines on the underarm are necessary, too (slashes X and Y).

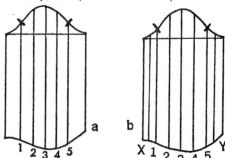

Fig. 277

SLEEVE STYLES WITH CIRCULAR FULLNESS

General Procedure

1. Start with the appropriate sloper or sleeve pattern.

2. Draw the necessary slash lines.

3. Slash and spread to the desired fullness at the cap *or* the wrist. Add the necessary length for puffiness.

4. Trace the pattern, correcting the style lines.

5. Where needed, construct the pattern for a sleeve cuff, band, or placket opening. See Chapter 14, "Sleeve Finishes."

6. Complete the pattern.

Following this procedure, try your hand at developing the patterns for the sleeves below.

Shirtwaist Sleeve with Fullness at the Wrist

Start with the basic shirtwaist sleeve pattern. See Fig. 278.

Fig. 278

Bishop Sleeve

Starting with the basic shirtwaist sleeve pattern (Fig. 276b), add fullness at the wrist. The bishop sleeve has more fullness and more length toward the back of the sleeve at slash line 5 (Fig. 279).

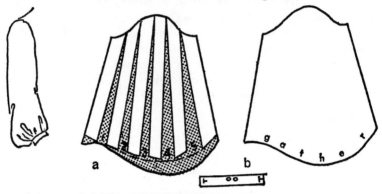

Fig. 279

Short Puffed Sleeve with Fullness at the Cap

The design in Fig. 280 is based on the short sleeve sloper.

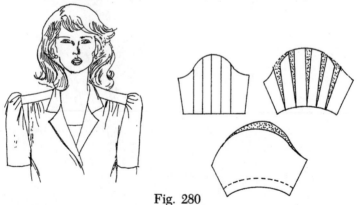

Fig. 280

Circle Sleeves

The ultimate in circularity for a sleeve is shown in Fig. 281.

Two concentric circles become the pattern for the sleeve in Fig. 281a. The circumference of the inner circle is the same length as the armhole.

Having the same depth and the same amount of fullness all the way around, this circle sleeve falls in a cascade from shoulder to underarm when set into the armhole.

Fig. 281

Should you wish to control the top-of-the-arm and the underarm lengths, develop the pattern from the short-sleeve sloper. Slash and spread until a full circle (Fig. 281b).

Several of such sleeves of varying lengths (perhaps of various colors) are a dramatic feature of an otherwise simple dress (Fig. 281c).

Fitted and Full

In all of the foregoing designs the circular additional fullness resulted from a slash-and-spread through the entire length of the sleeve pattern. However, fullness may be limited to one part of the pattern piece while the rest retains its original trimness. This type of fullness is characteristic of the bell sleeve and the leg-of-mutton sleeve.

Bell Sleeve

The bell sleeve fits smoothly across the upper arm and flares at its lower edge like a bell.

Hanging soft and free without the constriction of a band, the sleeve has the simplicity and innocence of an angel's sleeve in an ancient fresco—well, mostly. Consider the unangelic allure of the lacy bell sleeve in Fig. 282a.

Fig. 282

Tied once, twice, many times, its puffs evoke the splendor of medieval costume (Fig. 282b). What matter a dip into history if the result is dramatically the present?

It's a bell but there is no liberty at its edge. It looks charming when its edge (elasticized) is pushed up on the arm (Fig. 282c). An elasticized casing can produce a lovely self-ruffle (Fig. 282d). A band and button is another way to coax the bell into a self-ruffle (Fig. 282e).

How to Make the Pattern for the Bell Sleeve

1. Trace the full-length sleeve sloper. Remove most of the ease from the cap. Eliminate the elbow dart by extending it across the entire sleeve, folding it out, and fastening it to position. (In this full sleeve, the dart will not be necessary. Remember that the full, unfitted bodice or skirt did not need their darts either?) Trace the new sleeve pattern.

2. Draw a line across the upper part of the sleeve separating the part you wish to remain trim from the part you wish to be full (anywhere from underarm to above elbow). Square a line from each of its ends the length of the sloper. Draw vertical slash lines from the separating line to the lower edge of the sleeve (Fig. 283a).

3. Cut away the upper part of the sleeve. On the lower part of the sleeve, slash and spread for circularity to the desired fullness. The underarm tips of the upper and lower sleeve continue to touch. The center slash is spread a little more than the others (Fig. 283b). The drop between the two parts of the sleeve provides some extra length where needed when the arm is bent.

4. Trace the pattern. Correct the lower style line of the sleeve with a smooth, curved line (Fig. 283c).

5. Complete the pattern.

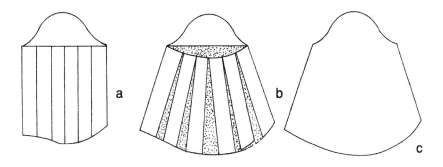

Fig. 283

Leg-of-Mutton Sleeve

Another out-of-the-past sleeve that comes and goes in fashion is the leg-of-mutton sleeve (Fig. 284). It is slim and fitted below the elbow, full and rounded at its cap.

Since this sleeve is quite fitted in the lower-arm area, you will have to decide what kind of closing you want before developing the pattern.

Part of the underarm seam may be zippered for a closing (Fig. 284-1). Should you choose to do this, start the pattern with a dartless sleeve sloper, the same kind used for the bell sleeve.

Or close the sleeve with a row of small loops and buttons (Fig. 284-2). For this type of closing, shift some of the elbow dart to the wrist at the little-finger position to serve as the opening. Shift the rest of the dart control as for gathers to the cap to be incorporated in the puff as in Fig. 284a.

1. Trace the appropriate sleeve sloper. Draw a line across the sleeve a little below the elbow separating the part you wish to remain trim from the part you wish to be full. Draw slash lines from cap to separating line (Fig. 284a). Cut away the lower part of the sleeve.

2. Remove most of the ease from the lower part of the sleeve by tucking the pattern to fit the arm.

3. Slash and spread the upper part of the sleeve to the desired circular fullness. The underarm tips of upper and lower sleeve continue to touch (Fig. 284b).

4. The rise between the two parts of the sleeve provides some extra length needed for puffiness. More puffiness may be added by drawing a freehand line that raises the cap still further (Fig. 284b).

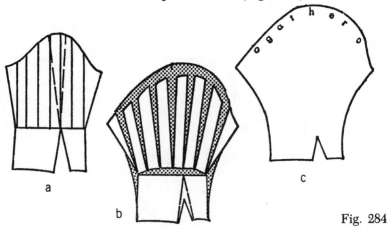

Fig. 284

284–1

284–3

284–2

5. Trace the pattern, correcting the angularity of the underarm seams with curved lines (Fig. 284c).

6. Complete the pattern.

Obviously, the leg-of-mutton sleeve must be made of a fabric firm enough to sustain its shaped fullness. In addition, the puff may be bolstered by stiff underlining or a sleeve pad or roll. An ingenious stiffening is the smocking in Fig. 284-3.

UP, OUT, AND AWAY

The leg-of-mutton sleeve is not the only sleeve that takes off in space. There are a host of others whose caps extend up, out, and away.

Here in Fig. 285 is a modification of the leg-of-mutton sleeve that has height and some fullness only in the upper part of the sleeve. The rest of the sleeve retains its slimness. Slash and spread a dartless sloper as illustrated. Remove ease to fit the arm snugly but comfortably.

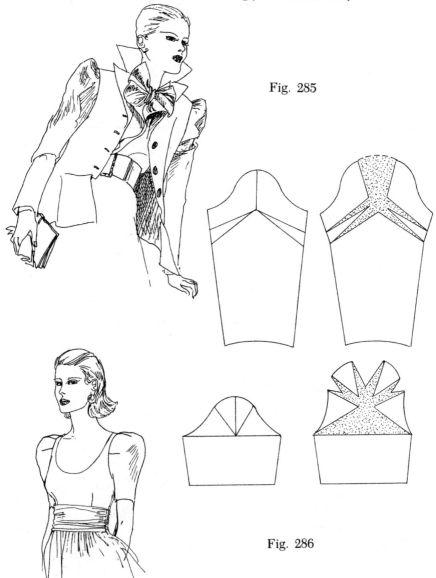

Fig. 285

Fig. 286

By the use of *darts or triangular folds,* a square look is achieved (Fig. 286).

The *sleeve with extended sleeve cap* consists of two parts—the extension and the original sleeve joined by a curved seam (Fig. 287).

1. Trace *two* short-sleeve slopers without cap ease. Use one for the extension (Fig. 287a), the other for the lower section of the sleeve (Fig. 287c).

Extension

2. On Fig. 287a, draw a style line across the sleeve cap as far down on the cap as you wish the sleeve to extend out from the armhole. Label A and B. Draw slash lines from style line to cap seam line.

3. Cut away the extension. Slash and spread it against a straight line, which becomes the new sleeve cap (Fig. 287b). The curved line becomes the seam line, which is stitched to the lower section of the sleeve.

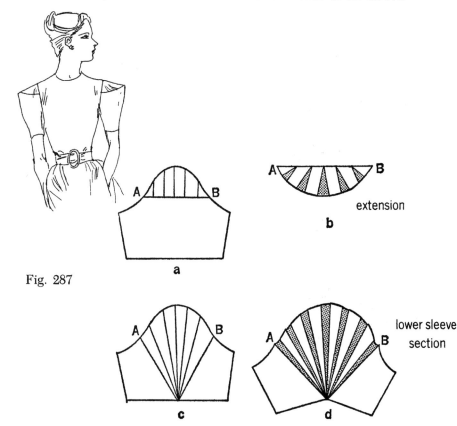

Fig. 287

Lower Section of the Sleeve

4. On Fig. 287c, locate the position of the style line on the cap seam line AB. Draw slash lines from the center of the hem to the sleeve cap. The first and last slash lines extend to AB.

5. Slash and spread so the seam line AB of the cap equals the seam line AB of the extension (Fig. 287d). Correct the angularity of the hemline.

Both patterns

6. Trace the patterns and complete them.

The *lantern sleeve* is developed by a similar procedure. From a natural shoulder it swells to rounded fullness at a style-line seam, then tapers to a snug lower edge. The widest part of the sleeve may be at any length you choose. The width may be anything from just flare (Fig. 288a) to the complete circles of the *barrel sleeve* (Fig. 288b).

1. Trace the sleeve sloper with ease removed from the cap.

2. If desired, shorten the sleeve. In a below-elbow-length style, eliminate the elbow dart.

3. Draw the style line that divides the sleeve into upper and lower parts. Cut the two sections apart on the style line.

Fig. 288

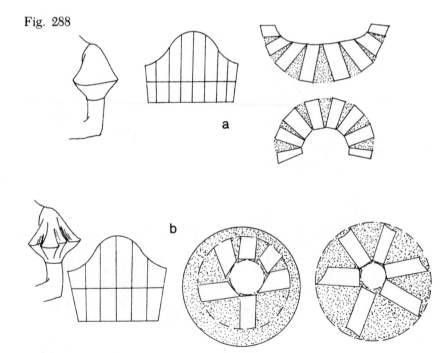

a

b

4. Slash and overlap or tuck the lower sleeve to remove excess fullness at the hem which must fit the arm snugly. Trace the pattern. It is this new lower-sleeve pattern which will be used for the added fullness.

5. Draw enough slash lines in both sections to provide an adequate guide for the seam lines of both upper and lower sleeves.

6. Slash and spread both upper and lower sleeves to the desired fullness. Make the style-line seams match in length.

7. Trace the patterns and complete them.

The barrel sleeve is very popular for children's clothing. It is so easy to iron when the circles are pressed against each other.

Whenever there is a seam, there is an opportunity to insert some trimming—piping, cording, lace edging, or braid. There is even a chance to modify the circular edges with interesting shapes—say, scallops.

SLEEVE STYLES WITH BALANCED FULLNESS

General Procedure

1. Start with the appropriate sloper or sleeve pattern.

2. Draw the necessary slash lines. Draw a guide line at right angles to them. It also helps in reassembling the cut-apart sections of the sleeve pattern if you number them.

3. Draw a guide line on a fresh sheet of paper long enough for the spread pattern sections.

4. Slash and spread the pattern sections to the desired degree of balanced fullness, with the guide lines matching.

5. Add length at the cap for puffiness. Add length at the lower edge of the sleeve when it too will be gathered for puffiness. When pleats are involved, fold the pattern in the direction the pleats will be formed. Trace the cap and lower edge of the sleeve, correcting the style lines as necessary.

6. Where needed, construct the pattern for a sleeve band, cuff, or placket opening. See Chapter 14, "Sleeve Finishes."

7. Complete the pattern.

Following the above procedure and the diagrams, make the patterns for the sleeves with balanced fullness which follow.

Short, Puffed Sleeve

For a sleeve with a puffed cap and free-hanging hem, see Figs. 289-1, 289a, and 289b.

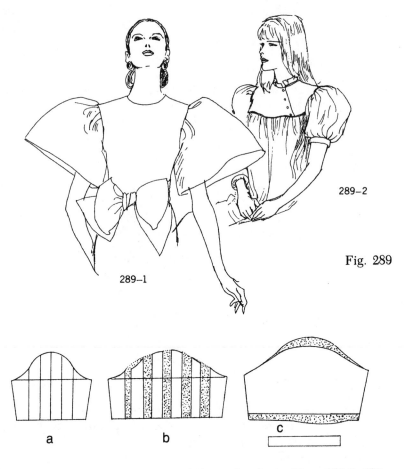

289–2

Fig. 289

289–1

a   b   c

For a sleeve with a puffed cap and sleeve band, see Figs. 289-2, 289a, 289b, and 289c. Note the slight extra length at the overarm position.

Short Pleated Sleeve (Fig. 290)

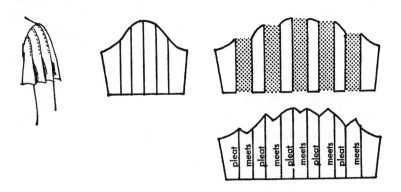

Fig. 290

Long Sleeve with Balanced Fullness at Cap and Wrist (or Hem)

Start this sleeve with the shirtwaist sleeve sloper. The type of balanced fullness need not be the same at the cap and wrist as they are in Fig. 291. One may be gathered, the other pleated as in the fashion sketch of Fig. 292.

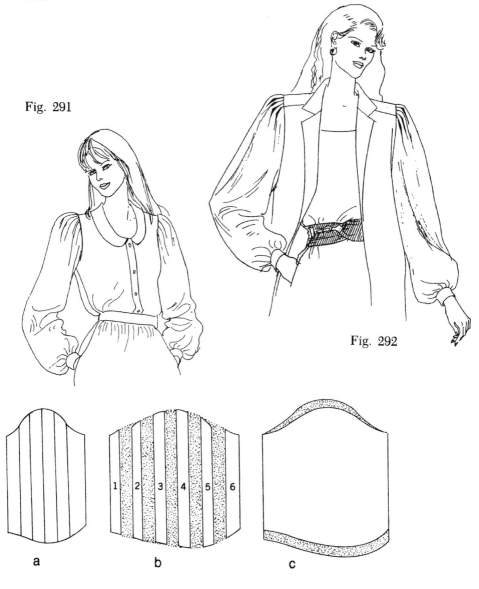

Fig. 291

Fig. 292

a   b   c

Fullness upon Fullness

1. Start with Fig. 291b. Slash the sleeve on the guideline, dividing it into cap and lower sleeve.

2. Arrange sections 1 to 6 of both cap and lower sleeve on a new guideline as follows (Fig. 293):

Cap: The sections are placed so they form a curve *above* the guideline— sections 3 and 4 are raised 1 inch above the guideline, sections 1 and 6 touch the guideline at the underarm seams, and sections 2 and 5 are placed between 1 and 3 and 4 and 6.

Lower sleeve: The sections are placed so they form a curve *below* the guideline—sections 3 and 4 are dropped 1 inch below the guideline, sections 1 and 6 touch the guideline at the underarm seams, sections 2 and 5 are placed between 1 and 3 and 4 and 6.

3. Trace the new pattern and complete it.

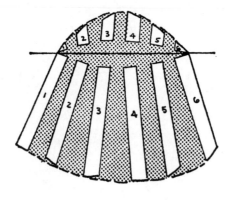

Fig. 293

DRAPED FULLNESS

As with bodices and skirts, sleeve fullness need not always be vertical. It may be horizontal or at an angle. When horizontal fullness is gathered or shirred, the effect is draped. Needless to say, use soft materials that drape well.

Here in Fig. 294 are a few construction patterns that show how to get draped fullness in a sleeve. Note that the additional fullness may be balanced or circular.

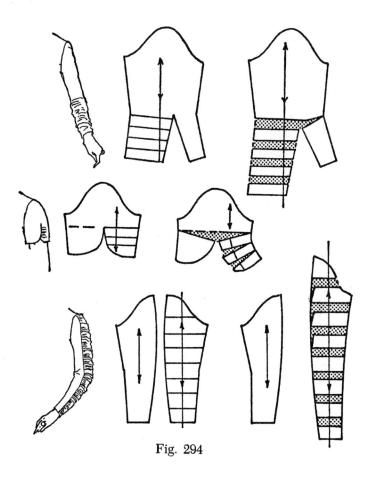

Fig. 294

SLEEVE DESIGNS VIA CONTROL SEAMS

Like other control seams, those of the sleeve offer possibilities for design, too.

The control seam may be a continuation of the shoulder seam (Fig. 295-1) or a style line of the garment (Fig. 295-2). Both are worked the same way.

1. Trace the one-piece long-sleeve sloper. (In these designs use the suit or coat slopers.) Draw the line for the control seam, dividing the sleeve into two parts. Extend the elbow dart to the dividing line. Place notches above and below the elbow dart (Fig. 295a).

2. Cut out the extended elbow dart. Slash the dividing line. Divide the elbow dart control three ways—between cap, wrist, and elbow, the latter to be used as ease. For subtle shaping of these designs, you may use less of the dart control at the cap and wrist, placed equally on both sides of the dividing line. Shorten the elbow dart and those in the control seam, if desired, for shaping. Establish the grain lines in each section (Fig. 295b).

3. Trace the pattern. Correct any angularity with matching, smoothly-curved style lines at the control seam (Fig. 295c).

4. Complete the pattern.

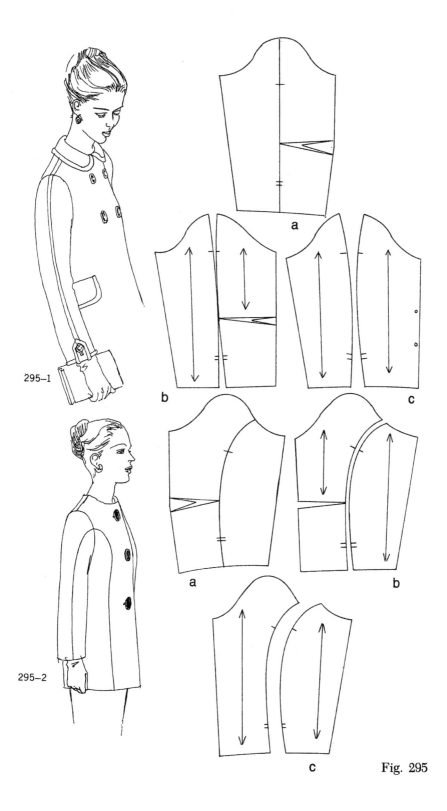

295-1

295-2

a

b

c

a

b

c

Fig. 295

Whenever there is a seam there is also an opportunity for some design detail. For instance: An extension for buttoning at a sleeve vent (Fig. 296a). Or some shape at a sleeve opening (Fig. 296b). It may even be that some style feature can be limited to one part of the two-piece sleeve. In Fig. 296c, flare is confined to the overarm section of the sleeve.

Fig. 296

SHOULDER-PAD ALLOWANCE

When a set-in sleeve design calls for shoulder pads, an allowance for them must be made in the pattern.

Bodice Adjustment

Raise and extend the shoulder half the thickness of the shoulder pad, both front and back. Draw a new armhole from shoulder to underarm. The new shoulder line meets the old at the neckline (Fig. 297a).

For instance, if the shoulder pad is ½ inch thick, then raise and extend the shoulder ¼ inch in front and ¼ inch in back.

Sleeve Adjustment

For a One-piece Sleeve:

1. Draw a slash line across the cap. Draw a line at right angles to it extending to the top of the cap (Fig. 297b).

2. Slash these lines. Raise the cap to the amount of the thickness of the pad. For instance, the rise is ½ inch for a ½-inch pad. Keep all cap points together (Fig. 297c).

The spread at the top of the cap automatically opens to the right amount to accommodate the pad. Locate a new shoulder notch at the center of the opening.

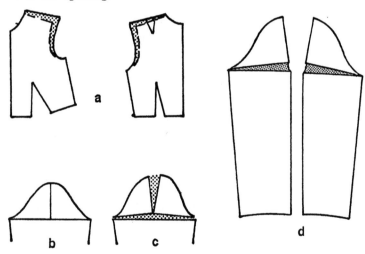

Fig. 297

For the Two-piece Sleeve with a Vertical Control Seam:

1. Draw slash lines across the front and back caps.

2. Slash and spread to the amount of the thickness of the pad (Fig. 297d).

SLEEVELESS DRESS OR BLOUSE

A sleeveless dress or blouse is not just one with the set-in sleeves left out. It is planned that way deliberately. See Fig. 298.

A garment with sleeves must have an armhole deep enough and a bodice wide enough to provide for ease of movement. Leave out the sleeves and you're left with a gaping hole too wide, too deep, and lacking in design. What's more, a part of your anatomy never particularly noted for its beauty is exposed.

In a sleeveless style, the underarm is generally built up however bare the shoulders and arms. If the design shows two versions (with or without sleeves), two underarm seams must be shown on the pattern—the lower one for the standard set-in sleeve, the higher one for the sleeveless style.

In this fashion period of pleasant exposure, the designers have been the best barers of good views.

Fig. 298

Fig. 298

ANYTHING GOES!

As you may have discovered in this chapter, the cap of a set-in sleeve may have any shape and any degree of fullness as long as it will fit into the armhole and hang in accordance with the design. The sleeves themselves may be as simple or as dramatic as your fancy dictates.

Chapter 13

Sleeves in One with the Bodice

It is easy to understand the universal and timeless appeal of sleeves in one with the garment. They are easy to cut, easy to sew, easy to wear. Catering as they do to comfort, they are the essential style ingredient of unfitted, loose, free-form shapes. The prevailing emphasis on such fashion makes them as good (and as necessary) today as they were in times past and in faraway places.

ALL OF BODICE JOINED WITH THE SLEEVE

Kimono Sleeve

The Japanese kimono, the spiritual ancestor of our own, has given its name to a whole group of sleeves that resemble it more in style and definition than in structure.

The Japanese kimono is a deep rectangle of cloth whose sleeve is stitched on at right angles to the main body of the garment (Fig. 299a). (Traditional Japanese fabric was loomed too narrow to cut the sleeve all in one with the garment.) Our kimono sleeve is more often cut at an angle that more nearly approximates the natural hang of the arm (Fig. 299b).

Between the right-angle sleeve of the Japanese kimono and the often near-vertical hang of our kimono sleeve are a whole group of deep armhole sleeves with varying degrees of fullness. The angle at which the sleeve emerges from the garment is determined by the way in which the bodice-front, bodice-back, and sleeve slopers are positioned to produce the pattern.

Fig. 299

Basic Kimono-Sleeve Pattern

1. Trace the bodice-front sloper. Trace the bodice-back sloper and shift the shoulder dart to the neckline—out of the way of the kimono sleeve construction. Trace the sleeve sloper. Divide it into front and back with a line from shoulder notch to wrist. Place notches on the dividing line. Cut out the slopers.

Fig. 300a

2. Place the bodice slopers in such a way that the shoulder seams touch at the neckline and are spread ½ inch apart at the armhole for ease.

3. Fold back the sleeve cap and place the sleeve sloper so that the underarm seams are an equal distance below the front and back armholes on the side seams.

4. Trace all three slopers in this position.

5. Draw a line connecting the point at which the shoulders meet at the neckline with the dividing line of the sleeve.

Fig. 300b

6. Cut out the pattern. Cut it apart on the dividing line.

7. Trace and complete the pattern.

This basic kimono sleeve pattern produces a fitted sleeve with restricted movement. Freedom of movement can be restored with the insertion of a hinge, or gusset (Fig. 301), or a deeper underarm style line (Fig. 302). The use of the sport-shirt slopers produces a loose sleeve (Fig. 303). Additional fullness from flare (Fig. 304) to full-blown (Fig. 305) can be added to any of the above.

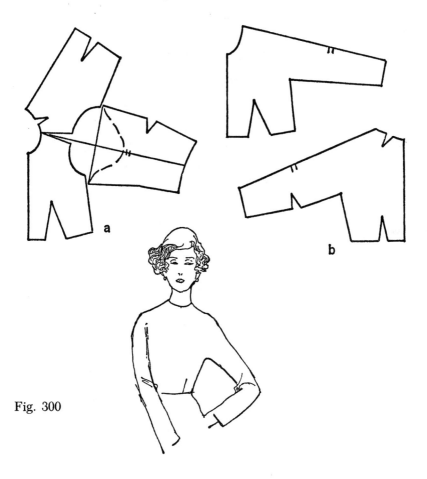

Fig. 300

Pattern for a Gusset

1. Draw a line from the underarm to the shoulder at the neckline (Fig. 301a).

2. On this line, measure up a distance equal to the length of one side of the gusset—small enough to keep it hidden on the underarm, say 3 to 4 inches. The pattern will be slashed to this point. Mark the end of the slash (Fig. 301a). (The gusset is inserted in this slash.)

3. On separate paper, draw two lines perpendicular to each other. Draw a diamond-shaped gusset each side of which is equal to the length of the gusset slash line (Fig. 301b).

4. Complete the pattern for the gusset.

The diamond shape is the basic gusset shape. However, you know enough about designers now to know they are never satisfied with just basic shapes.

There are many variations of gusset shapes. Here are two frequently encountered; a two-piece gusset for more precise underarm shaping (Fig. 301c) and one incorporated into the underarm section of a short sleeve (Fig. 301d). Be as inventive with a gusset as with any other part of a garment.

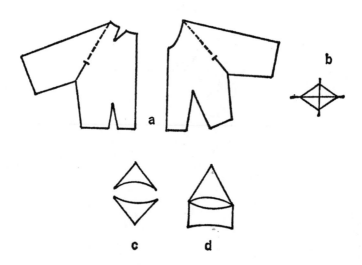

Fig. 301

The Deeper the Sleeve, the More Dramatic It Becomes

Draw identical curved lines from the side seams of the bodice to the underarm seams of the sleeves both front and back. The drop may be from just enough to provide movement without resorting to a gusset (Fig. 302a) or all the way to the waistline for the batwing design (Fig. 302b).

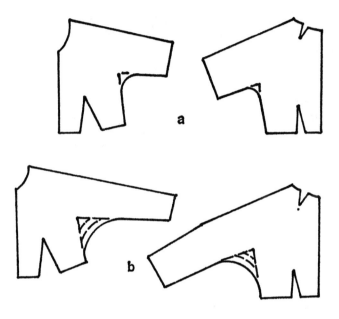

Fig. 302

Wide Kimono Sleeve

Whether short (Fig. 303-1) or long (Fig. 303-2), this loose kimono sleeve starts with the already wider sport-shirt sloper.

1. Trace and cut out the sport-shirt slopers—bodice front, bodice back, and sleeve. Divide the sleeve into front and back by drawing a line from cap to hem.

2. Place the bodice slopers so that the shoulder seams overlap at the neckline and spread 1 inch at the armhole. Place the sleeve sloper as illustrated in Fig. 303a. Trace the slopers.

3. Draw a line from the point of overlapping to the dividing line of the sleeve (Fig. 303a).

4. Trace the front bodice with its original neck and shoulder line continuing into the sleeve line. Trace the back bodice and sleeve in the same way (Fig. 303b).

5. Correct the angularity of the shoulder line with a curved line.

6. Complete the pattern.

Fig. 303

To add flare to the wide kimono sleeve, follow steps 1, 2, and 3 as for Fig. 303. Then draw slash lines, slash, and spread (Fig. 304). Continue as for Fig. 303 from steps 4 to 6.

Fig. 304

Not only flare but *full-blown fullness* can be added to the basic kimono-sleeve pattern. Just slash and spread (Fig. 305).

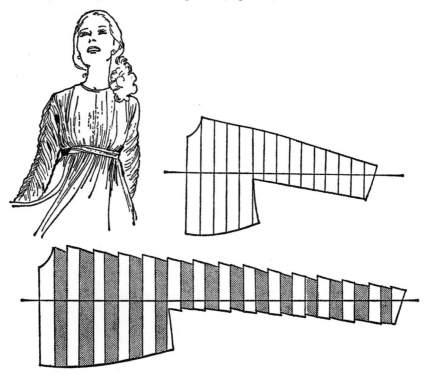

Fig. 305

Don't be alarmed at the size of the kimono pattern—particularly the long-sleeved or very full variety. Remember that you now have not only the bodice pattern but the sleeve pattern, too.

New Sloper Placement Results in New Designs

By changing the basic arrangement of bodice-front, bodice-back, and sleeve slopers, the design of the kimono sleeve can be varied. (You have already seen this in Figs. 303 and 304.)

Kimono Sleeve That Fits Close to the Body

1. Draw a right angle large enough to take the complete drawing.

2. Trace the bodice-front and bodice-back slopers so that the shoulders touch at the armhole and are spread open at the neckline. The center front is on the vertical line of the right angle. The center back is on the horizontal line (Fig. 306a).

3. Place the sleeve sloper so that it overlaps the bodices. The shoulder notch touches the bodice shoulders. The side seams of the bodice are equal in length. Trace the sloper in this position. Divide it into front and back with a line from cap to wrist (Fig. 306a).

4. Trace the pattern.

If the fabric to be used for this design is a plain linen weave, the pattern may be used as one piece (Fig. 306b). The center front is the lengthwise grain, the center back is on the crosswise grain, and the sleeve is on the bias. The shoulder shaping is accomplished by the dart that is formed by the placement of the slopers. It will fit better if the dart legs are curved. For the more usual front and back patterns, trace each separately (Fig. 306c). Correct the shoulder angularity with a curved line.

5. Locate the position for the gusset and construct it (Fig. 306c).

6. Complete the pattern.

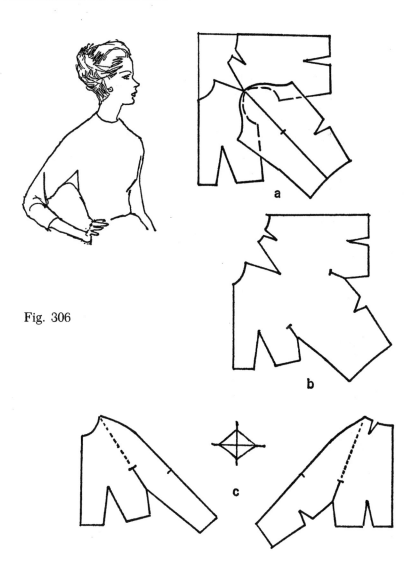

Fig. 306

Kimono Sleeve with Underarm Drapes

In soft fabrics, the drapes fall in free folds (Fig. 307-1). In stiffer fabrics, the folds can be arranged more formally (Fig. 307-2).

1. Place the bodice-front and bodice-back slopers so the shoulders touch. Trace them. Place the sleeve sloper so the shoulder notch touches the shoulders and the underarm drops below the bodice. Make certain that the bodice side seams are equal. Trace. Divide the sleeve into front and back with a line that is a continuation of the shoulder line (Fig. 307a).

2. Shorten the sleeve (Fig. 307a).

3. Draw deep underarm curved style lines both front and back (Fig. 307a).

4. Trace the front pattern. Trace the back pattern. Mark the shoulder point (Fig. 307b). Only the front pattern is shown in this exercise. The back is developed in the same way.

5. Draw slash lines from the shoulder point to the underarm on both front and back patterns (Fig. 307b).

6. Cut out the pattern. Slash and spread (Fig. 307c).

7. Trace the new pattern, correcting the angularity of the shoulder with a curved line. Draw the underarm curve (Fig. 307d). You may cut away the sleeve on a new style line from shoulder to hem as in Fig. 307-2. Or lay the fullness in soft folds as in Fig. 307-1.

8. Complete the pattern.

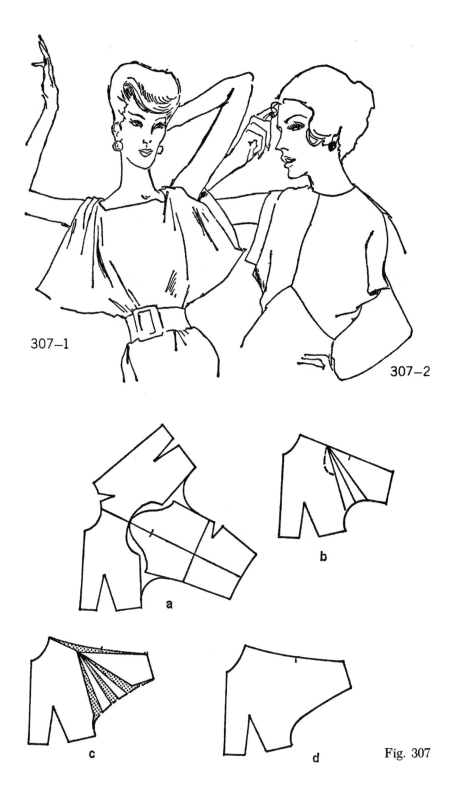

307–1

307–2

a

b

c

d

Fig. 307

Dropped-Shoulder Designs

The kimono sleeve is the basis of the dropped-shoulder sleeve. A great variety of designs are built upon it.

Here is yet another way to arrange the bodice and sleeve slopers (Fig. 308).

1. Place the bodice-front and bodice-back slopers so the shoulders touch at the armhole and spread open somewhat at the neckline. Trace the slopers in this position (Fig. 308a).

2. Place the sleeve sloper so that the cap touches the shoulder and overlaps the bodice at front and back. Trace the sleeve in this position. Divide the sleeve into front and back. Place notches on the dividing line (Fig. 308a).

3. Draw a line across the sleeve to shorten it (Fig. 308a). Place notches on the cross line.

4. Cut out the pattern. Cut off the lower portion of the sleeve. Cut the pattern apart on the shoulder seam (Fig. 308b).

5. Complete the pattern.

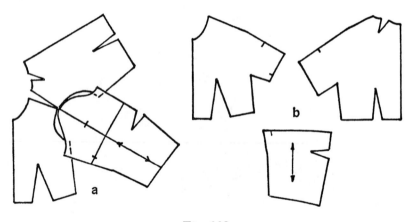

Fig. 308

The resulting short sleeve of the dropped-shoulder design is a perfectly satisfactory sleeve of itself (Fig. 309a).

If the sleeve is to be long, there is not much point in cutting the pattern apart merely to join it again, unchanged, with a seam. Make the separa-

tion meaningful by adding some design feature—perhaps a band of trimming at the seam (Fig. 309b). Or add fullness to the lower sleeve—
circular (Fig. 309c) or balanced (Fig. 309d).

Fig. 309

Juggle the Pieces

The variety of kimono sleeves in the foregoing designs are dependent on the relative placement of the bodice-front, bodice-back, and sleeve slopers. Glance back over this chapter and note the effect created by the placement of front and back slopers with:

1. Shoulders touching at the neckline and spread at the armhole.

2. Shoulders overlapping at the neckline and spread at the armhole.

3. Shoulders touching at the armhole and spread at the neckline.

4. Shoulders touching at the neckline and armhole while the sleeve cap is dropped below the armhole.

5. Shoulders open at the neckline and touching at the armhole while the sleeve cap overlaps the bodice.

It's like a game to juggle these three pattern pieces until one arrives at an interesting design.

Extended-Shoulder Designs

Very short versions of the kimono sleeve extend the shoulder line. So simple are these designs that the patterns for them can be made without the juggling around of slopers.

The *cap sleeve* is such an extended shoulder design (Fig. 310).

1. Trace the bodice-front and bodice-back slopers.

2. Extend the shoulder lines to the desired length of the cap. The cap should be only deep enough to cover the shoulders. If it is any deeper, it must be drafted by the regulation kimono-sleeve method.

3. Lower the armhole 1 inch to 2 inches (Fig. 310a).

4. Connect the extended shoulder to the lowered armhole. You may use either a straight line (Fig. 310a) or a curved line (Fig. 310b).

On some figures such cap sleeves have a tendency to strain and tear at the armhole. Try this design: skip Step 3; substitute for Step 4 the following: connect the extended shoulder to the waistline (Fig. 310c). Stitch to normal drop for cap sleeve.

Fig. 310

A *modified cap sleeve* is another solution for the problem of tearing at the armhole. This sleeve has the good features of both the cap sleeve and the sleeveless dress. The upper part looks like the cap sleeve, while the lower part retains the freedom of a sleeveless dress (Fig. 311-1).

Fig. 311a

1. Extend the shoulder line as for the cap sleeve.
2. Raise the underarm curve.
3. Draw the style line of the cap, bringing it to the raised underarm at or slightly below the usual notch position.
4. Designate the facing.

Fig. 311b

5. Trace the facing.
6. Complete the pattern.

In Fig. 311-2 the extended shoulder of the modified cap sleeve becomes part of an extended yoke. Yoke and underarm are faced separately. See also "Sleeve and Yoke in One Piece," page 414.

311–1

311–2

a

b

Fig. 311

PART OF THE BODICE JOINED WITH THE SLEEVE

Sometimes only *part* of the bodice is joined with the sleeve. A whole new group of sleeves stems from this procedure—the dolman, the raglan, the saddle or strap, and the yoke-and-sleeve.

Dolman Sleeve

While the kimono sleeve was *all* bodice and sleeve, the dolman sleeve is *part* bodice and sleeve. Whereas front and back kimono sleeves are joined by a shoulder seam, bodice and dolman sleeve are joined by a bodice seam.

The underarm of the dolman sleeve may be as deep as desired, often starting at the waistline (Figs. 312a and 312b). So do some kimono sleeves, and because of the similarity of silhouettes, such deep kimono sleeves are often called dolman (Fig. 312c). The true dolman, however, is a combination of sleeve and part of bodice.

Use the bodice-back sloper with the shoulder dart. When possible incorporate the dart in the style line.

Fig. 312

1. Place the bodice-front and bodice-back slopers so the shoulders touch at the neckline and are ½ inch apart at the armhole. Fold back the sleeve cap and place the sleeve so that the ends of the cap extend an equal distance below the front and back armholes on the side seams. Trace the slopers in this position (Fig. 313a).

2. Use the bodice dart control as gathers or unstitched control. An unfitted look is associated with this style. A stitched dart would greatly detract from the interest of the dolman-sleeve style (Fig. 313a).

3. Draw the style line for the dolman sleeve in a sweeping curve across the shoulders from the bodice-front side seam to the bodice-back side seam. Move the back-shoulder dart to the style line so that the dart legs become part of the line. This style line, like all style lines, can be any shape you would like it to be. Draw matching underarm curves from side seams to sleeves (Fig. 313a).

4. Cut the dolman sleeve away from the bodice at the style line. Cut out the bodice front and bodice back (Fig. 313b).

5. Divide the style line of the sleeve into quarters. Divide the underarm curve in half. Draw slash lines connecting the front and back quarter marks at the style line with the center point of each underarm curve (Fig. 313c).

6. Slash and spread about 1½ to 2 inches. This lengthens the underarm seam and provides more grace to the sleeve as well as more ease of movement (Fig. 313d). Trace the sleeve (Fig. 313e).

7. Complete the pattern.

Fig. 313

Strap-Shoulder Sleeve (Saddle Sleeve)

Use the shirt-sleeve sloper for this sleeve. Normal cap ease is unnecessary (indeed it would be inaccurate) for this construction. Shift the back-shoulder dart to the back neckline out of the way of the strap.

1. Trace the appropriate bodice-front, bodice-back, and sleeve slopers.

2. Draw the style line of the strap, as you would a yoke, across the shoulder of front- and back-bodice slopers. The total width of the strap should not be more than 3 inches. If it is wider, it will not fit the cap of the sleeve very well. Notch the strap front and back. Notch the shoulder seam (Fig. 314a).

3. Cut the yokes away from the bodice (Fig. 314b).

4. On the sleeve sloper, draw a lengthwise guideline passing through the shoulder notch and extending the length of the strap above the sleeve cap (Fig. 314c).

5. Place the front and back yokes so the shoulder seams meet on the extended line and the armhole ends touch the sleeve cap (Fig. 314c). Fasten in this position. As you can see, the combined yokes form the strap, which is attached to the sleeve cap.

6. Trace the pattern (Fig. 314d) and complete it.

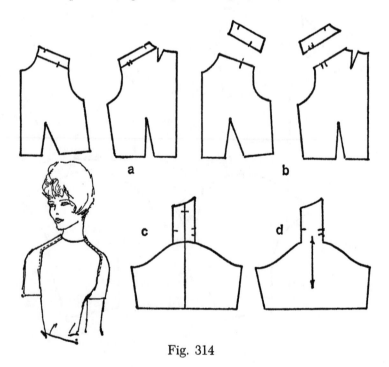

Fig. 314

Fullness added to this sleeve by way of pleats at the cap and gathers at the lower edge adds design interest (Fig. 315).

Fig. 315

RAGLAN SLEEVE

The raglan sleeve in all its design variations is a great favorite (Fig. 316). In coats and jackets, it is roomy enough to wear over other garments. In hard-to-ease fabrics there is none of the struggle there is in a set-in sleeve. It is a natural choice for a double-faced fabric or a reversible garment, since it involves none of the bulk or bother in constructing a set-in sleeve. With additional fullness in the sleeve and/or bodice it becomes enchantingly feminine.

The raglan sleeve is constructed on the same general principle as the strap sleeve. Such differences as there are in the development of the patterns stem from the fact that a larger section of the front and back bodices are cut away on the diagonal to form the yokes. This is the characteristic shape of the raglan sleeve.

There are two types of raglan sleeves. Type A is made by the same method as the strap sleeve. Type B is made with a shoulder dart.

The pattern for the bodice is the same for both types. Use the shirt-sleeve slopers.

Fig. 316

Part I—Bodice Pattern for Both Types of Sleeves

1. Trace the bodice-front and bodice-back slopers. Draw a diagonal style line—either straight or curved—from neck to armhole (Fig. 317a). Notch the style line and the shoulder line.

2. Cut the bodice yokes away from the rest of the bodice on the style lines (Fig. 317b).

3. Trace the sleeve sloper. Draw a lengthwise guideline passing through the shoulder notch and extending the length of the shoulder (Fig. 317c).

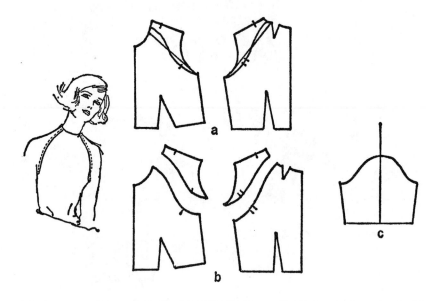

Fig. 317

Part II—Type A Raglan Sleeve

1. Place the front and back yokes together so that shoulder seams meet. Fasten with Scotch tape (Fig. 318a). This forms the strap.

2. Because of the length and depth of its curves, the strap cannot accurately fit the cap of the sleeve. Since no adjustment is possible on the strap, an adjustment must be made on the sleeve cap. Draw curved slash lines on the sleeve cap from the shoulder point to the underarm tips (Fig. 318a). (The cap now looks like a handlebar mustache.)

3. Place the sleeve strap on the sleeve cap so the shoulder line of the strap becomes an extension of the vertical sleeve line. The strap overlaps the cap about ½ inch at the shoulder (Fig. 318a).

4. Slash and spread the cap sections to meet the strap until the sleeve cap touches the armhole ends of the shoulder strap (Fig. 318b).

5. Connect the raised ends of the cap with the sleeve hemline. Correct the strap style line with a curved line to the underarm seam (Fig. 318b).

6. Trace the new sleeve pattern (Fig. 318c) and complete it. Note that the diagonal line of the raglan sleeve will have to be eased into the bodice.

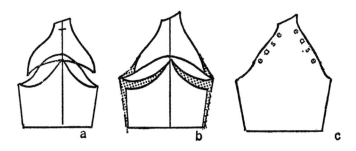

Fig. 318

Part II—Type B Raglan Sleeve

1. Place the front and back yokes on the corresponding curves of the sleeve cap. A dart will form at the shoulder (Fig. 319a).

2. Draw several slash lines from the armhole edge of the shoulder yokes to the front and back style lines (Fig. 319a).

3. Slash and spread, slightly raising and extending the underarm ends of the sleeve cap (Fig. 319b).

4. Connect the extended yoke tips with the sleeve hemline. Correct the yoke style lines with smooth curves (Fig. 319b).

5. Trace the pattern (Fig. 319c) and complete it.

The raglan sleeve may be cut and used in one piece as shown in Figs. 318c and 319c. These can become two-piece raglan sleeves by slashing the Fig. 318c pattern from neckline to hemline (Fig. 319d) and the Fig. 319c pattern from the dart point to the hemline (Fig. 319e).

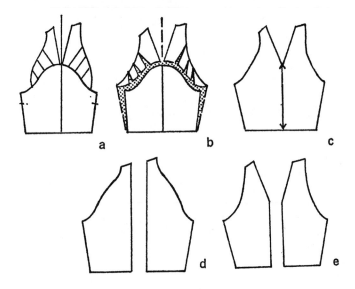

Fig. 319

Dart Control Variations

A dart is a dart is a dart. You may use the one in Fig. 319c in any way a dart can be used. Here a few suggestions.

Shift the dart control and use it for fullness at the hem (Fig. 320).

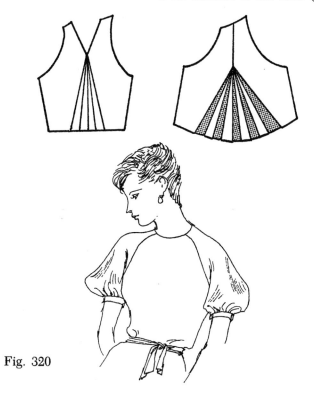

Fig. 320

Use the dart control in a seam (Fig. 321).

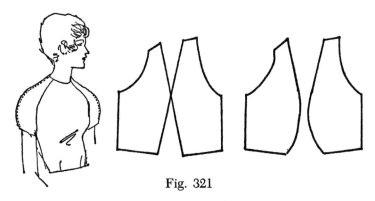

Fig. 321

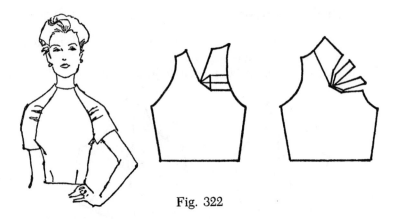

Fig. 322

Convert the dart control into multiple darts (Fig. 322).

In patternmaking, you see the same principles work in the same way wherever the same conditions prevail. There are just as many possibilities for designing with a raglan sleeve as with a set-in sleeve or no sleeve at all.

Sleeve and Yoke in One Piece

The strap-shoulder and raglan sleeves are examples of designs where sleeve and yoke are used as one piece. It is a frequent theme in design. Fig. 323 illustrates another type.

1. Trace the necessary slopers. Draw the yoke style line on bodice front and bodice back. Draw a lengthwise slash line on the sleeve, dividing it into front and back (Fig. 323a).

2. Cut out the patterns. Cut the yokes away from the rest of the bodice. Cut the sleeve apart on the dividing line.

3. Place the front yoke and front sleeve so they touch at the point of the yoke and are slightly spread at the shoulder. This positions the sleeve at a more comfortable angle for the arm (Fig. 323b). Do the same with the back yoke and sleeve, making sure that the angle of the back sleeve matches the angle of the front sleeve (Fig. 323b).

4. Trace the yoke-sleeve patterns, connecting them at the shoulder with a smooth, continuous, curved line. Trace the bodices (Fig. 323c).

5. Complete the pattern.

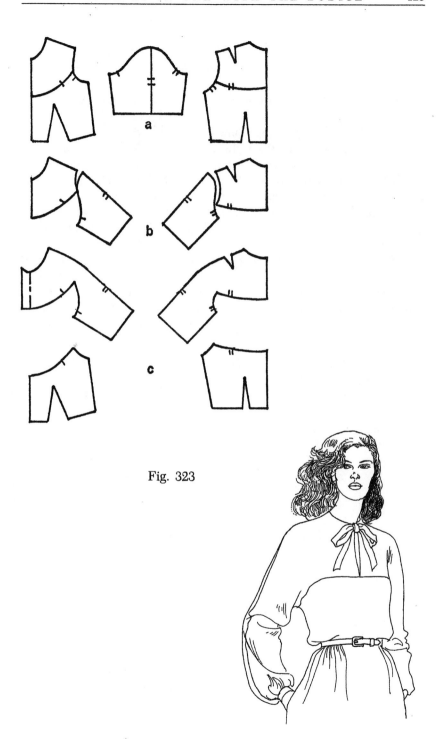

Fig. 323

Sleeve in One with a Yoke Panel

1. Trace the hip-length front and back slopers. Trace the short-sleeve sloper.

2. Draw the style line for the control seam and the yoke on the front sloper. Draw the style line for the control seam on the back sloper. Draw a line dividing the sleeve sloper into front and back (Fig. 324a).

3. Draw a right angle. Place the front and back slopers against the vertical and horizontal lines of the right angle. Place the sleeve sloper so it overlaps the front and back as illustrated (Fig. 324b). (This is the position for the slopers for Fig. 306.)

4. Trace the front yoke panel and front sleeve all in one. Trace the side front. Trace the back panel and back sleeve all in one. Trace the side back (Fig. 324c).

5. Cut out the patterns. Place the side front against the front yoke panel in position to divide the dart control between armhole and waistline. Establish the grain in the side front (Fig. 324d).

6. Cut apart the center-front pattern on the yoke line (Fig. 324d).

7. Trace all pattern sections, correcting the angularity. Complete the pattern.

To complete the pattern illustrated in the sketch, draft the neckline. Shape to suit. Add all necessary symbols and notations.

Fig. 324

Dropped or Extended Shoulder on a Yoke

1. Trace the bodice-front and bodice-back slopers. Trace the sleeve sloper.

2. Draw yoke style lines on the bodice-front and -back slopers. Draw a vertical line dividing the sleeve into front and back. Draw a horizontal slash line across the sleeve cap dividing it into upper and lower sections. Shoulder notch to slash line on the cap and shoulder to style line on the armhole are the same length (Fig. 325a).

3. Cut the sleeve apart into upper and lower sections (Fig. 325b).

4. Draw slash lines in each upper cap section (Fig. 325c). Slash to the cap but not through it.

5. Attach the front slashed cap section to the front armhole. Make the two touch from shoulder to yoke. This will automatically spread the cap to the right amount. Its style line should flow into the style line of the yoke. Fasten in this position (Fig. 325d). Do the same with the back.

6. Cut the yoke and cap away from the rest of the bodice. Trace the dropped-shoulder yoke. Trace the lower bodice (Fig. 325e).

[Actually this much of the pattern makes an interesting design all by itself. However, if this were all you wanted, it could be constructed much more easily by following the directions for the modified cap sleeve (Fig. 311). The style line of the yoke could be a continuation of the style line of the cap.]

To complete the pattern for this design you will need to adjust the lower sleeve cap to fit the spread of the upper sleeve cap now part of the yoke.

7. Draw a slash line across the lower sleeve from underarm to underarm. Draw two diagonal slash lines as illustrated (Fig. 325f).

8. Slash and spread until the new cap equals the combined lengths of the front and back yoke caps (Fig. 325g).

9. Trace the sleeve pattern, correcting the angularity resulting from the spread (Fig. 325h).

10. Complete the pattern.

Fig. 325

Wouldn't fullness added to the lower bodice and sleeves of this pattern make a glamorous blouse (Fig. 326)?

Fig. 326

ADD-A-PART

This business of cutting off a section of pattern and adding it to another opens up all sorts of interesting possibilities in creating new designs. The following are only a few of the inexhaustible variations but they will serve to illustrate how ingenious one can be in combining parts.

The front shirtwaist yoke becomes an extension of the back (Fig. 327).

Fig. 327

A raglan sleeve can be attached to a front—or back (Fig. 328).

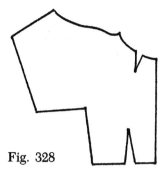

Fig. 328

A back bodice wraps around to the front (Fig. 329).

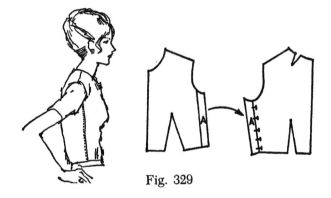

Fig. 329

A front skirt wraps to a back panel (Fig. 330).

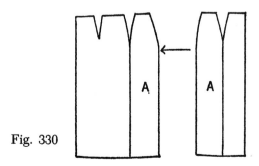

Fig. 330

All of which seems an appropriate way to "wrap up" this chapter.

Chapter 14

Sleeve Finishes

Be it set-in or all-in-one with the garment; short, long, or in between; fitted or full—the lower edge of the sleeve needs a fitting finish.

From the standpoint of design, the lower edge of the sleeve offers just as many and as varied opportunities for interesting treatment as the neckline. Choose one consistent with the design of the sleeve and the rest of the garment, the collar with which it is often paired, and the kind of fabric to be used.

SLEEVE HEMS AND FACINGS

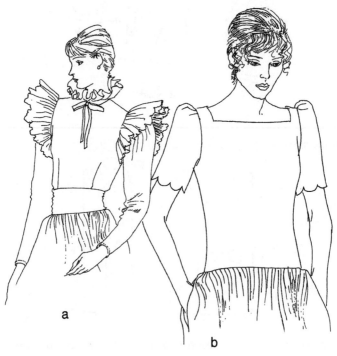

a

b

Fig. 331

The simplest and easiest way to deal with the sleeve edge is by a self-hem. If the sleeve itself is dramatic (Fig. 331a), this may also be the best way.

When the lower edge of the sleeve is shaped (Fig. 331b), a facing is necessary.

Fig. 332

Sleeve hems and facings are handled in the same way as those for necklines (see page 221).

Bias binding can also be used as a narrow hem.

DECORATIVE SLEEVE EDGES

Piping or cording can be inserted in the seam that joins sleeve edge and facing (Fig. 332a).

Banding—self or contrasting—added at the lower edge of the sleeve (Fig. 332b) or applied to the right side of the garment in place of hem or facing (Fig. 332c) adds design interest.

Romantic ruffles frothing at the wrist (Fig. 332d) call attention to beautiful hands and expressive gestures.

SLEEVE PLACKETS

When a sleeve is designed to fit close to the arm or wrist at its lower edge, some opening (placket) must be provided for easy access. Placket types range from the sturdy zipper closing to the fragile thread loop-and-button closing.

Since all sleeve plackets work equally well, select a type consistent with the design of the garment, the kind and amount of wear it is to get, and the character of the fabric. Plackets may be made in the opening left in a seam, added to a seam, or set in a slash or dart.

Remember that sleeves come in pairs so that right and left sleeves will open in opposite directions. Except for those incorporated in a seam, the openings are located toward the back of the sleeve in a line with the little finger.

IN-A-DART SLEEVE PLACKET

A wrist dart can be utilized for a placket (Fig. 333).

Draw the dart and its seam allowance. Mark the opening of the placket and the clip in the seam allowance slightly beyond the end of the opening. The seam allowance below this is formed into a narrow hem.

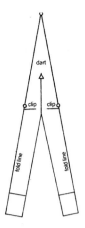

Fig. 333

IN-SEAM SLEEVE PLACKET

The in-seam placket makes a neat, flat finish. When the *closing is by zipper*, the finish is a strong one as well. Simply mark the opening for the placket on the seam line.

When a zipper is not available or is inappropriate for the material, the placket may be closed with *snaps or hooks and eyes* instead. Such plackets require the creation of an overlap and underlap. These may be extensions of the seam allowances (Fig. 334) or two strips of self-fabric on straight or bias grain.

On the pattern, mark the opening for the placket and the clip in the seam allowance slightly beyond it. Add the extensions for the overlap and underlap or provide a pattern for the strips of self-fabric in the necessary width and length plus seam allowances.

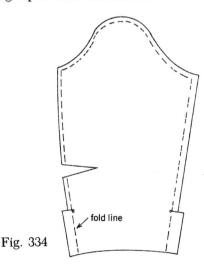

Fig. 334

SLEEVE LOOP-AND-BUTTON CLOSING

The loop-and-button closing may be made of thread, tubing, or braid.
Mark the position for the loops along the seam line of the front edge of
the closing and align the position of the buttons on the underlap with the
edge of the overlap. The underlap is an extension of the sleeve opening
(Fig. 335a). The overlap is a facing for the sleeve opening (Fig. 335b).

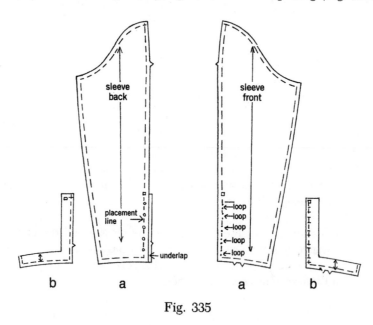

Fig. 335

LAPPED CLOSING WITH A ROLLED HEM

The lapped closing is another variation of an in-seam placket (Fig. 336).
It is used with a buttoned cuff. The opening is finished with a rolled hem.
When the cuff is attached, the placket is folded into a pleat for the closing.

On the pattern, mark the position of the 1⅜ to 1½-inch opening centered over a line that would extend to the little finger. Indicate the seam
line across the opening and slightly beyond its ends. Draw the clips at the
ends of the opening.

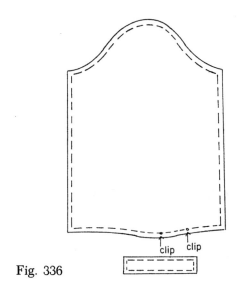

Fig. 336

clip   clip

SLEEVE VENT WITH SELF-FACING

The sleeve vent with self-facing in a vertical seam is typical of suit jackets and tailored coats with two-piece sleeves (Fig. 337).

Add extensions at the lower edges of the back seam of upper and under sleeves. On a medium misses' size, the extensions measure from 1½ to 1¾ inches wide by 3½ to 4 inches long. To this add seam allowances and hem. Draw the fold lines for the self-facings, hems, and the miters that join them. Show the position of the buttonholes on the overlap and the buttons on the underlap.

Fig. 337

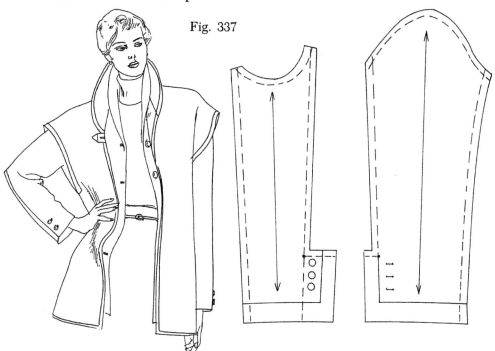

PLACKET IN A SLASH

When there is no convenient seam to use for the purpose, a placket can be set in a slash. This is generally at the little-finger position.

The finish can be as unobtrusive as a faced placket (Fig. 338a) or a continuous-bound placket (Fig. 338b). Or it can be as decorative as a tailored placket (Fig. 338c).

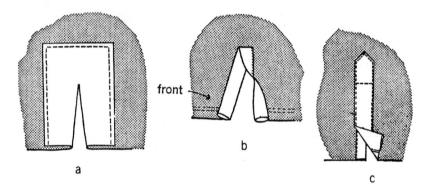

Fig. 338

The *faced placket* calls for a square or rectangular facing equal to the length of the opening plus generous seam allowances all around.

The *continuous-bound placket* requires a pattern for the binding equal to the length of both sides of the opening by twice the width of the finished binding plus seam allowances.

The *tailored placket* (French or shirt placket) for the sleeve is designed in the same way as the tailored neck placket (see page 289).

FINISH FOR FULL SLEEVES

When free-hanging, the fullness at the lower edge of a full sleeve can be finished in the same way as that of a fitted sleeve with a hem or decorative edging. However, there are a number of ways for controlling the fullness: tucks (Fig. 339a), buttoned pleats (Fig. 339b), ribbing (Fig. 339c), casings through which drawstring or elastic can be drawn (Fig. 339d), or casings that form ruffles (Fig. 339e).

Fig. 339

Tucks and pleats on a sleeve are formed in the same way as on other parts of the garment.

Ribbing can be attached to the sleeve seam allowance.

Any hem, tuck, facing, seam allowance, or applied strip or band can serve as a *casing* through which the elastic or drawstring is drawn. On the pattern, indicate the two rows of stitching (Fig. 340a) or the one row of stitching and one fold line that form the "tunnel" (Fig. 340b).

Make the casing as wide as the drawstring or elastic to be used plus ⅛ to ¼ inch for ease in drawing up the fullness.

Fig. 340

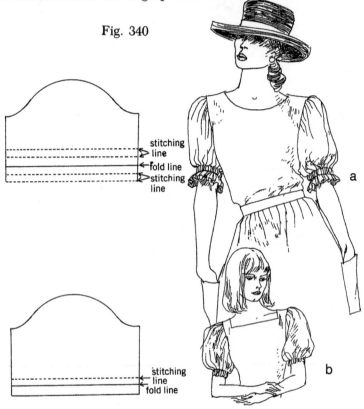

To create the *casing with a ruffle*, add an amount beyond the casing equal to twice the width of the ruffle for a faced ruffle. For a single-thickness ruffle, add only the width of the ruffle plus a separate strip for the casing.

CUFFS

Other than a hem, perhaps the most familiar finish for a sleeve is a cuff. What a collar is to a neckline, a cuff is to a sleeve.

Essentially, a cuff is a band of fabric attached to the lower edge of the sleeve as an extension of it. The band can be as simple as the cuff without a placket or as complex as the French cuff.

The band may be a rectangle of fabric, folded in half so the cuff and facing are cut in one piece on straight or bias grain. Or the cuff may be cut in two pieces—the cuff and its facing. This provides opportunity for shaped edges, for contrasting color or texture, and (for example, if there is a seam) for insertion of trimming.

BAND CUFF WITHOUT A PLACKET (SLEEVEBAND)

The band cuff is the simplest of all cuffs because no opening is involved. The cuff ends are joined. The band is attached to the gathered or pleated lower edge of the sleeve (Fig. 341).

Make the band long enough to slip over the hand easily (knuckle circumference plus ease). Make its width 1 inch to 1½ inches. Add seam allowances to length and width. Place notches to match those on the sleeve. Cut the cuff on a fold for a one-piece construction. The grain may be straight or bias.

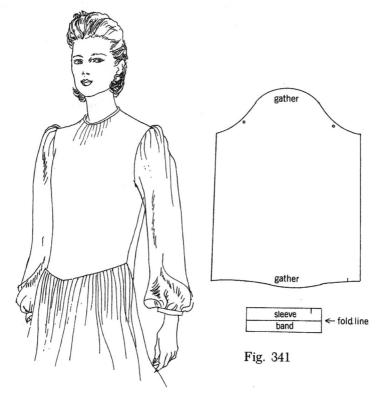

Fig. 341

BAND CUFF WITH A PLACKET

When there is a sleeve placket, the cuff ends may be lapped, extended, or flush with the placket edges. In a lapped band cuff, the front end is flush with the front placket edge while the underlap projects from the back placket edge.

1. Determine the length and width of the cuff. Add an extension to the back end. Indicate the underarm of the sleeve with ⚬ (Fig. 342a). Add seam allowances. Place notches to match those of the sleeve. Mark the grain line.

2. If the band is to be faced, cut four—two for each cuff. If the band is to be cut in one piece, double the width and cut two. Mark the fold line (Fig. 342b).

3. Mark the buttonholes on the overlap and the position of the buttons on the underlap.

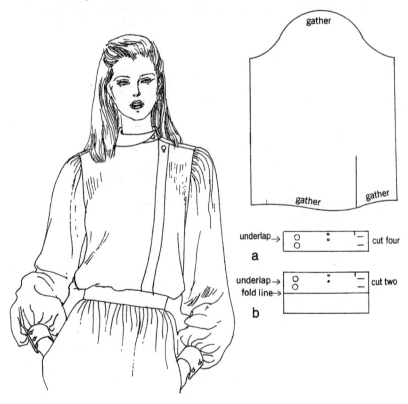

Fig. 342

BAND CUFF WITH EXTENDED ENDS

For the band cuff with extended ends, develop the pattern as for the band cuff with a placket. Add extensions to *both* front and back ends. In Fig. 343 the cuff has been set on a shortened sleeve.

Fig. 343

FRENCH CUFF

In the French cuff both front and back ends are flush with the placket edges. A wide, faced band turns back to form a double cuff. There are four buttonholes on each cuff fastened together in pairs through which cuff links are passed.

1. Shorten the sleeve an amount equal to the width of the cuff.

2. Make the length of the cuff equal to the edge of the shortened sleeve. Double the width of the cuff. Add ½ inch to the turnback end of it in order to hide the seam which joins cuff to sleeve. The edges of the turnback may be square (Fig. 344a) or rounded (Fig. 344b).

3. Mark the buttonhole placement an equal distance from the fold line.

4. Trace the facing exactly the same as the cuff. (This cuff is an exception to the rule for seam-roll allowance since all edges of the cuff are visible.)

5. Complete the pattern.

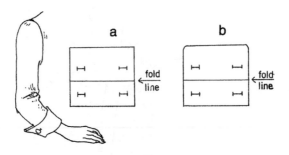

Fig. 344

SLEEVE WITH WIDE, FITTED BAND

The sleeve with a wide, fitted band is designed on the lower portion of the sleeve sloper. In the full sleeve of Fig. 345, the band, like a yoke, provides a trim fitted look that contrasts with the fullness above.

1. On the cut-out sleeve sloper with the cut-out elbow dart, shift the dart control to the position for the sleeve opening (Fig. 345a).

2. Close the dart temporarily as for a bulging pattern. Draw the style line for the fitted band as for a yoke. Notch the style line and the underarm seam. Label sections 1 and 2 (Fig. 345b).

3. Cut the band away from the rest of the sleeve. Slash the dart line. Separate the two sections (Fig. 345c).

4. Join sections 1 and 2 on the underarm seam so the band may be cut as one piece (Fig. 345d).

5. Remove the excess ease by slashing and overlapping the band to fit the lower arm snugly (Fig. 345e).

6. Trace the pattern (Fig. 345f). Add a closing extension. Face each band.

7. Complete the pattern.

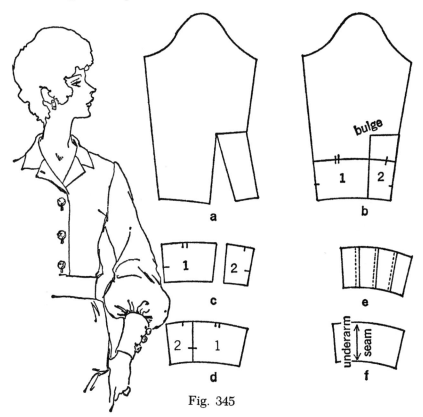

Fig. 345

TURNBACK CUFF

The turnback cuff rolls back to cover the base of the sleeve. It can be an extension of the sleeve or a separate cuff.

The circumference of this cuff at its outer edge (at either fold line or seam) should be somewhat larger than the sleeve to which it is to be attached so that the cuff will stand away from the sleeve. How much circumference ease is needed depends on the thickness of the material. Start with ½ inch and adjust as necessary.

To negotiate the turnback there also should be sufficient length from the outside edge (style line) to the inside edge. The amount necessary depends on the weight and texture of the fabric.

A two-piece turnback cuff should be larger than its facing to assure sufficient material to encircle the sleeve smoothly. Once more, the amount necessary depends on the weight and texture of the fabric used.

Short-sleeve Turnback Cuff

1. Start with a short sleeve pattern that has a straight hemline. Mark the width of the cuff on the sleeve (Fig. 346a).

2. Fold the pattern on the hemline and trace the cuff.

3. Unfold the pattern and draw in the cuff (Fig. 346b).

4. Add length to the cuff for the turnback. Add ease to the underarm seams starting at the outer edge of the cuff and tapering to the hemline (Fig. 346c).

5. For facing in one with the cuff, fold once more at the new lower edge and trace the cuff and sleeve hemline.

6. Unfold the pattern. Draw in the facing. Mark a hem allowance at the lower edge of the facing in an amount that will be covered by the cuff when turned to wearing position (Fig. 346d).

7. Mark the hemline of cuff and facing. Mark the cuff fold line. The facing hemline becomes the turnback line. When the completed cuff is turned to position, the hem is blindstitched in place.

8. Complete the pattern.

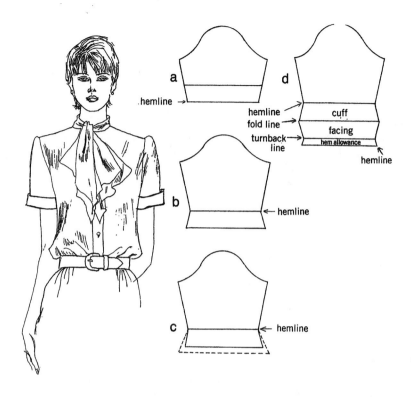

Fig. 346

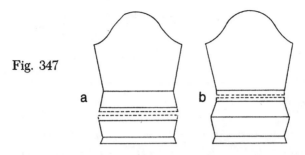

Fig. 347

Should you wish a separate facing, cut the pattern apart along the fold line and add seam allowance to each edge (Fig. 347a).

Should you wish a separate cuff, cut the pattern apart at the sleeve hemline and add seam allowance to each edge (Fig. 347b).

A separate cuff or facing offers opportunity for use of different grain, color, or texture of fabric. It may be cut on the straight grain or the bias. The latter shapes better around the sleeve.

If a separate turnback cuff has a shaped style line, its ends are brought together not at the underarm as would be done with a plain band but at a point in line with the little finger as in the long-sleeved turnback cuff (Fig. 348-2).

Long-sleeve Turnback Cuff

When the long sleeve is a full one (Fig. 348-1), the cuff pattern is developed in the same way as a short-sleeve turnback cuff. The pattern for a turnback cuff on a long fitted sleeve (Fig. 348-2) is developed as below.

1. Trace the long-sleeve sloper. Straighten the hemline. Mark the width of the cuff on the sleeve. Draw a line from the elbow dart to the little-finger position (Fig. 348a).

2. Fold the pattern on the hemline. Trace the cuff and the little-finger dart line. Unfold the pattern and draw the cuff and the dart line (Fig. 348b).

3. Cut out the pattern. Cut out the elbow dart. Slash the little-finger dart line and shift the dart control to it. Shorten the dart.

4. Add similar shaped style lines for design interest and ease in the opening created by the little-finger dart. Add ease at the underarm seams starting at the cuff edge and tapering to the hemline. Correct the sleeve seam distorted by the closing of the dart (Fig. 348c).

5. The original hemline of the sleeve becomes the turnback line. The cuff facing duplicates the extended cuff plus a hem allowance above the hemline in an amount that will be covered by the cuff when turned to wearing position. Locate the facing on the sleeve (the broken line in Fig. 348d). Notch the outside edge (Fig. 348d).

6. Trace the two facing sections. Label them 1 and 2. Join the sections at the underarm (Fig. 348e). Since it is the facing which becomes the

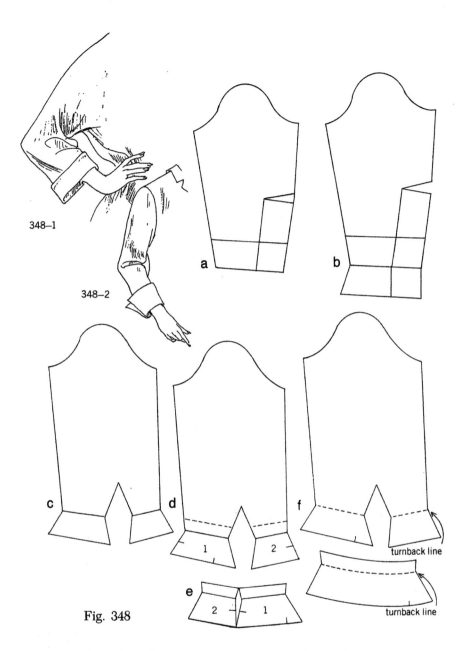

348–2

a

b

c

d

e

f

1   2

2   1

turnback line

turnback line

Fig. 348

upper surface when the cuff is turned back, add at least ⅛ inch to all outside seams as an allowance for rolling the joining seam to the underside.

7. Trace the complete facing, ignoring the shaped section at the underarm which remains as ease for the turnback. Correct the angular lines with smoothly curved lines (Fig. 348f).

8. Trace the sleeve with its extended cuff. Mark the turnback line (Fig. 348f).

9. Complete the pattern.

Fig. 349

For a similar *turnback cuff on a full sleeve* (Fig. 349), cut two of the facing pattern of Fig. 348f. Add seam allowance at the edge that will join the sleeve and notch it.

Like other parts of garments, cuffs may also have additional fullness like the flared, turndown cuff of Fig. 350 or a buttoned extension as in Fig. 351.

Flared Turndown Cuff

1. Trace the fitted-sleeve sloper. Decide how much of lower sleeve is to be flared and draw the dividing line. Notch it. Draw slash lines on the cuff section (Fig. 350a).

2. Cut the cuff away from the sleeve. Slash and spread it at the hem edge to the desired fullness (Fig. 350b).

3. Trace the spread cuff for the facing (Fig. 350c). Trace it a second time for the cuff itself and add ⅛ inch to all outside edges (except that which joins the sleeve) for a seam-roll allowance.

4. Complete the pattern.

Why not try a flared collar to match?

Fig. 350

FITTED CUFF WITH A CLOSING OVERLAP

1. Trace the fitted-sleeve sloper. Draw the style line for the cuff. Show the closing line AB, the overlap beyond it with the position of the button and buttonhole, and the underlap line CD. Label section 1 which will include the extension for the overlap. Label section 2 which will include the underlap (Fig. 351a).

2. Trace section 1 and line AB. Trace section 2 and line AB. Add ¼-inch ease to each underarm seam (Fig. 351b).

3. Cut out sections 1 and 2. Join them on the underarm seam (Fig. 351c). Trace this for the cuff facing.

4. For the cuff itself, trace Fig. 351c. Add ⅛-inch allowance on all outside edges for the seam roll.

5. In a separate cuff, the grain is usually centered over the top of the hand. In this case, line AB meets that requirement so it becomes the straight grain.

6. Complete the pattern.

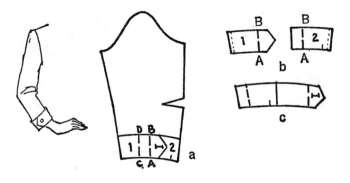

Fig. 351

DETACHABLE CUFFS

Detachable cuffs provide a removable, washable trim when used over a sleeve or an existing cuff (Fig. 352a). A band cuff, simulating a shirt cuff that extends below the sleeve edge adds a crisp, fresh touch (Fig. 352b).

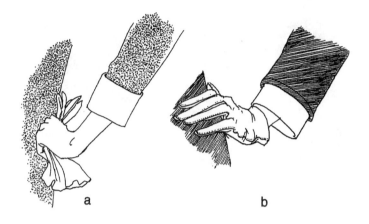

a   b

Fig. 352

The Cuff That Goes Over a Sleeve or Other Cuff

The detachable cuff in Fig. 352a must fit both the measurement of the outer layer that goes over the sleeve or other cuff and the measurement of the inner circumference of the sleeve.

Cut the pattern for the cuff to the necessary length and width at its outer edges and taper to the inner circumference of the sleeve.

The cuff may be worn with free ends or with a slit at the outer end.

The Cuff That Extends Below the Sleeve

Cut the pattern for the band cuff in Fig. 352b to fit the inner circumference of the sleeve and wide enough so its edge may be deep within the sleeve edge.

The completed cuff is slipstitched to the inside of the sleeve.

WHEN IT SEAMS APPROPRIATE

A cuff seam, too, can be gussied up with ruffles, lace, or insertions of any kind—when it seams appropriate (Fig. 353).

Fig. 353

THE END OF THE BEGINNING

The end of this chapter marks the end of your introduction to pattern-making. You've come a long way—all the way from being frightened by a dart to making a complicated pattern. Now you must go on to study, investigate, experiment, perfect.

Even were you never to make a complete pattern of your own, as much learning as you have acquired in the course of this book would still be valuable. Thoughtful performance always deepens your understanding and appreciation of the problems involved in any skill.

You understand painting a little better when you have tried to paint; music a little better when you have tried to play an instrument; farming a little better when you have struggled with a vegetable patch. Undoubtedly, in the future you will regard all patterns, both your own custom-made ones and the commercial ready-made ones, with a little more appreciation and respect for the time and knowhow that go into their creation.

Chapter 15

Remnants

Everyone who sews knows all about remnants, those wonderful leftover bits and pieces of material too precious to discard, too small to make a whole big thing of.

Authors have remnants, too—important bits and pieces of information too diverse to lump under one heading, not quite large enough for each to merit a chapter of its own. That's a fair enough description of this last chapter.

SEW IT SEEMS

The grandest plans on paper may be totally unworkable in fabric! Many a dream dress has died a-borning on the drawing board. It is not enough to know the principles of designing and the techniques of patternmaking. One must also know whether the design so artfully conceived and the pattern so painstakingly constructed can actually be put together. A knowledge of sewing is invaluable to the patternmaker.

One does not expect the designer or the patternmaker to be a skilled dressmaker or tailor. However, a reasonable background in the techniques by which design ideas are translated into finished garments will vastly improve the designs, the patterns, and the garments.

DRAPING

Draping is the oldest and longest continuous means of designing clothing. Understandably so. One can see the garment literally take shape in the hands.

Any art is limited by the character of its medium. There are things you can do with clay that you cannot do with wood, with watercolor that you cannot do with oil paints, with fabric that you cannot do with paper, even with one fabric that you cannot do with another. In draping one works directly with a fabric. This is an enormous advantage. It is so often difficult to visualize in a flat pattern the flow of a line in cloth or to tell from a diagram whether the fit will be all one desires.

Inevitably all sewers as well as designers resort to some form of draping. If the design doesn't work out as you conceived it, somehow, it seems very natural to take it in hand and make it do what you want it to do.

There are some great designers who develop their designs by draping directly in the fabric they plan to use for the garment. For them the color and texture of the fabric are the source of inspiration. Others work from sketches handed over to patternmakers and drapers for interpretation. Still others work out their own patterns.

There is no doubt that an understanding of patternmaking is a great boon even to a draper. For the home sewer, often a combination of the two methods—drafting and draping—is an excellent way to work out a design. Every sewer who has done any fitting (and who has not?) has done some draping whether she was aware of it or not.

HERE'S WHAT YOU'LL NEED FOR DRAPING A NEW DESIGN

An eye for line, proportion, balance, detail.
Hands free to coax or caress the cloth into shape.
The courage to cut into cloth.
Fabric to inspire you.
A patient model or a dress form on which to do the draping.
You'll also need: sharp scissors, lots of pins, some ½-inch cotton or twill tape, tailor's chalk, a yardstick or tape measure, a full-length mirror. (Somehow one can get a better perspective on the design in a mirror.)

LET THE FABRIC TELL YOU WHAT IT WANTS TO DO

A dress is only as exciting as the fabric that makes it. There is certainly no dearth of beautiful fabric today. The only real problem in selection is what of the vast and gorgeous array to choose.

Once having chosen your fabric, pay some attention to it. It has a mind and character of its own. It practically tells you what it wants to do. Don't fight it.

Fabric falls with the grain. No matter how you cut it or force it into other positions, in the end it will fall with the grain. If you misuse the grain, you may end up with unexpected and perhaps unpleasant results.

Most fabrics hang best with the vertical grain. Pleats and soft folds always hang best on the vertical grain. The horizontal grain can be used for trimming, for contrast, for areas that do not need to be closely fitted to the figure.

Bias grain has great elasticity. It can be molded to the body. Use it wherever roundness or curviness is sought without darts or seams to do the shaping: collars, sleeves, belts, bodices with little shaping, skirts when easy movement is desired. Use it for decorative effect in drapery and soft folds.

The texture of a fabric may dictate the design. Obviously, stiff fabrics cannot do what soft fabrics can and vice versa.

HAVE THE COURAGE TO CUT

To do any draping you must have the courage to cut. If you're apprehensive about cutting, then draping is not for you. Better stick to patternmaking. Of course, you're fearful you'll make a mistake—cutting is so final! Just remember it's only fabric. If you ruin it, there are miles and miles more of the stuff. It's the release from fear of making a mistake you need most of all.

If your fear is based on the expense or the uniqueness of a particular fabric that cannot be replaced, then use an inexpensive fabric of a similar degree of drapability, unbleached muslin in a suitable weight, cotton, or voile.

LEARN TO USE YOUR HANDS

The eye dictates the line. The fabric tells you where it wants to go. The hand must follow these orders.

Learn to use your hands to smooth the material over the body (or form) until the fabric eases into position. Feel the design in your fingertips. Manipulate the fabric until the effect is what you want.

HALF A DESIGN IS OFTEN BETTER
THAN THE WHOLE DESIGN

It is practically impossible to drape two sides identically. It is only a rare individual who has so sure an eye or so steady a hand. Only machines duplicate exactly. In handwork, there is always the element of human error.

Work out the design on one side of the figure. (An asymmetric design would be the exception to this rule. Even in such designs there are details that must be balanced on both sides.) Refine the design, perfect the fit, true up the pattern, and duplicate the second side.

SUGGESTED PROCEDURE FOR DRAPING

1. Experiment with the placement of any plaids, stripes, checks, or design motifs. Decide how you wish to use the grain of the fabric.

2. Start with an approximate length and width of fabric for the design you have in mind. Allow sufficient material for any fullness, sleeves in one with the garment, turnback facings, hems, lapels, etc.

3. Anchor the fabric at strategic points: center back, center front, neckline, waistline, hips, or any special place in the design. Pin the fabric to the dress form, the underdress of your model, or to a length of tape placed as a base where needed.

4. Working around the figure, pin the fabric into darts, folds, fullness, or drapery. Cut the cloth into sections at control seams and style lines and pin them together. See that the front style lines flow naturally into the back.

5. Cut away any excess fabric at the neck, shoulders, armholes, and side seams. Be sure to leave seam allowances. Clip all curves to the seam line (the line on which the garment will fit when stitched).

6. Check the grain, the shaping, the ease, and the outline seams.

7. Remedy any wrinkles, bulges, gaping, or strain that need correction. Bulges at dart points mean that the dart is too large. Wrinkles (excess or drooping fabric or folds) may mean that more dart control is needed. "Hiking up" or "poking out" may mean that more dart control is necessary or that more length is needed or both. Don't throw the grain off by too much dart control in any one dart or seam. Keep the grain balanced on both sides of a seam or there will be pulling or puckering when stitched.

8. Mark the center front and center back with rows of pins or with tailor's chalk. In the same way, mark the shape of the neckline, the shoulder seam, the armhole, and the side seams.

9. Determine and mark the waistline. Determine the approximate length of the garment, allow for a hem, then cut away the excess fabric.

10. Cut a length of material (on grain) to drape around the neck for a collar. Lap the collar neckline over the neckline of the garment, clipping as necessary to release the curve. Trim away excess material at the neckline. Mark the neckline of both collar and bodice. Check the stand, the roll line, and the fall of the collar. Cut the collar style line.

11. Cut a length of material for a sleeve. Placing the cloth on grain, drape it around the arm. Pin the underarm seam from the armhole to a little above the elbow. Lap the cap over the armhole. Pin in small tucks or folds to represent the ease in a set-in sleeve cap. Pin the cap into the armhole. Trim away any excess material. Clip as necessary. Check the grain and adjust as needed. Mark the seam line on the sleeve and the garment. On both sleeve and garment, mark the shoulder and front and back notches where arm and body meet. Now pin in the elbow darts. Pin the rest of the underarm seam.

12. Decide the placement and size of buttons, pockets, and trimmings. Paper cutouts or scraps of cloth pinned to the garment will give some idea of the effect. Perhaps you would prefer to draw these directly on the muslin.

13. Be mindful of the fact that the garment is yet to get interfacing and/or underlining, facing, lining, and perhaps an interlining. The lines of the garment will be sustained by all of these but they will make the garment fit a little more snugly when they are applied. Be sure to allow sufficient ease.

14. Experiment, pin, cut. Experiment, pin, cut. Experiment, pin, cut.

15. When the draped garment is completed, remove it from the form or figure, mark in any way still necessary, unpin the garment, correct any jumpiness of the pins, and true all lines with drafting instruments. Make certain that all corresponding seams match in length, that pairs of dart legs match in length. Do anything that will complete the pattern.

16. Transfer the design of each section to pattern paper. Cloth does not make for a trustworthy pattern. It is too easy to force into a layout without due regard for shape or grain.

Add all the pattern symbols that will make for accurate layout, cutting, and stitching.

PATTERN GRADING

Grading is the process by which a pattern may be increased or decreased to the next size. The change is *gradual* rather than in one place, hence the term "grading."

Grading is also *proportionate* rather than uniform. This is because, in growth, the bony structure of the body does not increase in the same amounts as the fleshy parts. Therefore, there is less differential in bony areas than in fleshy areas as patterns are graded from one size to another. Fig. 354 suggests where the pattern changes are made and the generally accepted amount and placement of grades for misses' and women's sizes.

In industry, grading is now generally done by computers.

For the occasional needs of the home sewer the following methods work well. There are two: the split or tuck method (Fig. 355) and the shift method (Fig. 356). Use whichever method seems easier for you.

Grading directions are for the basic sloper sections. If you grade the sloper before you do your pattern designing, the changes will be easy enough. If you grade the pattern after the designing, it will be a little more complex. Decide how these overall amounts can be allocated in the number of pieces that make your total pattern. Just remember that all pieces that join must have similar adjustments.

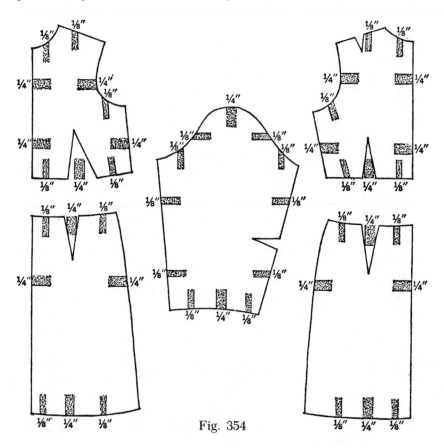

Fig. 354

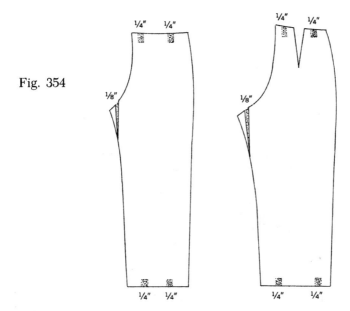

Fig. 354

SPLIT OR TUCK METHOD

To Make the Pattern Larger, Slash and Spread

1. Slash and spread the pattern in the places and to the amounts indicated in Fig. 354.

2. Fill in the open spaces with tissue (Fig. 355a).

To Make the Pattern Smaller, Slash and Overlap or Tuck

1. Slash and overlap or tuck the pattern in the places and to the amounts designated in Fig. 354.

2. Scotch tape to position (Fig. 355b).

Fig. 355

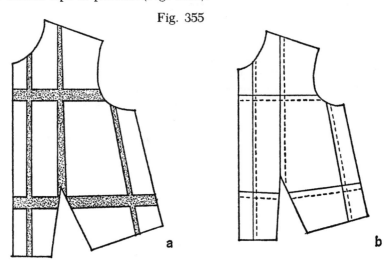

a   b

SHIFT METHOD

To Make the Pattern Larger

Fig. 356a. Draw a new center-back line. Place the center back of the pattern along this line then shift it up ¼ inch from A to B. Trace the B corner.

Fig. 356b. Always keeping the center back of the pattern parallel to the new center-back line, shift the pattern out ⅛ inch. Trace the neckline to C.

Fig. 356c. Once more, shift the pattern out ⅛ inch. Trace the shoulder to D.

Fig. 356d. Shift the pattern down ¼ inch to E (notch). Trace from D to E.

Fig. 356e. Shift the pattern out ⅛ inch. Trace the armhole from E to F.

Fig. 356f. Shift the pattern down ¼ inch to G. Trace the corner at G.

Fig. 356g. Shift the pattern down ½ inch and trace the waistline from G to A.

Fig. 356h. This completes the grade.

To make the pattern smaller by this method shift the pattern back rather than out in the same amount.

Grade each of the pattern pieces in the same way to the amounts suggested in Fig. 354. This is a faster method (once you get on to it) than the slash-and-spread or the slash-and-overlap (or -tuck) method though the latter may be a little easier and more accurate for inexperienced graders.

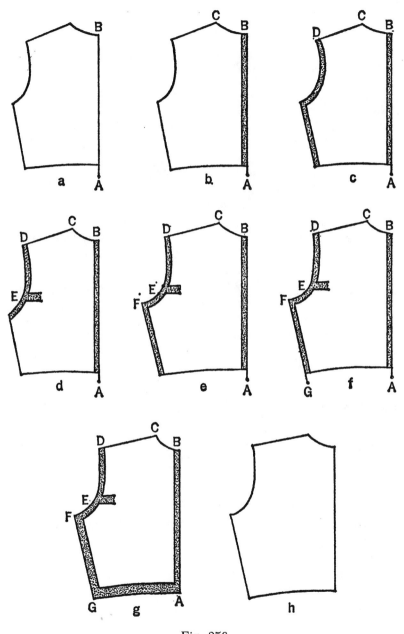

Fig. 356

LET'S MAKE THE PATTERN!

Comes a time when one is anxious to put together in one great pattern all the separate learnings and skills acquired during the study of this book. How to go about it?

Here is a suggested procedure.

1. Design the garment.
2. Select the appropriate sloper.
3. Collect all the materials you will need to draft the pattern—paper, instruments, sketch, and any pertinent information.
4. Draw the style lines.
5. Decide the shaping. Deal with the dart control accordingly.
6. Add fullness where necessary.
7. Work out each part of the pattern as directed in this book. You may use this book as you would a cookbook. Open to the proper page for the recipe.
8. Cut and fit a trial muslin (see page 457). Make any needed changes. Transfer any changes to the pattern.
9. Line up the pattern and complete it.
10. Work out an economical layout for cutting (see "Pattern Puzzle," page 458).

Often it is helpful to develop the pattern in a smaller scale until you have solved all the pattern problems. Then tackle the full-scale pattern. It is quite a thrill to see this complete full-scale pattern materialize.

WHERE DO DESIGN IDEAS COME FROM?

Designing a garment, like any other creative activity, deals with the expression of an idea—not just any idea, but *your* idea. That is not to say that if you want to design a pattern for a dress, you must invent something absolutely brand new, something never seen before. All of us, even as great designers do, build on what has gone before.

Actually, for every one of the few famed giants of design—those who lead the way—there are countless others who, with less acclaim, make very significant contributions to fashion. And there are literally millions of people who have worthwhile and original ideas.

The same sources of inspiration are there for all. Some are more able— by talent, by training, and by the very habit of creating—to view, to select, to interpret, to adapt, to organize, to present as much of the past, as much of the present, and as much of themselves as will give their work their own unmistakable imprint.

You've heard it said that there is nothing really new—there are only new ways of looking at old ideas. Creative as Dior was, even his most widely heralded contribution was only a "New Look." It is this "new look" that any of us can take from past styles or existing trends. When filtered through our own individuality, this gives us the right to say "This is my idea." This is as true of creating a design for an article of clothing as of creating a poem or a song or a picture.

Well, then, where do the design ideas come from? Anywhere, everywhere. A picture in a magazine and a painting in a museum. A glimpse in a window and a glance at a book. A candid camera shot of a celebrity or an unknown young woman hurriedly crossing the street. Some yardage of irresistible fabric and a piece of jewelry that needs a proper setting. A fashion report in the newspaper and a description overheard on a bus. A memory out of the past and a dream of "taking a flier" at that daring new thing from Paris or London or Tokyo or Milan or New York or wherever.

A WORKING SKETCH

Clip pictures of designs that appeal to you for color, line, and detail. Make a sketch of something you've seen that you particularly like. You don't have to be an artist to do this. You need only a kind of pictorial shorthand that shows style line, proportion, seams, darts, and decorative details. For you, a work of art is not important; a working sketch is. Note the silhouette, the proportion and relationship of its various parts, the important style lines, or any special features that attract you to the design.

INFORMATION, PLEASE

Analyze the design for details. For drafting a pattern, a general observation is not enough. Every aspect must be specifically and carefully considered.

1. Where is the shaping? How is the dart control used? Is there one dart or several darts? Are the darts straight or curved? What direction do they follow? Do any of the style lines conceal the dart control? Which are the decorative seams and which the control seams? Do any of the darts enter a control seam? How much dart control is needed for a "relaxed

look"? What is the best place for additional dart control for a very fitted garment? Does the dart control appear as a dart, a tuck, a dart tuck, a pleat, gathers, shirring, or smocking?

2. Is there fullness in addition to the dart control? Where is the fullness? How much fullness is there? In what form does the fullness appear? Where should the pattern be slashed? How much shall the slashes be spread?

3. Which are the important style lines? Where do they start and where do they end? How much above the waistline? How far from the center line? How much in from the side seam? How much below the neckline? How far above the knee? Below the knee? Where in relation to the hip? Where in relation to the armhole? Where on the shoulder seam? Does the style line of the bodice continue into the skirt? Does it include any part of the sleeve? Are the style lines curved or straight? Are they simple lines or complex lines? What direction to the line? Is it repeated in any way?

4. Where is the straight grain? (If you are copying a picture or dress, the grain line is an important clue to its construction, especially if there are several sections to the pattern.) Where is the straight grain on each piece? Where is the straight grain on the sleeve? Is the sleeve on the bias? Where is the straight grain on the collar and cuffs, the pockets, the peplum, the panel, the decorative band?

5. Are there any decorative features of special interest? Are there buttons or bows? Where are they placed? How large are they? Is there any trimming? How much trimming? What kind of trimming? How is it applied?

6. What kind of neckline does the garment have? Is it raised or lowered? Is it asymmetric or formally balanced? What neckline for the front? For the back? Is there a collar? What type of collar? How large is the collar? How much stand? What is the style line of the collar? Is it made of contrasting material or self-fabric?

7. What kind of sleeves, if any? Are they short, long, or in between? Are they set-in, kimono, raglan, dolman? Are they fitted, puffed, bell, full, rippled, cape?

These features are by no means all that could be noted, but they will serve to give you some idea of the kind of detailed observation that is required to determine the type of construction for each part of your pattern. As you train yourself to see these many necessary things, you will have the happy experience of discovering just how much there is to see when you look at a design.

You will find that by the time you have completed gathering the information you need for your pattern (as nearly in your judgment as you can at this stage; more questions will pop up as you work along), you will have a pretty good idea of how to proceed.

TRIAL RUN: THE MUSLIN MODEL

In industry every new model gets a trial run. This is essential for getting all the "bugs" out of the design. You, too, will need to give your pattern a trial run. Your test is a muslin model (or a model of any material appropriate to the design) made from your completed pattern.

The muslin will give you a good idea of how the garment will look when made up. It will reveal whether your pattern produces the effect you have in mind.

Try the muslin on your dress form, yourself, or the person you are making the pattern for. Usually half a muslin garment is sufficient for testing. Sometimes, however, you cannot judge the effect unless you have a complete muslin for a collar, for instance, for a double-breasted, or asymmetric garment, or fullness for any special effect.

You may be tempted to skip this step, but don't, particularly at the beginning of your patternmaking experience. You may find that you want to make changes in your design as well as in your pattern. Perhaps the pattern is too wide or too skimpy. Maybe the sections don't match. It could be that the darts or seams don't line up. Perhaps the fit would be improved if parts were cut on the bias rather than the straight grain. You may find the proportions are not pleasing. Or that a style line needs shifting. You may sadly discover that while the original was perfectly enchanting on paper, it's a fright in fabric.

Try, Try Again

Don't be discouraged. Practically no one hits it right the first time. Some correction is almost always necessary. This is the stage in which your pattern is perfected. Pattern companies and manufacturers spend a great deal of time on this muslin sample. If they're lucky, they perfect it after a second or third time. Sometimes it takes even a fourth and fifth try.

All of this entails many consultations among the stylist, the fashion artist, the draper, the patternmaker, and the sample maker. An error could be very costly for these people. It could be for you, too. A test muslin may save you an expensive or favorite length of fabric or many hours of finished sewing on a garment that turns out to be a dud.

It's a Pattern!

Make the corrections on your pattern which the muslin fitting indicates. Make certain that you have a pattern for every part of your design, from the tiniest to the largest piece. Trace the perfected and completed pattern. Add the seam allowances and all the necessary symbols. Make any notations on the pattern that will help in assembling the garment. You may want to jot down some sewing directions for any particularly difficult or tricky part.

PATTERN PUZZLE

Commercial patterns give you a layout chart and the yardage requirements, in addition to the pattern and sewing directions. When you make your own patterns, you will have to work these out for yourself. A study of commercial patterns can be quite helpful in this matter.

Laying out the pattern pieces is like playing with a big jigsaw puzzle. All of them must be so placed that the various shapes fit (reasonably) against each other, with a proper respect for the grain of the fabric. All this must be accomplished with the least amount of material, for economy's sake.

Wherever possible cutting is by twos: either two of a kind or two halves (to be joined by a seam for a whole) or a half pattern placed on a fold of fabric (to become a whole when unfolded). This makes for accurate cutting and marking.

First place the largest pieces or those that must lie along a fold of fabric. Arrange the smaller pieces in the spaces left. Fit shapes against each other, locking them wherever possible. Be sure to observe the grain line when placing the pieces.

When the fabric has a nap, pile, or directional weave or print, arrange all pattern pieces so they go in the same direction—neck to hem.

When you are satisfied with the layout, make a little working chart.

Possible Pattern Layouts

The standard layout arrangements are the following: lengthwise fold, crosswise fold, open double, open single (full width), double fold, partial fold, combination folds.

A *lengthwise fold* layout (Fig. 357a) is the one most frequently used.

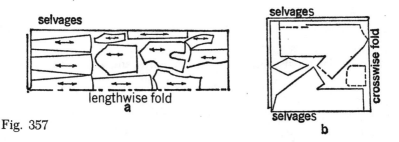

Fig. 357

A *crosswise fold* layout (Fig. 357b) is for fabrics without nap or directional design and for pattern pieces too wide to fit half the width of the fabric.

An *open double* layout (Fig. 358)—two thicknesses of full-width material—is for fabric with a nap, pile, or directional design and for patterns too wide to fit half the width of the fabric.

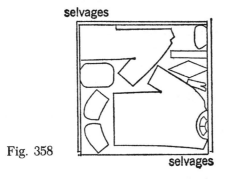

Fig. 358

An *open single* layout (Fig. 359) is for asymmetric and bias designs which must be cut individually. The layout is on a single thickness of fabric opened right side up to full width for the complete pattern.

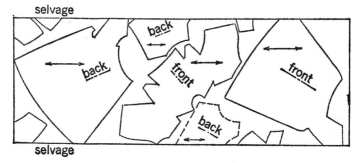

Fig. 359

A *double fold* layout (Fig. 360) is used when each of several pattern pieces need to be cut on a fold, for instance, both the center front *and* the center back of a skirt.

Make two lengthwise folds along the straight grain, with selvages facing each other. Keep the distance equal from fold to selvage.

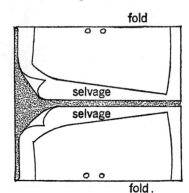

Fig. 360

A *partial fold* layout (Fig. 361) is used when both a narrower lengthwise fold and a single layer are required.

Make one lengthwise fold on grain (determined by the widest pattern piece that must fit in the space) with the selvage placed an equal distance from the fold throughout the length.

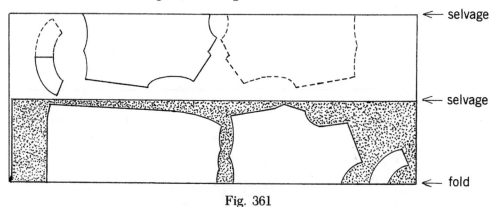

Fig. 361

There are all sorts of *combination* layouts possible (Fig. 362). Part of the garment may be placed on one type of layout, a second on another, and so on.

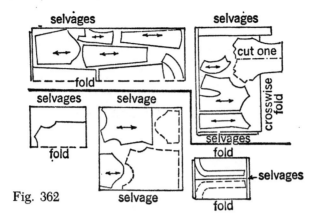

Fig. 362

If a pattern piece is shown extending beyond a folded edge (Fig. 363), it means that this piece must be cut in that space after all the other pieces have been cut and the remainder of the cloth is opened out.

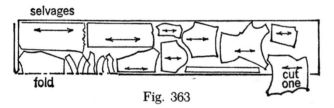

Fig. 363

A complete pattern indicated by dotted lines means it is to be used a second time (Fig. 364). A complete pattern, half shaded or half solid lines, half dotted lines (Fig. 364) is cut from folded fabric in that space.

You can save a lot of confusion in layout if you cut a complete pattern when it is necessary or cut two patterns when they are to be used twice.

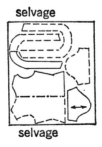

Fig. 364

How Much Yardage?

It is a good idea to keep on hand several lengths of pattern or wrapping paper cut to the standard widths of fabric—35 inches, 39 inches, 44 or 45 inches, 54 inches, 60 inches. Have them long enough to test the yardage necessary for your design. Mark the edge which corresponds to the selvage. Fold the paper in the appropriate manner. Lay out the pattern pieces with the grain parallel to the selvage. Measure the amount needed to complete the pattern.

They've Got to Fit!

You may have to do a bit of juggling to fit all the pattern pieces in economically, with due regard for the grain, nap, pile, direction of fabric design—all this within the confines of the standard fabric widths. If the pattern doesn't quite fit the fabric width or length, several changes may be made in the pattern.

1. Piece the pattern. Make sure the grain of the piece is the same as the grain of the section from which it was cut. Whenever possible, try to piece in some place where the joining seam will be inconspicuous or where it will be lost in a fold of the material.

2. Remove some of the fullness until the pattern fits the width of the fabric.

3. Shorten the pattern where and if possible.

4. Eliminate any expendable detail.

5. Change the grain on certain pattern sections. Facings, yokes, pockets, collar, cuffs, sleeves—all are possibilities.

6. Combine the fabric with other fabric for contrast of color or texture. This may be done for facings, insets, yokes, panels, or wherever consistent or effective in your design.

These changes involve a certain amount of restyling. Sometimes interesting ideas emerge because of limitations. Often the result is an improvement over the original. (At least you can try to persuade yourself that this is so.)

When your pattern and layout chart are completed, fold them neatly or roll them up. Store them in any manner convenient for you. It is well to attach a picture or sketch of the design so you will know just what that precious bundle of paper represents when you finally do get around to using it.

"I MADE THE PATTERN FOR THIS MYSELF!"

Now your pattern is really complete. Between you and your astonished public remain only those comparatively slight details involved in assembling your materials (fabric and findings) and assembling your garment (the sewing-fitting-ripping-sewing). Just think how proud you will be when you announce, "I designed and made this myself." And while your friends are clucking admiringly, you can further stagger them with a certain ostentatious modesty when you say quietly, "I made the pattern for this myself, too." You are sure to be the center of attention from that moment on whenever you make an appearance.

BARGAIN PATTERNS

The experience of making your own patterns will unquestionably affect your attitude toward commercial patterns. While freeing you from your dependence upon them, your new knowledge will also make you more appreciative of what they have to offer.

You get in each pattern envelope a style created by a talented and often big-name designer. It is the fruit of much experimentation, much consultation, much perfecting by a staff of experienced technicians. It includes a listing of all the materials necessary for production, step-by-step directions for sewing, suggestions for suitable fabrics, and even, in some cases, a label to add prestige. You certainly must agree that you are getting a bargain.

FREEDOM OF CHOICE

Will what this book offers you make you abandon the use of commercial patterns? Of course not. Make your own patterns when you wish. Use commercial patterns when the designs appeal to you. You now have the freedom to choose.

Often you can start with a pattern that basically has the features you want. That can be a timesaver. Then change any features which will bring the design closer to your own ideas or make the design more becoming to you. The knowledge of pattern construction will provide you with new confidence in handling commercial patterns. You will find that you are no longer fearful of changing the position of a dart or the line of a seam or of eliminating a detail or adding or removing some fullness. Your knowledge of patterns will even help in the actual sewing. You will understand why and how pattern pieces are joined in a particular way. You will be emancipated from that little sheet of printed instructions.

There is a great deal you can learn from a commercial pattern. Study the shapes of the pattern pieces and try to analyze how they were arrived at. Note any particularly ingenious use of pattern principles. Examine the layout charts carefully for hints on the best use of your material. Build up a library of commercial patterns that have interesting design details you may want to incorporate with your own ideas. Handle the commercial pattern as you would any other piece of research material. It has important information that you can use creatively.

YOU'LL NEVER BE THE SAME!

The experience of making your own patterns will inevitably result in your seeing fashion with a new eye. It will be difficult for you to be merely a passive observer. No longer will you just sit quietly daydreaming on bus or train. You will be trying to figure out how to make the pattern for a dress or a suit or a coat that you see and admire on someone else. A new fashion book will send you flying to your paper, pencil, and scale models. Watching a movie or a television show will become a mental exercise as you trace the lines and solve the problems of pattern construction of the heroine's clothes long before she solves her own problems. You will enjoy a wonderful new sense of power that comes with discovering that you can produce just what you want to wear!

Patternmaking, fascinating as it is in itself, is merely a means to an end. The larger end is the creation of works of beauty. In this instance, happily, that beauty may adorn you.